CUBA AND THE POLITICS OF PASSION

Damián J. Fernández

THE POLITICS OF PASSION

 University of Texas Press, Austin

First edition, 2000

Requests for permission to reproduce material
from this work should be sent to Permissions,
University of Texas Press, Box 7819, Austin, TX
78713-7819.

⊚ The paper used in this book meets the minimum
requirements of ANSI/NISO Z39.48-1992 (R1997)
(Permanence of Paper).

Library of Congress Cataloging-in-Publication Data
Fernández, Damián J.
Cuba and the politics of passion / Damián J.
Fernández
        p.   cm.
Includes bibliographical references and index.
ISBN 0-292-72519-1 (alk. paper) —
ISBN 0-292-72520-5 (pbk. : alk. paper)
    1. Political culture—Cuba.   2. Cuba—Politics and
government.   I. Title.
JL1010 .F47   2000
306.2'097291—dc21   00-024153

CONTENTS

PREFACE

This book does not begin with this sentence. It started years ago, in 1979, when as a senior at Princeton I walked the streets of Havana during a week-long visit. It was the first time I had been in Cuba since my family and I left in 1963. The experience was emotional and revealing; revealing perhaps because it was emotional. The Cuba I felt did not match the Cuba I had studied in class and read about in books. Something was missing in the political science texts on the topic. This book, two decades later, is an attempt to explain to myself and others what that was.

After years of study and several other visits to the island, I identified what was missing as *lo informal* (the informal). The literature on Cuba presented a political system and a social system detached from each other and far more formal than what I encountered during my trips. Far from being a characteristic exclusive to one or another set of scholars, formalism was pervasive in a field of study otherwise marked by pronounced cleavages. With time I have come to recognize that the bias toward formality runs deep in the intellectual history of modernity; it is not confined to the study of Cuba. Like the bulk of political science scholarship, the literature on Cuban politics has focused primarily on national and international structures and formal institutions. Even when scholars have emphasized (or overemphasized) the role of leadership, *lo informal* has not been considered. Informal social practices, the interactions among individuals in everyday life, and their political import have been neglected or rendered invisible. The resulting portrait of what constitutes the social and, by implication, the political has been rigid, inhuman, and much more "rational institutional" than what is true in the day-to-day experience of Cubans.

In the standard academic perspective the Cuban people have appeared as either agents or objects of politics, confined to the categories "masses" or "classes," but not as feeling beings with affective social networks that thrive in the non-state-regulated sphere. The emotional impact of politics and the relevance of emotions for politics have been absent as analytical categories. Even personal testimonies, so much a part of the revolutionary literary experience—for instance, Oscar Lewis's famous *Four Lives: Living the Revolution*—do not tell the story fully, as the emotional is not made explicitly political. Given the emotional outpouring the revolution of 1959 elicited, and continues to elicit inside and outside the island, even among academics, the absence of the politics of informality and the politics of emotions is nothing short of remarkable.

My concern with social informality and its impact on state-society relations led me to pose a number of questions regarding the feelings and norms expressed in that arena of daily life. What are the codes of the informal? What are the sources of its political culture? What constitutes its hardware, its networks? What impact do informality and the emotional have on formal politics? How do formality and informality intersect? What do they reveal about the limits of state power vis-à-vis the society? What light do the informal and the politics of emotions shed on human action? These queries forced me to consider the sociopolitical role of emotions in the Cuban case. Intuitively I had felt this was important, yet it had remained unspoken as scholars pursued "objective" analysis. Speaking about the emotional was a bit suspect, "soft," "flaky," passé, marginal at best. From the contemporary hegemonic political science paradigm of power and interest, emotions are a nontopic.

As I am of Cuban origin my interest in the affective was seen as especially questionable by the standards of a discipline that asks us not to get too close to the emotional and, most of all, not to become involved with our subject matter, perhaps valuable advice if one were a therapist. From the dominant perspective "others"—racially, intellectually, physically, sexually, and morally "inferior"—rely on emotions rather than on reason. But a passionless discipline cannot make sense of the passions that compel individuals to act politically the world over, from Algeria to Zimbabwe, from Argentina to Yugoslavia. In the United States and in Europe issues such as immigration, civil rights, abortion, ethnicity, and national identity inflame passions. In the Cuban case the political passion exhibited by Cubans and non-Cubans regarding revolutionary politics rivals only human passion for passion. Yet passion has remained outside the parameters of political science, at least in modern scholarship.

After realizing the importance of the sociopolitics of emotions, I set out to find why there was such silence on the issue in political science. This book is the product of what I found in the process, a process that was much more inductive than deductive. What I (re)discovered in a multidisciplinary literature (from the founding fathers of liberalism to recent works by Mansbridge, Lutz, Solomon, Frank, Fukuyama, and Holmes, among others) challenges the reductionist perspective of rational choice theory. The (re)discovery warranted a fresh, if not entirely new, approach to the study of politics: one in which emotions would be reconsidered and reincorporated; one that would not subsume all human action under a narrow rubric of self-interest; one that would not divorce the emotional from the rational or the affective and subjective from the instrumental and institutional; one that would bring together the nonmaterial (including the affective) and the material; one that would be affectively embedded, placing the individual with his or her affective networks in the broader institutional, cultural, and economic context.

This book proposes such an approach. It attempts to bring the emotions back in, or better still, to bring them out—for they have been there, hidden and unrecognized—while not discarding rational choice or falling into the classical dichotomy of reason versus passion. I present a way to reincorporate the emotions into the study of social politics based on the "new romanticism" in philosophy and social constructivism in anthropology. Reason and emotion are understood as mutually reinforcing, culturally intertwined, and significant for the social and, therefore, for the political world. The approach seeks to bridge the divide between assumptions of individualism and institutionalism by attending to connections of affective and cultural embeddedness.

Cuba and the Politics of Passion tells two main stories. The first is the hitherto untold story of the role emotions play in politics, a story that has a modern and a late modern subtext. It is the story of social politics with emotions considered, particularly what I call the politics of passion and the politics of affection. Through this narrative I attempt to contribute to a revisionist interpretation of politics generally and of Cuban politics specifically by incorporating the fundamental, but not exclusive, role that affection and passion play in the political, a theme that since modern times has all but disappeared from the discipline. The book offers a dimension complementary to other approaches, not a substitute for them. It does not argue that material and other nonmaterial factors do not matter, nor does it argue that emotions play the primary role in political developments in Cuba or anywhere else. Quite the opposite: structural, geographic, institutional, personal, historical, and international variables are indispensable for political explanations. My interest is to rescue a lost story and retell it through the Cuban case, in so doing broadening our understanding of the political.

My approach is a political-cultural one—with an emphasis on the affective—that intersects with state-society relations. It is informed by a variety of other approaches and disciplines, ranging from feminism to sociology, from anthropology to philosophy. I hope to contribute to the appreciation of the politics of emotions and informality and their impact on sociopolitical change and stability. The rediscovery of the politics of emotions in the Cuban case will shed light on several other topics, namely, social revolutions, charismatic authority, informality, and civil society, as well as on current debates regarding modern assumptions about politics and society.

The second story this book tells takes place over time in a specific locale —Cuba in the twentieth century. This is the Cuban political story with emotions considered. I write about Cuba for a variety of reasons. First and foremost, because it interests me in very personal ways and because I have studied it longer than any other country. Second, it was through the Cuban case— Cuba on the ground—that I found *lo informal* and the politics of emotions. The Cuba I encountered in 1979 and the one I have come to know in the diaspora led me to pose the theoretical questions the book attempts to answer.

The political culture of Cuba provides fertile ground for an analysis with emotions brought in. The island's history allows us to compare the sociopolitics of passion and affection under two political regimes—a capitalist democracy (1902–1959) and socialism (1959 to the present)—and during the revolutionary struggle that culminated in 1959. Democracy, socialism, and revolution require similar, yet distinct, emotional infrastructures. By comparing them, we can reach conclusions as to the continuity and discontinuity of the politics of passion and affection, the modalities they assume, their impact on different political systems, and how they, in turn, are affected by political and economic structures.

This is not an especially happy story, for it is a tale of a people who have aspired to political modernity in terms of sovereignty, nationhood, statehood, and democracy (in both its liberal and socialist variants) and who continue to dream of a better tomorrow despite the disappointment their aspirations have met in the past. Reality in Cuba, as in most other places, has not matched the lofty normative expectations of modern constructs. As I argue here, the politics of affection and passion challenge our understanding of what is and is not modern.

The two story lines—that of the politics of emotions and that of Cuban politics with passion and affection considered—are interwoven, forming an account of how the modern paradigm is an incomplete perspective through which to understand and feel politics in specific contexts. The partiality of the traditional rational choice perspective and of political modernity broadly writ stems from the neglect of the most immediate human dimension, the affective. In the realm of sentiments the presumptions and notions of modernity find their greatest theoretical and practical challenges. Humans relate to the world affectively through their culture. Emotions, especially in a social context, express interests and make interests understandable to others, even if at times emotional intensity might work against the achievement of those interests. In daily life the line between the emotional and the intellectual is much more blurred than the reason/passion dichotomy suggests. If the creations of modernity—the nation-state, for instance, which Max Weber defined as a community of sentiment—fail to provide sentimental satisfaction, they do so at their own peril. We must, therefore, reassess our understanding of political modernity by considering the place of emotions in societies, eschewing simplistic oppositions along the way: the rational and the affective, the traditional and the nontraditional, constructive and destructive emotions.

Affection and passion, their norms and their networks, do not disappear in modern societies, or in those such as Cuba that, according to some, are not modern enough. The affective is an integral part of the human, the cultural and the social, expressed differently—that is, with particular norms, roles, and modalities—in specific contexts and with multiple paradoxical consequences for political order. The emotional is not prepolitical but merely political.

The modern account of politics is partial in that it dismisses competing and coexisting epistemologies and ontologies. The Cuban experience shows that divergent political cultural paradigms coexist, shaping the course of a society in unexpected and unforetold ways. The resilience of alternative and "traditional" ways of relating to the social world is an integral part of this story. What is modern and what is not become hazy, as modern notions—such as revolution—are propelled by nonmodern forces such as religious zeal and affective bonds.

In some ways this book also tells the story of the author, as most books do. Contrary to currently fashionable claims that the author is dead, he or she never is, even if the "I" does not appear at the beginning of sentences and despite an inevitable degree of intertextuality. This story is part of my own story as I deal with issues of reason and emotion, of desire and disenchantment, of modernity and antimodernity, of civility and incivility, of nationalism and internationalism, and of exceptionalism and universalism. The Anglo-Saxon message, transmitted to me on more than one occasion—not to be emotional or judgmental, and not to take things personally—always struck me as a bit absurd, if not outright dehumanizing. Now I understand that to be or not to be emotional is an expression of culture. To express your emotions is also to make judgments on reality and to interpret that reality personally (the only way I know how). Now I know that modern socialization is in no small measure an attempt to render individuals unemotional (capitalism and its political order seemingly require it), impersonal (by allegedly divorcing the private from the public), and nonjudgmental. This doctrine of the good modern subject, detrimental as it is to a holistic interpretation of human action (not to mention its noxious message on how to live life), has insidiously influenced the way we study and approach our field. This book is my way of responding to and challenging that epistemology and ontology.

After a brief review of why passion (almost) disappeared from political science, Chapter 1 offers a reinterpretation of the role of the affective in politics. It argues that emotion and reason should be understood as supplemental rather than oppositional categories of human behavior; emotions have their reasons and their interests. Only by incorporating the emotional can we get a fuller picture of the "reasons" people act the way they do. Most modern approaches to politics assume or presume an emotional infrastructure that is never explicitly explained but which is decisive in constructing, maintaining, and destroying political order, as the Cuban case shows. Two specific manifestations of the politics of emotions are presented and defined: the politics of passion and the politics of affection. Without feeling and thus understanding both, one would be unable to interpret how Cuban politics have been shaped socially and culturally, and one would miss the reasons for and the interests behind the emotional intensity of Cuban politics through time.

In the first chapter I set out the main argument of the book, that the combination of the politics of passion—politics construed as a moral imperative for absolute ends—and the politics of affection—politics based on an instrumental logic in which anything goes, justified by who you know and who you love—helps to sustain *and* subvert the institutions of modern nation-states. In the long run societies marked by the politics of passion and the politics of affection are caught in a cycle of pursuit of lofty goals that come to naught as those collective goals are undermined by the politics of affection. The tension, if not outright contradiction, between absolute ends for the collectivity at large and immediate instrumental personal objectives leads to the undoing of modern norms and institutions.

Chapters 2 and 3 provide a revisionist interpretation of Cuban political culture (with emotions considered) and of Cuba's political history (from colonial times to the 1990s) from the counterpoint of the politics of passion and affection. Chapter 2 highlights the importance of three paradigms, the liberal, the corporatist, and *lo informal*, in shaping Cuban aspirations and reality over time. It also analyzes the cultural codes that underpin the politics of passion and affection in the Cuban context. The chapter rediscovers an intellectual tradition of the Cuban Republic that argued in typical positivist fashion that the island's political culture and its affective dimension corroded civility and democratic practice. Finally it places the political culture of passion and affection in the larger economic and political context of the island.

Chapter 3 traces the politics of affection and passion in tandem with structural factors throughout the twentieth century, focusing on the Cuban Republic (1902–1959) and the revolution (1959 to the present). It analyzes how passion and affection contributed to erect, uphold, and destroy political order over time, providing in the process a new outlook on Cuban politics by connecting the politics of passion and affection with the economic, national, and international situation through time. By bringing together the emotional and the material, the politics of emotions are shown to have their own affective, instrumental, and material logic.

Chapter 4 focuses on the early years of the revolution of 1959. The revolution was a modern project that promised a utopia for the nation at large. It was an affair of the heart: it relied on passion and affection to carry out its agenda of radical social change. On the one hand, politics became a quasi-religious crusade for moral absolutes that would redress the injustices of the past; on the other, politics were highly personalized, relying on the affective connection between the rebels and the people and between the charismatic leader and the masses. Fidel, the maximum leader of the revolution, generated fervent feelings akin to religious devotion among many. Strong affection bonded him and the people, in part, but not only, because of the economic policies his government implemented on behalf of the majority of the population. The revolution's political program can be conceptualized as a moral crusade pursued partly through the instrumental means of the politics of affection. Combined, the politics of passion and affection had contributed by the 1980s to the gap between promise and practice in Cuban socialism.

Chapter 5 analyzes the difficulty of reproducing the politics of passion by exploring state-youth relations since the 1960s. Whereas their parents and grandparents were compelled to support the revolution for subjective and material reasons, succeeding generations started to judge the regime based on performance rather than on promise, on standards of efficacy and efficiency rather than on passion and affection. The gap between theory and performance undermined revolutionary fervor. The young, disappointed with the public and the official, started to find in the private sphere and in the informal alternative sources of identity, meaning, community, and economic survival.

Chapter 6 addresses the informal sphere of daily life, where the politics of affection bring people together outside the channels of the state and the socialist economy. The politics of affection and its networks have undermined slowly the tenets of the official ideology and the governability of the system, especially through their role in the informal economy. In *lo informal* individuals develop hidden transcripts and form groups that stand on their own emotional infrastructure with their own normative aspirations. These developments are harbingers of sociopolitical change.

In Chapter 7 I examine the process of change under way in Cuban society and its implications for transition and posttransition politics. I pose a basic but neglected question in the study of transitions and civil society in one-party states: From where does civil society emerge? The answer is to be found in affection and its networks. I argue that civil society will emerge from the politics of affection, from *lo informal,* as well as from the state itself. While the emergence of civil society outside the control of the state and the Communist Party will spur change, the politics of passion and the instrumentality of the politics of affection will tend to manifest themselves once again in the future. In short, political transition does not mean necessarily social or cultural transformation. The political culture of the island does not bode well for liberal democracy in the long run.

Like revolutions, transitions are affairs of the heart. Political change will not come easily with an economy in shambles, high expectations, and a nation that might continue to be divided over foundational issues. Aspects of the country's political culture, namely, the politics of passion and affection, will reappear, perhaps with a vengeance, calling into question the civil character of civil and political society in Cuba. The conclusion is not as optimistic as many would like, because I do not foresee a rainbow at the end of the road, a deus ex machina. (And, I hope, there will be no caudillo to save the day.) The best I hope for is that the civility of civil and political society will be strengthened as a result of lessons learned from the past. But this is a difficult and unlikely outcome that implies changing the manner in which Cubans tend to relate to each other, to official state institutions, and to politics in general.

In the Epilogue I offer a sketch of how the politics of passion and affection have been manifested in the Cuban diaspora. The analysis shows that the politics of passion and affection have been reproduced in a different context and have contributed to the economic and political profile of Cubans in the United States. The Epilogue underscores the resilience of the affective codes of Cuban political culture, presents their multiple positive and negative effects, and suggests how the politics of passion and affection might change and remain the same as the exiles become Cuban-Americans. Finally, I offer concluding remarks on bringing the emotions back in to the study of politics and what the Cuban case teaches us in this regard.

As I finish this book in early 2000, the politics of passion are burning bright once again. This time the reason behind them is Elián González. Six-year-old Elián was found on an inner tube adrift in the Atlantic, north of Miami, two days after the boat that he, his mother, his stepfather, and several others used to escape Cuba had capsized. Of the eleven people on board, only Elián and two others survived; the boy lost both his mother and his stepfather. Shortly after his rescue, Elián went to stay at his paternal great uncle's home in Little Havana. Days later his father and the Cuban government demanded that Elián be returned to the island. His Miami relatives, backed by notables and ordinary citizens, refused. What was initially and fundamentally an issue for immigration authorities, or at most a custody battle, became a moral crusade in which two sides of the same nation—a group of Cuban-Americans and the Cuban government—were competing for their own version of righteousness: where and with whom does Elián belong? Here or there, us or them, right or wrong, good or evil? The Elián González case is a living metaphor for the politics of passion. The Cuban government mobilized thousands of Cubans to demand Elián's return from his kidnapping by the Cuban-American "mafia." Cuban-Americans took to the streets to manifest their support for the child to stay in Miami, so as not to be sent back to the "Cuban hell." Both sides became locked in the pursuit of contending absolute moral imperatives, fighting for the future of the child as if it were the future of the nation. As usual, the politics of passion shrouded political interests and sectoral agendas. For Cubans here in Miami and there in Cuba, the new century and the new millennium began the same way they ended. For better and worse, passion continues to define the way Cubans pursue politics.

ACKNOWLEDGMENTS

I would like to acknowledge the contribution of several individuals and institutions to this book. The College of Arts and Sciences and the Latin American and Caribbean Center at Florida International University (FIU) offered financial support at various stages during the project. FIU's Cuban Research Institute, through its Ford Foundation grant, made it possible for me to undertake research in Cuba. The School of International Studies of the University of Miami was my host during the sabbatical semester in which portions of the manuscript were completed. I especially owe a debt of gratitude to Lesbia Varona at the Cuban Collection and to the late Enrique Baloyra, who facilitated my appointment as visiting scholar there.

Several friends and colleagues read and commented on earlier versions of the book and particular chapters, and I thank each of them. I am especially grateful to Marifeli Pérez-Stable and Juan del Aguila for their intelligent comments and suggestions on an earlier draft of the manuscript. I also extend my gratitude to my graduate assistants over the past years, especially Luis Foianini, whose attention to details and knowledge of the computer world is much greater than my own.

I am grateful for the support of the staff at the University of Texas Press, especially Theresa May, who liked the project from the beginning, and Sheila Berg, a superb editor. I am grateful also to the staff of the International Relations Department at FIU.

The book's shortcomings are, unfortunately, my own.

CUBA AND THE POLITICS OF PASSION

1

BRINGING BACK THAT LOVING FEELING

Passion, Affection, and Politics

Cuban politics have revolved around two poles: the politics of passion and the politics of affection. The heart of the politics of passion is the crusade for absolute moral ends for the community at large. The politics of affection respond to a different beat: an instrumental and affective logic that justifies breaking the norms of the state to fulfill personal needs (material and otherwise) as well as those of loved ones. Contending logics aside, both share an emotional intensity that has marked Cuban political history. Before exploring the sources, meaning, and impact of the politics of passion and affection and how they have been expressed through time on the island, a fundamental theoretical question must be posed: What is the role of the emotional in the political?

This is one of the oldest questions in the study of politics, yet scholars have disregarded the topic, particularly in the latter part of the twentieth century. The emotional has become invisible as every political action has been subsumed under the rubric "rational interest," a notion that seems to preclude affect. The demise of the politics of emotions as an area of inquiry predates contemporary times.[1] Even in posing the question today one runs the risk of being considered outdated, or worse, marginal to the serious business of political "science." Be that as it may, affection, passion, and emotions in general constitute the proximate cause of much of what is social and political. This is not to imply that "impersonal" forces such as institutions and structures are unimportant or even of secondary significance. On the contrary, all organizations are much more personalized than one usually presumes and have their own networks of affection, if not their own passions.

A reconsideration of the politics of emotions does not entail a substitute for other explanations but a complement to them, for politics are determined by multiple causes—material and nonmaterial—in tandem, not by single, mutually excluding factors. The attempt to bring the emotions back in to the study of politics stems from my interest in telling part of the story that is missing and telling it in an engaging way (i.e., with feeling). By embodying politics with feeling people, I hope to challenge some commonly held conceptions about modernity, rationality, politics in general, and Cuban politics in particular.

The disappearance of passion from political science has hurt our understanding of politics. Without passion one is hard pressed to make sense of the intense feelings that motivate people to engage in (or at times disengage from) a political campaign, or of the emotions that politicians and social movements evoke, stir, and use as one would a material resource. If we agree that the affective is one of the principal motivations, if not the main one, for human behavior, we should conclude that emotions have political import in a number of important ways. The literature, however, usually presumes the emotional without explicitly articulating it. Perhaps the task at hand is not so much to bring emotions back *in* as to bring them *out* and *back* from where they have remained hidden for centuries.

Bringing the emotions out and back in to political analysis carries added and unexpected benefits. To find the role of emotions in politics is to discover the realm of the informal, of the usually invisible and neglected: the everyday practices and networks of individuals that coexist with and bypass formal institutions. This realization helps to embed individuals in their affective and cultural context and thereby bridges the gap between an approach that assumes an atomized individual pursuing self-interest and one that presents institutions as determinants of behavior.[2] Without accounting for (or feeling) the politics of emotions and the informality of social relations, the study of state-society relations misses a vital dimension that helps to explain the emotional infrastructure of political change and continuity. Emotions in their social cultural setting reflect the community's outlook, its normative map. They are indicative of political culture, that is, the values, norms, and affective codes that influence how people in particular groups relate to politics. Moreover, emotions are instrumental in creating the trust, affection, and personal connections that are necessary to live in community. Social life has an emotional infrastructure, and so do political systems. The point of departure of this book is that social life and political life are intimately tied and mutually influencing. To understand the political broadly writ one must start with the social.

In society one finds formal as well as informal practices and institutions in which men and women participate on a daily basis. The informal ones rely on networks of affection and on their politics, which in turn have a variety of repercussions on governability, civil and political society, and the state.

The argument does not discredit rationality and self-interest as the basis of decisions or politics in general. It does, on the contrary, add another element by arguing that rationality and emotionality are not diametrically opposed, as the classical dichotomy would have it. One could refer, as I do throughout this book, to an "affective rationality" to redress the reductionism implied in rational self-interest, bringing the affective to a central, if redundant, place in defining both rationality and interest. The emotions expressed by groups and collectivities regarding social matters are value judgments that indicate likes and dislikes, frustrations as well as aspirations and demands. They make sense (i.e., they are logical) in a particular setting at a particular time. Contrary to the traditional modern perspective that emotions are destructive of political order, I argue that emotions help to erect and sustain it as well. Contrary to the notion that the emotional is prepolitical and noninstrumental, I argue that the affective is foundational as well as instrumental.

This book offers a look at the sociocultural basis of politics through the prism of emotions, specifically in the Cuban case. Although the topic of emotions and politics is a broad one, two distinct manifestations of the emotional foundation of politics seem particularly important: the politics of affection and the politics of passion. The politics of passion and the politics of affection have motivated individuals and collectivities in their social pursuits over time. Each has a strong affective character, but they differ in their logic and language as well as in their agents and scope. Together they have contradictory effects on national politics and social life. Both modalities of the politics of emotions have considerable impact on political change and continuity as they intersect in a variety of ways. The two terms help to explain past, present, and, most likely, future trends in Cuban politics. Without incorporating affection and passion, any account of politics in Cuba, as in most other places, would be anemic and incomplete.

Hiding Your Emotions

If in the final analysis individuals are the protagonists of politics, why has the dominant paradigm of political science—the rational actor—and most other approaches to the discipline neglected emotions? Surprisingly the neglect is only apparent. A review of the literature reveals that the emotional has a long genealogy in the study of politics going as far back as classical times. The founding fathers of liberalism also confronted the issue directly. Even in contemporary times the politics of emotions are present, if unseen, in most political science texts. As rational choice and self-interest became the dominant perspective, the emotional was rendered invisible, implicit, and unrecognized, but it never disappeared from the literature altogether.

The reductionist view that humans are motivated by a narrow definition of rational interest (whether political or economic) robs humans of one of their principal qualities: their ability, and propensity, to experience the world through emotions and feelings. As Albert Hirschman uncovers in *The Passions and the Interests,* between the seventeenth and the eighteenth century, during the rise of capitalism—and contributing to its expansion—the notion of passion was replaced by the notion of interest. Emotions and feelings, known then as passions, came to be perceived as noxious to the proper orderly conduct of political and economic capitalist affairs. Thus they needed to be harnessed or redefined to legitimize the pursuit of material gain, which up to that point had been considered sinful. While passions came to be associated with unruly human impulses that would lead to social conflict and economic decline, interest became synonymous with rationality and the ability to rein in the irrational. Interest and rationality, in turn, would be conducive to peace and material progress for individuals and nations alike. Interest was passion controlled for constructive ends (capitalism and the new liberal order). What was initially a normative projection by a number of thinkers including Adam Smith—that "negative" passions should be checked and replaced by virtues or "positive" passions and transformed into interest—was later standardized as the principal assumption of economists and political scientists: humans are rational beings motivated by the pursuit of self-interest.[3] An economicist view of political "man" started to dominate the study of politics.

Early modern thinkers, not to mention classical writers, underscored the role of emotions in creating as well as in destroying political community. Adam Smith, the founding father of modern economics, considered sentiments, specifically what he called moral ones, indispensable for the proper functioning of society.[4] Even given the fact that some of the most influential thinkers of the past—Durkheim, Burke, and Weber, among many others—acknowledged the importance of affection in bonding community together, with time the discipline of political science disciplined us to become good modern subjects who would eschew feelings for interest, notwithstanding that this interpretation of modernity is a partial and contested one.

An alternative perspective of modern subjectivity relishes the sentimental as part and parcel of the self-expression of the individual and the community, but this one never received recognition in the study of politics. On the contrary, as the field "grew" two almost simultaneous developments secured the preeminence of the dominant interpretation: the advent of computer-based quantification in social science research and the attention devoted to the less-developed countries after World War II. These two developments underscored the "value" of objectivity and rationality not only for scientific pursuits in the social sciences but also for economic and political progress.

More was lost than gained by excising the emotions from political "man." Binary thinking reduced the complexity of the issue to simplistic positive and negative categories. Reason was civilized; passion was primitive. Reason was modern; passion, traditional. Reason was public; emotion, private. Reason was scientific; emotion, prescientific. Reason was active; passion, passive. Reason was controlled; passion was uncontrollable (whereas one is in control of one's reason, one is overtaken by passion). Reason was masculine; passion was feminine. Interest was political; emotion, prepolitical. In the process emotions were portrayed as the province of (and for) less civilized beings, women and others—namely, non-Western European others. Therefore, emotions were in need of control.

Not everyone accepted the new dogma, though. Unlike many of his contemporaries, Rousseau celebrated passions as natural and good, as the expression of the noble savage. Rousseau notwithstanding, most thinkers of the time (and still many today) considered that only white, educated, male property owners were to be trusted with the conduct of public affairs, or with their own, because of all others' reliance on the sensual and the sentimental. Emotionality made others irrational, as rationality was opposed diametrically to affectivity. The construction of the nation-state, the definition of citizenship, the division of power in society, and the expansion of colonialism had an emotional, racial, and gendered subtext.

Modern projects such as nationalism, ironically, relied primarily on feelings, not reason or imagination exclusively.[5] Emotional attachment to a place, its symbols and myths, and the sense of solidarity with strangers (i.e., co-nationals) were the cornerstone of national identity. Revolution, another modern notion, required more than cost-benefit calculation to spread its fire; it demanded affect and disaffect. What, if not affection, is the basis of the rallying cry "Fraternité"? In his revisionist interpretation of liberalism, Stephen Holmes claims that classical liberalism was not only concerned with self-interest, but with fairness above all: the universal equality of rights.[6] This moral assumption has empathy at its core, which is conducive to trust and community.

Modern political theories have implicit, and partial, presumptions about the emotional makeup of individuals. Classical liberalism and Marxism, the two most influential political philosophies of the modern era, centered their analyses on modern assumptions about human beings and their motivations. While both regard individuals (or social classes, in the case of Marxism) as rational, fundamentally motivated by interest, both also acknowledged passion, if secretly. Holmes claims that "passion and constraints, irrational motivations and institutional limitations," are the two poles of classical liberal theory.[7] A similar argument can be made in the case of Marxism. The recognition of exploitation and the overthrow of capitalism by the working class required an emotional (and moral) reaction. The implementation of socialism also demanded a new emotional infrastructure, much different from the one on which capitalism was based. For someone so intent on exploring the meaning of capital, it is surprising that Marx did not uncover the emotional capital on which preideologies and ideologies rest. Capitalism depended, and continues to depend, on the instrumentalization and restraint of passion to work and for work. The layout of the factory, whether in the traditional Ford-style plant or the postfordist model, requires discipline, the (self-)control of labor, and unemotional workers.

As Holmes argues, "The rise to dominance of the concept of self-interest (by the 19th century) was due to disenchantment with aristocratic ideals and the dogma of original sin. In the process the tradition of moral psychology was neglected and self-interest replaced it, particularly because it served the democratic and egalitarian aspirations of both liberalism and Marxism."[8] Constraint overcame passion. Yet both liberalism and Marxism need people to feel, to hope, to expect, to desire, if the theories are to "work." Both implicitly acknowledge that sentiments are powerful forces that play decisive roles in political affairs and that different political institutions foster and require different emotions. Whereas some emotions may compel individuals to sympathize with their neighbors, others make it possible to kill the boss in a factory takeover. Without these emotions, liberalism and Marxism could not stand.

Although both theories rely on what can be called an implicit emotional infrastructure to sustain their prescribed forms of authority and the behavior they presume and expect from individuals, neither incorporates affect explicitly in its analysis. As good products of modernity, both theories are afraid to show emotion. The Cuban case illustrates that emotions and feelings— expressed specifically in the politics of affection and the politics of passion —have been among the main challenges that the normative constructions of liberal democracy and Marxist-Leninist socialism have had to confront in practice. Sentiments have been largely responsible for the establishment of democratic and socialist forms of government on the island as well as for many of the obstacles both types of regimes have faced in their attempt to regulate state-society relations. Emotions are both destructive and constructive of political order. Not mere by-products, emotions are constitutive forces as well. They not only help to shape politics, they are also shaped by politics. The relationship between socioeconomic and political structures and emotions is interactive, mutually influential.

Bringing the Emotions Back In and Out

Part of the reason that emotions virtually disappeared as an area of inquiry in political science was that they eventually came to be perceived as negligible in modern polities, as having a negative impact on political order, and as being the remnant of a moral tradition that had less and less of a place in the discipline. But emotions did not exit altogether; they remained off center stage. Several scholars who focused on the process of modernization in traditional societies continued to address the topic, if indirectly. As important as their contributions were, they offered a partial discussion grounded on the metanarrative of modernity and its traditional binary outlook. What remained of an erstwhile energetic debate on the politics of emotions in the seventeenth and eighteenth centuries revolved around binary categories in which the first concept is positive and the second one is negative: reason versus emotion, order versus disorder, modern versus traditional, rational versus irrational. Instead of a dichotomous and exclusionary analysis, what is called for is a reconciliation of reason and emotion that illuminates how individuals bundle them together and how political action is influenced by both.

Since the 1950s modernization theory, influenced by Weber and liberalism, has argued for what can be labeled the depersonalization of politics and society. It proposes industrialization, rationalization, and secularization as the route to progress. Modernization called for the replacement of particularistic norms (i.e., affection for family members) by universal principles (i.e., merit). Emotions and sentiments were seen, once again, as obstacles to progress. On the road to modernity countries were prescribed a larger dosage of reason and a diet of emotion.

Several of the early writers on political psychology and comparative politics in the second half of the twentieth century went against the grain by identifying ways in which affect was relevant to politics without necessarily prescribing an abandonment of emotional expression. At about the same time political sociologists and anthropologists in the United States and elsewhere studied the roles and meanings of friendship, specifically in relation to the formation of coalitions and corporate ties.[9] Others pioneering in the field of political psychology took into consideration not only personality traits but also feelings to explain leadership types.[10] Harold Lasswell, in *Power and Personality,* presented a list of personal attributes that would contribute to democratic character. Some of the traits he listed, for instance, trust and lack of anxiety, had an affective and emotional basis.[11] Although this strand in the literature was never fully adopted, it offered insights into the significance of the affective that are well worth rescuing.

Several scholars reconsidered the importance of the emotions in modern forms of government. In *The Civic Culture,* Gabriel Almond and Sidney Verba concluded that democracy, more than just a set of formal institutions, "is a matter of attitude and feeling." [12] They argued that while "politics must not be so instrumental and pragmatic that participants lose all emotional involvement in it . . . the level of affective orientation to politics ought not to become too intensive." [13] Their statement presumes that politics is somehow an autonomous phenomenon that one can shape at will, that the political is disembodied from people who feel, that all political issues that threaten the system can be controlled or decharged, and that only in a blanket of lukewarm emotional balance does democracy work, which is not clear in practice. From this perspective, similar to Harry Eckstein's, too much emotion threatens normalcy, equilibrium, and sanity.[14] This is a reflection of modernity's fear of the affective, which is traceable back for centuries. But what is most noteworthy is that the recognition of the affective, with notable exceptions, did not lead to major theories or to its acceptance as fundamental in politics. What persisted was framed within the modern notion that emotions were noxious to political stability and development, especially if they were not kept in check.

One partial exception is Lucian W. Pye's groundbreaking study on political culture. In it he argued that affective orientation—the feelings about the system, its roles, officials, and performance—and the valuative judgments people made about the government, including how they felt about the political system, not only cognitive orientation, shaped how the public related to the political.[15] Pye's approach not only incorporated but also emphasized the impact of the affective on the political. He argued that the "political sphere is not sharply differentiated from the spheres of social and personal relations" [16] and concluded that "the affective or expressive aspect of politics tends to override the problem solving or public policy aspect." [17] I take these propositions as points of departure to bring the emotions out of hiding and interpret state-society relations in Cuba.

Pye's scheme, however, falls into the standard dichotomy that portrays Western and non-Western societies as polar opposites. Whereas in modern Western societies politics are dominated by issues of public policy, in non-modern societies politics are affective and expressive. Politics in the former are an "emotionally satisfying drama," according to Pye.[18] What Pye fails to recognize is that all politics in modernity have an emotional subtext (i.e., the feelings people experience in relation to the arrangement of authority in their society) and an emotional infrastructure that help to sustain the system. Politics are not exclusively based on day-to-day bureaucratic and technocratic performance, even in the most modern societies. Affective attachment to the system is crucial for governability and legitimacy. Especially in moments of transition, in crises, and when dealing with issues of morality or foundation, all politics are emotional dramas, satisfying or otherwise. The postmodernists are right in claiming that politics is performance (especially in the age of television and computers), although politics is much more than a mere spectacle. Feminists are also on target when they argue that the political is personal, although they do not make explicit the argument about the emotional. In practice, and contrary to what early comparativists schematized, the affective and the rational are not far removed from each other in either modern or traditional societies.

The dual society theory seems to rule out sentiments in modern societies. No one expressed this perspective better than Weber in his theory of the rationalization of modern societies and the resulting disenchantment of the world. Modernity, according to Weber, was the process through which enchantment was replaced by science and instrumental rationality. Instrumental rationality in modern societies was supposed to be operationalized through apersonal forces, namely, the bureaucratic conduct of social life. Social relations would be steered by universal norms rather than by sentiment, personal connections, or particularistic criteria. The world is objectivized as a result, and magic (or enchantment) disappears. This is, according to Weber, the price we pay for modernity. But in moments of crises charismatic leaders who appealed to the emotional could emerge, which is precisely what occurred in Cuba in the late 1950s, as Chapter 3 explains. Despite rationalization, Weber acknowledged that affective bonds were necessary for creating and sustaining society. The emotional was never far from the surface of modern politics.

Weber's dichotomous view of rationality and society failed to appreciate how the affective *and* instrumental rationality may come together in the politics of affection. In them, means and ends logic is fused with affection through functional affective networks of friends and family members. Instrumental rationality does not necessarily replace value-rational logic, as Chapter 2 shows in the Cuban context. On the contrary, both types of logic coexist in modernity; their coexistence can undermine, as well as help to erect, modern projects such as democracy and socialism. Modernity has its own "enchantments" that replaced premodern "magic." Notions of sovereignty, nationalism, revolution, democracy, and socialism all entail at least partial utopias, teleology, and some dosage of "enchantment." These modern constructs share an emotional charge derived from their religious origins and their normativity that imbue them with passion.[19]

But the hegemonic perspective in the political science literature is that of an affectless human being in a rather emotionally bland political system. From analysis to normativity is one small step: modernity seems to require relatively unfeeling subjects in an autistic but technocratic social system; otherwise disorder and decline are just around the corner. This conclusion fails to assess what occurs in most, if not all, societies. Contrary to accepted interpretations, the political import of the emotional is not exclusive to traditional polities. In industrial and postindustrial societies emotions also play a vital role in mobilizing individuals, in determining who gets appointed to positions of authority, in establishing networks, and in legitimizing government policies. In all societies one finds affective intent behind the pageantry associated with power. Technocracy, with its rules of impersonal efficiency, is not enough.

The modern rationalization of the individual in social theory has resulted often in a dehumanized or disembodied scholarship that is also partial in its conception of the politics of emotion. Contraposing emotion and reason exaggerates their oppositional relationship. Associating emotion with instability and antimodernity obscures as much as it illuminates. A theory of human action must take into consideration "rational self-interest" (defined in the standard perspective as maximization of the optimum) *and* emotions. Even using the language and logic of rational choice, it is easy to see that feelings can "invest" the material and the nonmaterial with different "values" for different people.[20]

The reductionism entailed in the rational actor model misses vital aspects of human action and, more significant, neglects that "the most important bases of choice" and "the majority of choices" are "affective and normative" rather than rational and self-interested.[21] Even scholars who have questioned the rational choice paradigm forget the emotional when they argue that "when people think about what they want they think about more than just their narrow self-interest."[22] The missing piece is that people do more than just think; people feel. Feelings reveal dimensions of the actor and his or her world.

Emotions of love, hate, anxiety, frustration, and hope are partially socially constructed, are expressed socially, and thus have political causes and consequences. Recent contributions from philosophy, feminism, and poststructuralism, particularly by scholars who are questioning the predominance of the rational choice model and the reason/passion dichotomy, help to usher the emotional back in to the political.

Defining the Emotions

Before bringing the emotions out of hiding and back in to the study of politics, we must define them, which is not an easy or uncontested task. Part of the definitional challenge stems from the fact that emotions have psychological and biological dimensions, in addition to the sociocultural ones that this book addresses. Emotions can be understood (1) functionally (as ways through which individuals deal with their environment); (2) existentially (as an expression of ways of being; i.e., one is emotional, one is affectionate); (3) as tendencies or dispositions (i.e., one tends to react with anger); (4) as preferences (i.e., a taste); and (5) as products, by-products (i.e., reactions to external circumstances), or events (i.e., the manifestation of rage at a particular moment).[23]

The slippery nature of the concept is compounded by the wide range of affects that it covers. No single schema for classifying emotions is universally accepted. Some scholars consider emotions passive (i.e., involuntary—one is overcome by grief), others active (i.e., voluntary—one acted with anger), and yet others both. The difficulties associated with "emotions" are magnified when one attempts to use the concept in the study of politics. Emotions are not only motivations for action, or mere orientations to politics; they can be conceived as power in some cases. Not only do they contribute biologically to physical power, they can also incite individuals to act in ways they would not ordinarily feel capable of. Emotional appeal serves as a sort of human capital, as others might support individuals who are perceived as trustworthy and sensitive. Emotions can also serve as commitment devices. As Robert Frank writes, "Being known to experience certain emotions enables us to make commitments that would otherwise not be credible."[24]

Definitional problems notwithstanding, I approach emotions from a cultural and philosophical perspective that reconciles the affective and the rational. In line with the anthropologist Catherine A. Lutz's theoretical framework, emotional meaning is mediated and structured by cultural systems and social and material environments. Emotion concepts are "elements of local ideological practice," and their expression "involves negotiation over the meaning of events, over rights and morality, over control of resources—in short, involves struggles over the entire range of issues that concern human groups."[25] Although the concept of emotion is caught in the dichotomies nature/culture, mind/body, and thought/action, which both simplify and complicate the definitional issue, I agree with Lutz that "emotion retains value as a way of talking about the intensely meaningful as that is culturally defined, socially enacted and personally articulated. It retains value also as a category more open than others to use as a link between the mental and the physical . . . and between the ideal . . . and the actual world. . . . And it retains value as a way of orienting us toward things that matter rather than things that simply make sense."[26]

Emotions are embedded in culture, insofar as individuals are socialized, live in community, and express themselves in relationships. Through socialization the individual is provided with cues as to how and when to manifest love, anger, dissatisfaction, jealousy, guilt, and shame, among many other sentiments. Cultures differ in the way they express these and in the propensity to manifest them. Neil Smelser writes, "Cultures and worldviews may value or devalue either the instrumental or the expressive mode, or both; may ignore one or the other; and may regard the two as complementary, mutually exclusive, or antipathetic."[27] The standard interpretation holds that since the Protestant Reformation social life in the West has been increasingly instrumentalized and rationalized, at a cost to the affective side. This does not mean that the emotional is absent in its multiple sociopolitical manifestations, or that the affective does not have its share of instrumental reason.[28]

Political cultures and political institutions legitimize certain affects (e.g., admiration for authority) and not others. Political systems also differ in the affective responses they seek in individuals. Yet all states and societies use rituals that call on feelings to muster support and cohesion. Rituals such as pledging allegiance to the flag carry a strong emotional undercurrent for practical purposes. Even when the emotional charge might be lost through repetition, it can be reenergized in specific moments, such as the outbreak of war. Although in all political systems emotions are important causes and consequences of politics, emotions play a stronger role at different times and places, due not only to culture, but to factors such as regime type, leadership style, economic situation, and international forces.

My argument rests not only on the social constructivist notion of the emotions but also on the new romanticism in philosophy.[29] From this perspective, first and foremost, passion and reason are not divorced. Emotions are choices, if sometimes hasty ones. Insofar as emotions are always about something, they are intentional. Since they have a purpose, they can be explained by reason. Second, passions are in essence judgments about the world, not uncontrollable eruptions from the human heart. These judgments, expressed affectively and perhaps effectively, are usually normative and moral. Rather than distort reality, emotions are interpretations of reality. Third, as a consequence of the above, emotions are indicative of our interests and our purposes. They are at the heart of our reasons. Fourth, reality is interpreted subjectively. According to Robert Solomon, "What is called reason is the passions enlightened, 'illuminated' by reflection. . . . It is our passions, not our reasons (and surely not nature), that constitute our world, our relationships with other people and, consequently, our *Selves*." [30]

What distinguishes emotional responses from other types of behavior (if such a separation is ever feasible) is that emotions are usually "urgent judgments[,] . . . emergency behavior[,] . . . in a situation in which usual intentions are perverted or frustrated; an unusual response is necessary." [31] Emotional control is a way to stop oneself from judging quickly. One can change the emotional response by changing the context or changing somehow the observer of the situation (i.e., by providing more information). But even "cool deliberations" entail some degree of emotionality. By and large, emotional responses, like most of what we call "thinking," are based on prejudice or preconceived notions to which one resorts to understand the world. [32] Usually emotions have short-term purposes. They are closely related to beliefs and normative criteria that are usually not verbalized. Beliefs, desires, and emotions are intimately bundled together. They are both an individual and a collective phenomenon.

Part and parcel of this theoretical grounding is the acknowledgment that a holistic theory of human action would not only incorporate the affective dimension of individual and collective behavior but would recognize as well that rationality and emotions are neither necessarily nor always polar opposites. Rationality and emotionality relate in ways other than exclusively oppositional. If rationality is defined in the most common Western fashion, emotions certainly can influence our view of maximization as an individual's ability to assess costs and benefits and maximize the latter while reducing the former. The concept of self-interest, the handmaiden of rationality, has been shown to carry affective dimensions at times explainable by cost-benefit analysis and at times not. [33] Jürgen Habermas's conception of rationality is enlightening in this regard: "Actors are behaving rationally so long as they use predicates such as 'spicy,' 'attractive,' 'strong,' 'terrible,' 'disgusting,' and so forth, in such a way that other members of their life-world can recognize in these descriptions their own reaction to similar situations. If, on the other hand, they use valuative standards in such a peculiar way that they can no longer count on a culturally established understanding, they are behaving idiosyncratically." [34]

From a positivist perspective, however, emotions and rationality do not always go hand in hand. By coloring the assessment of a situation, emotions shape behavior and influence external developments in a way that can be detrimental to our own purposes. Jon Elster argues that "emotions may lead to wishful thinking and thus, in typical cases, . . . to false beliefs about the world. This will also lead to a smaller degree of satisfaction of the goals dictated by these very same emotions. Beliefs born of passion serve passion badly." [35] In other words, intense emotions can distort cognition and, consequently, misdirect individuals in achieving their goals. Ironically Elster's positivist argument vindicates emotions by resorting to them as an explanatory variable as it establishes that aspirations are guided by the superego, which in turn is sustained by feelings. [36] What should be clear from this discussion is that individual and collective interests, identities, desires, and feelings, and how they are pursued instrumentally and affectively, are mixed together in convoluted combinations, not easily distilled from one another.

Emotions and the Politics of Community

Belonging to a large social group, such as a nation, requires affective attachment. In this fundamental way the emotional is necessary for political order. Societies in which large numbers of people lose their affective connection to the collectivity or are not integrated into any broad social association are candidates to experience a host of social problems. William Kornhauser concluded that "the atomized society invites the totalitarian movement which provides both pseudo-authority in the form of the charismatic leader and the pseudo-community in the form of the totalitarian party." [37] Although insightful, Kornhauser's conclusion fails to see that seemingly atomized societies contain multiple networks that exist in the informal sphere of daily life and provide attachment at a different social level.

If the national community does not fulfill the individual's need for identity, meaning, and material well-being, smaller-scale associations will take a preeminent place in fulfilling those needs. Usually smaller groups (factions, kinship groups, client-patron relations, networks of friends and associates) are based on affection to a greater extent than "interest" groups or national associations. Affection is an important factor in shaping the contours of trusts and by extension those of politics and the economy. The ability to form associations depends on mutual trust. Although trust may begin with small groups (usually groups that share some bonds of affection, as Chapter 7 argues), it can be generalized when individuals share a core set of values, norms, and institutions, particularly if they are perceived to promote collective interests rather than strictly personal ones.[38] Trust, therefore, is both a cause and an effect of specific social arrangements. Societies and cultures differ as to the extent of social trust and the value placed on cooperation beyond primordial groups. Societies are said to be well endowed in terms of social capital when they manifest a rich associational life.[39] Low-trust societies (those with poor social capital) tend to be characterized by weak and fragmented civil associations and rigid and bureaucratic legal systems. They confront serious obstacles in establishing political community at the national level, particularly in the absence of a strong state. In the economic sphere predominance of family businesses and stunted economic growth are an indication of low-trust societies. Where there is security and trust, corporations emerge; where insecurity predominates, coalitions arise.[40]

Loss of affective attachment to the system has serious implications for the national community and for government.[41] Unconnectedness beyond family and friends usually results from lack of generalized social trust and affective attachment to the nation-state and the organizations of civil society. While "we" feelings allow for reciprocity in small groups, they do not necessarily translate into the broader solidarity implied in a nation. On the contrary, familism and *amiguismo* (relationships based on friendship) can undermine its institutional bases while exacerbating the personalistic politics of affection. Edward Banfield coined the term "amoral familism" (an unfortunate choice of words) to describe the predominance of kinship as a source of moral concern and the absence of civic responsibility in southern Italy.[42] In the Latin American case, Glenn Cuadill Dealy argues a similar point. He concludes that a two-track moral code is responsible, on the one hand, for the lack of public civic consciousness common throughout much of the region and, on the other, for the love and fraternity characteristic of private personal relations. Whereas public affairs are conducted on the basis of expediency and opportunism, private matters are guided by an ethos of empathy and piety. The public realm, devoid of familiarity, is marked by distrust and potential hostility, which explains the difficulty in sustaining political stability.[43]

Recognizing the existence of the binary logic of the public and the private renders understandable that Latin Americans and other peoples deal with the demands of modern social life not only with trepidation but also by attempting to make the public familiar, by personalizing the impersonal. The process requires establishing networks of friends, family members, and patrons (or clients) within and without the institutions of the state and the formal economy that constitute the fabric of the politics of affection. These personal relations provide instrumental assistance and affective comfort in the face of the bureaucracy of the modern state, the economic demands of capitalism, and the anonymity of institutional life, usually by circumventing official norms. What is not recognized by the actors is that their private actions have serious public consequences, as the politics of affection are based on norms other than those that modern nation-states are supposed to represent and uphold.

The Politics of Affection

The politics of affection revolve around who you know and who you love. Ties of friendship, kinship, pseudokinship (i.e., *compadrazgo*), and clientelism bind individuals together in small groups. These personal relations constitute the basis of solidarity and the preconditions for social order.[44] Yet the politics of affection rest on norms that run counter to modern normativity. In practice the "premodern" norms of affection coexist with modern ones, albeit sometimes in tension. Affection broadly defined acts as the glue for primary group formation where membership is restricted to familiarity. As with other groups, hierarchy and reciprocity are combined with instrumental interests. Membership in the affective group, or in what I call the networks of affection, sets boundaries between us and them, providing a source of identity, meaning, and possible economic activity. Trust, personal choice, dependability, mutual acceptance, and understanding are features of affective networks. Solidarity, trust, and cooperation in the politics of affection are based on particularistic rather than "universal" criteria.[45] Cooperation tends to be greater within the group than without.[46] The politics of affection represent eunomic tendencies in society.

Although primarily based on affection, the politics of affection tend to intersect with instrumental or economic interests and functions. Goran Hyden found a similar combination of economy and affection in rural Africa, which he encapsulated in the term "the economy of affection."[47] The economy of affection describes the productive and redistributive network operating between families and friends that does not depend primarily on profit or on personal self-interest but rather on collective well-being.

Although the politics of affection are present in every society, their cause and effect are more significant in some as a result of cultural, governmental, and economic factors. In periods of economic crisis, structural adjustment, and reduction of welfare benefits, the politics of affection will expand in support of the economy of affection, by creating informal safety nets for friends and family.[48] In situations of scarcity clientelistic relations multiply and strengthen, for they not only serve as a hedge against uncertainty but may also satisfy affective needs. As Ayse Gunes-Ayata argues, clientelism is a form of privatizing public relations.[49]

The expansion of the politics of affection is related to the cycles of shifting involvements that Hirschman identified. Hirschman argued that as people's expectations regarding participation in collective pursuits are dashed, they will exit the public sphere to enter the private, devoting themselves to individual and family pursuits. As they enter the cycle of the personal, these individuals seek to exercise freedom from formal politics.[50] This has happened in a variety of political systems, ranging from the United States and other parts of the industrialized modern world to the former socialist states and Cuba.

The "retreat" to the personal has serious political consequences. The groups that engage in the politics of affection can act in ways that reaffirm the social order by promoting values and activities that support general goals of the system, or they can challenge the status quo by diverting resources from the state to members of the group or by promoting ideals and practices counter to the officially sanctioned ones. In contexts in which individuals are alienated from the political system, the politics of affection usually entail a rejection or bypassing of the institutional and the official.

Rather than a retreat from the public, the politics of affection coexist with formal politics and, in the Cuban case, permeate the public, blurring the border between them. They are functional insofar as they are a strategy to deal with specific challenges of modern life.[51] In settings in which social trust is weak, the politics of affection take a stronger hold because they appear as "real," "positive," "meaningful," and "pure," compared to the more institutionalized, impersonal, and detached social relations. They provide members with a sense of belonging and spirituality that is difficult to find elsewhere. Stuart Eisenstadt and Louis Roniger write, "The search for such pristine trust and intimacy and for real participation in pristine meaning, for pure dialogue, becomes most fully articulated in situations in which the potential for breakdown of the extension of trust develops, and in situations of transition from one institutional realm to another. . . . [T]his potentiality develops especially when such realms are structured according to different principles and entail dissimilar ways of interweaving trust, meaning and instrumental and power relations."[52] But the politics of affection are not exclusively an effect of social breakdown. Although these sorts of politics tend to erode institutional social rules and roles, they can facilitate their operation.

In the personal realm, alternatives and preferences are articulated. If access to the arenas of political decision making is unavailable or denied, particularly in closed regimes where the gap between promise and performance seems unbridgeable, the tendency is for the politics of affection to become a subversive force. Eventually individuals may want to formalize the informal and deprivatize the private by posing it as an alternative to the formal, staid public authority. The values underpinning the politics of affection would then become the moral basis with which to reconstruct power relations for society at large.[53] What James C. Scott has labeled "the hidden transcript" is developed in the private sphere of the politics of affection.[54] The hidden transcript captures the feelings of subordinate groups regarding their superiors and the political order. Elaborated among friends and trusted individuals, it remains undisclosed until the moment that someone dares speak truth to power. The infrastructure of the politics of affection, its networks, and its alternative worldview make the hidden transcript possible.

The process through which the hidden transcripts of the politics of affection becomes public is not inevitable or linear. Structures of opportunity — reduced risks and greater incentives — may in fact determine when the private becomes public, but one of the important dimensions of the politics of affection is that of serving as a depository of discontent and alternatives. As a consequence the politics of affection tend to have a corrosive impact on legitimacy, governability, and efficacy. Indirectly and slowly they contribute to a new order.

But the politics of affection are not necessarily or principally oppositional to the status quo. Networks of affection may sustain politics as usual. Clientelism, for instance, can arise as a backlash to the impersonal norms and bureaucracy of modern society and yet coexist with the "modern" political system.[55] It is not unusual for individuals to have dual allegiances to their family and friends, on the one hand, and to the society and the nation, on the other. Neither is it uncommon for them to assume double standards of behavior to deal with both sets of demands, as the Cuban case demonstrates. Moreover, the politics of affection provide the political system with flexibility, with a safe space for disaffection to be kept in check, and with mechanisms that allow for the provision of material and nonmaterial goods that the state does not supply. Precisely for these reasons, the incongruence between the politics of affection and institutional politics may coexist for long periods, especially if there is no institutional crisis or if the government is willing to resort to force if organized opposition emerges. Even facing breakdown, regimes can muddle through as the politics of affection remain circumscribed to the "private" sphere or coexist with political institutions without challenging them directly.

In sum, the politics of affection are part of the social capital of the society, but they can also erode social capital. They can contribute to stability and subvert it as well. They tend to render governability more difficult while facilitating the permanence of the system. These are the central paradoxes of the politics of affection, pointing to the need to explore in specific contexts how they manifest themselves, what their consequences are at particular moments, and what intervening factors determine the different outcomes.

The Politics of Passion

While the politics of affection are the stuff of private everyday life, even when they permeate the public sphere, the politics of passion are public and extraordinary. A specific cultural orientation to politics exists that charges issues with high intensity, contributing to what can be called the politics of passion. But the politics of passion are not merely a cultural construction of a given society. They are the expression of deep-seated foundational, material, and moral issues that elicit affective engagement. The politics of passion are both form and substance: they revolve around crucially important matters and are a way of conducting politics.

The politics of passion are defined by intense affectivity and personal engagement combined with a normative agenda driven by a moral imperative. They generally arise from potentially divisive "foundational" issues that establish the nature of the political community, who belongs to it, how it should be governed, and what its core of values should be. The politics of passion embrace the individual's and the collectivity's sense of self-worth, honor, and dignity. The politics of passion are usually motivated by codes of ethics and by normative frameworks influenced, at least indirectly, by religion.

The combination of personal affect and moral imperative makes politics passionate, rendering pragmatism, technopolitics, mediated solutions, and stability less tenable. The pursuit of moral absolutes imbues politics with idealism and intensity. The logic behind the idealism of the moral imperative is quite different from the instrumentalism of the politics of affection. But similar to the politics of affection, the normative search for absolute ends results in a situation in which individuals justify any means to pursue their "morally higher" ends.

The politics of passion conceive the political game as winner takes all, zero-sum. Their stakes are highest, not infrequently life and death, inclusion or exclusion from the political community, honor or dishonor. The absolute ends of the politics of passion demand social solidarity and rely on the convergence of the social with the political. Within the logic of the politics of passion, opponents are more than adversaries; they are enemies, traitors, evil, and inhuman. Loyal opposition is impossible; the middle ground is untenable. Passion, in this case, both polarizes politics and is an indication of the polarization of politics.

The methods of the politics of passion are varied, but they always resort to hyperattachments to symbols, myths, and values that carry with them an emotional and moral charge and a formidable affective impact on individuals. The principal instrument of the politics of passion is the language they speak. First, and above all, it is a language (both literal and symbolic) that people understand through personalization and affect. It makes sense because it is based on collective norms, aspirations, and symbols. It is authentic, employing cultural codes that do not necessarily translate intelligibly to outsiders. Second, it is a language that appeals to the senses as well as to the sense of social morality. People feel the language of the politics of passion; they feel it to be right or wrong. Third, it is the simple and comforting language of Manichaeism; good and evil are as easily distinguishable as night and day. No confusion is possible. The "we" is good; the "they" is evil. Inclusion in and exclusion from the community are determined by its logic. Fourth, it is teleological. The discourse of passion is simultaneously oriented to the past and to the future; like nationalism and religion, it often merges both. Although the politics of passion are grounded in the past, they chart the course for a utopian future that the community allegedly has always been destined for. Fifth, it is a metalanguage that provides meaning and identity to collective existence. Even when the specific issue at hand might not be an epistemological or ontological one, the language of the politics of passion addresses it as such. The politics of passion always speak the language of epic romance.

Communities in periods of crisis, redefinition, and transition from one order to another are especially susceptible to the politics of passion. Societies trying to redress a past injustice, especially if it relates to ethnicity, relations with an outside power, or the prevalence of an "imported" and therefore apparently inauthentic and immoral worldview, are prone to the politics of passion. The politics of passion are conducive to the emergence of charismatic leaders and are the medium of charismatic authority. While economic dislocation fans its flames, the politics of passion are culturally produced, reproduced, and experienced.

Affection and Passion Combined:
The Challenge to Governance and Civility

The politics of affection and the politics of passion combined render politics deeply affective. The coexistence of the politics of passion, with its logic of absolute moral ends for the collectivity at large, and the politics of affection, with its logic of hyperinstrumentality at the micro level of individuals and networks, is dangerous. The conjugation of both will tend to undermine governance by the nation-state. If prolonged, the combination will tend to produce an uncivil society in which pervasive personalism (with its implied exceptionalism) in social-political relations and high affectivity over issues will undermine civility, consensus, and official institutions. Legal equality and standard operating procedures are fragile in such contexts. The political stakes increase to the point that compromise is elusive. Such societies tend to manifest instability, corruption, mass politics, persecution of nonconformists, and support for charismatic authority. A strong state is usually necessary to impose order and control polarization and fragmentation. Uncivil societies are shaky foundations on which to establish democracy, for incivility tends to subvert compromise, negotiated solutions, and the possibility of a loyal opposition.

A strong state, however, is not a guarantee against the tendencies of incivility; nor does a strong state eliminate the politics of affection and passion. In authoritarian political systems the state itself is frequently the standard-bearer for the politics of passion. States, especially authoritarian and totalitarian ones, are frequently a product of passion, not only an instrument to abate political passion, and use passion to mobilize support. But, even when born of passion, states attempt to rationalize life and perform their functions in a bureaucratic and instrumental manner. The politics of passion and the politics of affection within and without the state pose a challenge to the state's ability to achieve its bureaucratic goals.

The combination of passion and affection is not always detrimental though. Both can contribute to the establishment of new social projects, including modern ones, as Chapter 3 shows. The instrumentality of the politics of affection can be conducive to political and economic innovation (particularly family businesses) and tends to accentuate the autonomy of social actors from the state. Cuban politics and society, as the next chapters show, have been caught between both these logics, with important consequences for the political system and the economy as well.[56]

Affection, Passion, and the Informal

The politics of affection and the politics of passion thrive in the informal, in the nonlegal, in the nonofficial institutional, in everyday social interaction. Although "informal," these relations and practices have their own "forms" depending on local material and cultural factors. Informality is found in all social settings, including bureaucratic institutional ones, but it does not conform to the norms of modern organizations. It exists behind the facade of standard operating procedures. Informal practices are part and parcel of what Victor Turner calls "liminal phenomena," at the boundary of institutional life.[57] Meanings are contested precisely at borders. Barrington Moore recognized the liminal nature of the relationship between rulers and ruled: "What takes place . . . is a continuing probing . . . to test the limits of obedience and disobedience."[58]

Most social sciences have neglected the liminal spaces and practices, the realm of lo informal, in the same manner in which they have omitted the emotions. Locating the emotions helps to uncover the informal and vice versa. Sociologists and anthropologists have studied key aspects of informality, for instance, friendship. Economists have turned their attention to the informal economy in the past two decades.[59] But with the exception of the literature on informal resistance[60] and patron-client relations,[61] political science has not incorporated the informal "basic stuff of social life" into general approaches to the discipline.[62] Informal groups and behavior intersect with the formal structures and roles of society: "We need to know how the formal roles are modulated by informal customs and practices and how far they feature in the meaning structure of peoples' everyday lives. Social science has an obligation to reiterate a study of everyday practice of social life with the commonly expressed theory of it."[63] To neglect the informal, therefore, is to disregard the origins of many of the practices that affect state-society relations and the embeddedness of individuals and institutions. To dismiss the informal is to miss the emotional, the heart of politics.

Conclusion

One of the weaknesses of traditional approaches to politics since the advent of modernity is that they do not take into consideration the emotional and the informal in everyday social relations and how they relate to the political. An approach that brings together political culture—with emotions included—and state-society relations can help to bridge the gap in the literature. But such an approach demands disciplinary eclecticism. Methods and readings ranging from anthropology (field observation) to the humanities (literary criticism and semiotics), from philosophy to popular culture and economics, must be used to study the emotions and the informal and their political significance. A measure of "disciplinary" informality is not only necessary but refreshing as well.

The study of politics with emotions brought in and out is a valuable approach on a number of counts. First, if we are interested in behavior, we should be concerned with what motivates it. Passion and affection motivate a good measure of social action and group formation. Second, passions and emotional reactions reflect and interact with the social-political "reality." They tell us about the state of affairs in a particular context and what people feel affectively and morally—what is meaningful to them. Third, the emotions are windows to political culture. Emotions are expressions of moral judgments. They reflect beliefs and the moral codes of the people and their society. Passions are expressed socially and culturally; their rationality is contextual. Different cultures have different emotional styles and different emphases in their emotional repertoire. Fourth, emotional responses are a way of coping with critical situations. Therefore, the study of politics with emotions considered is an especially valuable approach to crises and transitions. Passion and affection are contributing factors in constructing and destroying social and political order. Fifth, passions are rarely divorced from the exercise of reason. Passions and affections have their reasons, their power, and their instrumentality.

By incorporating the emotions, we are embodying the actor of politics fully, not partially. This approach allows for the subjective as well as the objective sources of behavior. Although the emphasis is on the emotions, the interpretation is not monocausal, for it highlights the interaction of the affective with the material and ideational and the individual with the institutional. The attempt is to rescue the liminal and place it, along with other factors, at the center of political analysis. By doing so, this political cultural approach with emotions brought in makes explicit what has been implicit and invisible for very long. As a conduit to the study of the nonofficial, which is at least as important as the official, the approach promises to shed light on the interrelationship between the formal and the informal by allowing us to understand what happens at the edges of state-society relations.

This approach integrates the micro with the macro; the "high" politics of the state with what has traditionally been called the "low" politics of society, although the hierarchy is not maintained in this book. The formal/informal dynamics of state-society relations, a theme that runs throughout the following chapters, reveal forces of change and continuity in political systems. However, one of the main challenges for modernists who approach politics from the perspective of emotions arises from the difficulty in establishing cause and effect (not to mention the problems associated with data collection). But this is also the advantage of the approach, for emotions are both cause and effect of politics. The relationship between the external structures and the individual's emotions is interactive.

We now turn to Cuban politics from the vantage point of passion and affection.

2

WITH
FEELING NOW

The Political
Culture of Cuba
Reconsidered

What are the sources of the politics of passion and affection in Cuba? How have they manifested themselves in the country's political culture, and how have they influenced political developments over time? What impact have they had on the society, the state, and the economy? I begin to address these questions by providing an overview of Cuban political culture with emotions considered. The politics of emotions reveal ways in which Cubans perceive and pursue politics as passion and affection and how these have been mediated by Cuban political culture, especially by *lo informal* and the material conditions on the island. The tension between the two modalities of the politics of emotions conspired to undermine many of the central projects of political modernity on the island. But the sociopolitical impact of the affective has not been exclusively corrosive. By the 1950s the politics of affection and passion laid the foundation for another modern project, revolution. The revolutionary state initially relied on the politics of passion and affection and later encountered the challenge they pose to institutions and policies.

Why have the two overarching political projects pursued in Cuba this century, liberal democracy and socialism, failed to meet expectations? Political culture and its emotional codes are partly responsible for the outcome, but only partly. A more complex and multicausal set of factors, domestic and international, economic and noneconomic, has contributed to the disappointing results of political modernity. In proposing a partial cultural answer to that question, I join an old intellectual tradition in the West and in Cuba.

For centuries Cuban intellectuals (at least since Father Felix Varela in the nineteenth century) have been voicing remarkably similar concerns about the problems Cuban culture poses to politics. Although I rediscover this critical intellectual tradition that became very pronounced in the early half of this century, my perspective is revisionist insofar as it focuses on political culture with a twist—the affective aspect of it, the passion and affection at the heart of Cuban politics—rather than on structural factors (such as the economy, class, or the relationship with the United States) or cultural factors devoid of feelings.

My discussion breaks with the canon in two other ways: it does not carry explicitly or implicitly a teleology of Cuban politics, and it argues that emotions have multiple effects both constructive and destructive of political order, not only negative ones as it is commonly presumed. By adopting this perspective, I question the modern divorce of feelings from reason and emotions from politics. The analysis points to the state's limits in controlling society and to the emotional subtext of social politics.

Cuban Political Culture: Three Paradigms in Tension

While the Cuban people have aspired to the project of political modernity since at least the nineteenth century—the creation of a nation, a state, and a civil society in the context of democracy—Cuban culture carries alternative normative and instrumental standards that collide with modernity. One of the most dramatic features of Cuban political history has been the chasm between the ideal and the real.[1] This chasm is not exclusive to the island, but why has it been so pronounced in its politics? The chasm has resulted from material constraints and from competing and coexisting political cultural frameworks among Cubans. Together three major cultural paradigms—the liberal, the corporatist, and *lo informal*—construed politics, on the one hand, as a moral crusade for absolute ends—the politics of passion—and, on the other, as a personal instrumental quest—the politics of affection. The politics of passion and the politics of affection are scripted into the political culture of the island in this fashion. They have been reproduced with slight variation over time depending on ideological, economic, and sociopolitical factors. Continuity is the predominant tendency though. The politics of affection and passion have defined the character of politics in Cuba. They are offshoots of the political and economic issues confronted in the process of constructing a nation-state. The politics of passion stem from one main source: moral judgments regarding the gap between what is and what ought to be in the political and social spheres.

The politics of affection are a product and the producer of the pervasive informality in the social sphere, and they reflect the weakness of formal institutions in addressing the needs of the Cuban people.

The tense coexistence and confluence of the liberal, the corporate, and the informal produced over time a particular manner of relating to the social and the political that, although typically Cuban, shared similarities with other areas of Latin America and the world. Modern liberal aspirations (and inspirations) have a long history on the island, dating back to the eighteenth and nineteenth centuries. Liberal ideology reached the island's shores from Europe and the United States, shaping the ways in which elites spoke and thought about the future of their country. Democracy and national sovereignty were the hallmarks of liberal ideals. Political modernity packaged a series of notions regarding the individual and "his" rights as well as projects for the society at large. Individual rationality and self-interest went hand in hand with the autonomy of social organizations in a free market economy. The modern liberal expression of political community was the sovereign state. The state would be the bureaucratic expression of the rationalization of modern life.

The central goals of political modernity proved to be intractable. Colonialism, and later neocolonialism under the tutelage of the United States, made sovereignty impossible well into the twentieth century. In practice other modern projects, such as liberal democracy and a civic-minded citizenry, did not live up to the norms prescribed by the paradigm either. Liberalism, nonetheless, imprinted the island's politics with a series of ideals to be pursued. The elusive nature of the quest would become evident immediately after independence (1902), throughout the Republic (1902–1959), and later under socialism (1959–present).

Modern aspirations came to naught because of their inherent idealism in conjunction with a host of economic, national, and international factors. Liberal values clashed with and were subverted by a corporatist cultural legacy. Based on the political philosophy of Saint Thomas Aquinas, among other Catholic thinkers, and with roots in Aristotle, corporatism was essentially monistic and patrimonial. The corporatist paradigm, a remnant of Spanish colonialism, endorsed the notion of law, order, stability, and elite leadership through a centralized bureaucratic authority—the state—that would rule over, and in coordination with, sectoral groups hierarchically and organically integrated. Each group had rights and responsibilities dictated from above. The state, along with the private sector, would play a defining role in the economy and would supply a modicum of goods to all. The economic paternalism of the corporatist state—with its implied concept of familial responsibility—influenced and continues to influence Cubans' expectations of the state. From this perspective, the state is a source of moral and economic benefits.

The ultimate purpose of corporatism was to safeguard social harmony in an effort to sustain a healthy body politic able to provide the "good" (i.e., moral, ordered, and prosperous) life as defined by theologians and moral philosophers. The state, therefore, was not only a moral construct but carried an explicit moral imperative as well. Idealism, reflected in universal ethical principles designed to create an earthly summum bonum, not the *plurum bonum* of the Protestant tradition, permeated the corporatist worldview. Corporatist utopianism provided a cultural foundation for politics as a crusade for moral absolutes, which the 1959 revolution pursued.[2]

The adoption of Marxism-Leninism as the official ideology of Cuba in 1961, two years after the triumph of the revolution, did not represent as big a cultural watershed as initially expected or hoped for by the leadership. The theoretical underpinnings of Marxism are not as far removed from other modern constructs as one would assume. Neither is Marxism in practice totally dissimilar from corporatism (i.e., in procuring mobilization through mass organizations, in valuing social harmony over individual self-interest, in promising a utopia). In Cuba Marxism-Leninism was able to rest on long-standing aspirations for modernization, social equity, order, and sovereignty (vis-à-vis the United States) and on the romanticism of Cuban political culture since the colonial era, later fostered by José Martí, the founding father of the nation. Marxism offered a material and moral utopia for the community at large. Although specific dimensions of political practice changed after 1959, the cultural bases of Cuban social politics sustained its traditional foundation, which rested on liberal, corporatist, and informal norms. The implementation of Marxism by a charismatic leader—whose authority derived in large measure from the politics of passion and affection, as the next chapter shows—provided continuity in political culture despite a change in official ideology and form of regime. The moral imperative and the instrumental logic of Cuban politics continued after the revolution, as did the informality of everyday life.

The Forms of *Lo informal*

Corporatism's emphasis on hierarchy, collective harmony, and regulation in society contradicts modern democratic notions (i.e., self-interest and the conflictual nature of social relations) and neglects the informal conduct of individuals in daily life. *Lo informal* is closer to a pattern of behavior (with its own logic, norms, vocabulary, economic rationality, and emotional infrastructure)

than to an explicitly articulated intellectual framework. Informality undermines the tenets of the first two paradigms by challenging institutional rationalization and regulation of life. Despite its sociopolitical importance, the
informal has been largely ignored because it is less visible and apparently
amorphous and thus difficult to study. But the informal has its own forms and
norms; *lo informal* can be considered an informal institution.

In Cuba *lo informal* was reproduced over time as a way of dealing with,
if not circumventing, the demands of the colonial regime to satisfy the material and nonmaterial needs of the self, the family, and the community. The
informal thus rests essentially on an affective rationality. African slaves, for
example, resorted to informal modes of resistance to carve out a space for
their own religious practices. Religious syncretism, in which Catholic saints
became identified with Yoruba counterparts, allowed slaves to conform out-
wardly to their masters' demands for piety while holding on to their own
beliefs. In a similar resort to informality, islanders participated in the black
market and personal networks in the informal economy at a time when the
Spanish Crown was attempting to monopolize trade. What I label *lo informal* is associated with what others call the Machiavellian dimension of Latin
American culture, identified by rebelliousness, localism, and lawlessness.[3]

Through time *lo informal* has assumed new modalities in response to
political and economic regulations, changing chameleon-like but not losing
its principal character. Informality does not clearly distinguish between the
affective and the rational as modern theories do. From the perspective of the
informal, the private is the basis for the public. It values the personal touch,
the role of person-to-person contact, and the bond of affection among family
members and friends above the impersonal norms of the state. What you feel
is real and immediate, not distant and abstract. The needs and desires of those
you know and love are more important than the principles of official norms
and institutions. People have hearts; institutions do not. Those you know and
love help to fulfill material interests, while the apersonal forces of the state are
unreliable at best and an obstacle at worst.

Informality is an epistemology and ontology of sorts based on personalism, on *simpatía* (likability), *confianza* (familiarity that leads to trust), and
ser buena gente (being a nice person). Its main tenet is personal exceptionalism and particularism due to affection. *Lo informal* is composed of groups of
individuals who know and like each other, the networks of affection through
which the politics of affection are manifested. These groups bring together
peers, superiors, and subordinates. Insofar as horizontal and vertical interaction is seemingly harmonious and patron-client relations are highly person-

alized, the networks of the informal resemble corporatism. But unlike corporatism and liberalism, the agents of the informal are the small group in the quotidian. Its tools are instrumental, flexible, partial, and ascriptive, although it has its share of moral and affective logic. Its sphere is the liminal.

Informality depends on the possibility of bending the rules and bypassing legal norms because I/you am/are special and real. Its capacity to rationalize each and every action on the basis that what is most important is to satisfy one's needs and those of our loved ones seems infinite. Precisely because of its immense capacity to justify what could be considered self-serving, the normative foundation of informal behavior usually suffers from civic myopia; it fails to see what is beyond the networks of affection and disregards in the process the significance of institutions for the common good. Although *ser informal* (to be informal) is not usually a positive trait in Cuban society, there is a benign appreciation or tolerance of it. Informality is commonly contrasted with the staid and the formal, the pedantic. The moral base of informality is personal exceptionalism, affection, love, and *ser buena gente,* which require spontaneity, flexibility, and relaxation of official norms to accommodate particular needs and wants. From the perspective of *lo informal,* love and affection should come first. This is a humanistic component—if limited to those one knows and cares about. The informal is thus intimately tied to the emotional.

Informality, and the pivotal role affection assumes in it, generates a particular worldview and specific ways of regulating social relations that do not conform to the rationalization of modernity. *Lo informal* renders life more manageable, tolerable, and malleable primarily by undoing the basis of ideal modern societies as postulated by theoreticians and presumed by officials of the state, although government officials are not exempt from its codes. The penchant for informality has been characteristic of Cuban political culture since the colonial era, marking the politics of the island with a distinctive flair.

The term "informal" has two main definitional variations: a state of being and a way of being. The first refers to things and the second to people. The first definitional nuance is the traditional one in the study of "informal" practices such as the black market (the informal economy). In Cuba, specifically, the second definition, to be "informal," means to be undisciplined, unserious, unreliable, a bit against the "proper" forms, amorphous. In both senses, *lo informal* is not unrelated to the *choteo* (mockery), a peculiar Cuban brand of humor.

The *choteo* is part and parcel of the informal "paradigm." Its comic peculiarity is that it targets authority, with the purpose of undermining hierarchy, order, and regularization, central values of corporatism and liberal modernity.

The *choteo* deauthorizes authority by debunking it and constitutes a form of rebellion. It is undisciplined, unserious, even if the business at hand is of the utmost importance. It reflects contempt for and cynicism about higher-ups and the institutions of society. In the world of the *choteo* individual exceptionalism and personal attachments are valued above the personal rules and distant norms of bureaucratic order. The purpose is to use humor as a way to privatize social relations by making them accessible, at least momentarily, by bringing the people and the institutions that stand above the common folk down to the level of the popular, of the streets, of "us." This is *choteo*'s equalizing effect.

The *choteo*, as dissected by Jorge Mañach, is a form of folk wisdom that goes hand in hand with quick wit, improvisation, and irrespectability. It is impressionistic, giving quick biting glances at reality. It shuns long-winded analysis of a situation, because it detests any excess of formality. In its form of social critique, emotional reactions constitute analytical deliberation and its judgment of the immediate world. The *choteo*'s impressionism can lead to precipitous and passionate, if not dogmatic, reactions.[4]

The *choteo* breeds jocular contempt for impersonal norms, the hallmark of modernity, as well as for ordinary people and leaders. The space of the *choteo* is social and public, for it always requires an audience of sympathetic ears who will understand the punch line and the sociocultural references. Above all, the *choteo* is an expression of disenchantment. Those who engage in it realize that nothing is totally sacred, believable, or honorable. The romantic idealism of Cuban culture finds a counterpoint in the *choteo*. Whether the *choteo* is the cause or the effect of public disappointment is not clear; it is probably a bit of both. While the political history of the island provides adequate material from which the *choteo* can craft its peculiar humor, the *choteo* contributes to the erosion of legitimacy of institutions and leaders. It renders social relations relaxed but guarded at the same time, because anyone can *chotear* (mock) as readily as they can be *choteado* (mocked).

Informality at the grassroots has a paradoxical impact on governance. While it establishes trust and collaboration among small groups of individuals and allows for the manifestation of divergent passions, interests, and identities, it undermines larger associations whose membership is not limited to personal contact. Some of the affective aspects and the networks of the informal are important to the foundation of a civil society. The seeds of civic "virtue" and civic associations are to be found in a similar emotional infrastructure of solidarity and trust. The challenge is how to translate the norms of the informal into ones that help to bind individuals into larger organizations and into community.

While informal practices are functional for those engaged in them (i.e., they provide satisfaction of needs, material and otherwise) as well as for the government (i.e., they reduce bottlenecks and less overt opposition), participation in the informal socializes individuals in a culture of illegality. It accustoms them to break the law and thus undermines the tenets of the regime and foments incivility. The logic of the informal is to obey when one has to—at least by keeping the appearances—and not to comply as often as possible. Since the informal is the terrain of the familiar and malleable, it offers a margin of autonomy for the individual, but its consequences can be noxious to the formation of a civil society. Informality tends to foster unregulated competition between groups and limit cooperation within small ones. The ramifications are many: difficulty in establishing a political community with equal rights for all, obstacles to the development of civil society, widespread anomic tendencies, and antagonism.

Informality may be seen as resistance to the state, but it is not always conscious resistance. As the next chapter argues, although informality has been present in both the democratic and the socialist periods in Cuba, its forms, intensity, and impact are different in each. The consequences of informality in both periods are basically identical: governmental efficacy and legitimacy are eroded and society exhibits tendencies toward incivility. Informality takes hold because it offers multiple ways of coping with the imposition of the state, the constraints of the economy, and the alienation of modern society.

Nation, History, and Emotion

Cubanidad (Cubanity) has a deep emotional current, as Anthony Maingot has pointed out.[5] The emotional charge in Cuban national identity stems from the juxtaposition of collective aspirations and realizations. The gap between the real and the ideal is a product of the normative clashes of Cuban political culture and the limitations imposed by the economy. From very early on in Cuban republican history, observers blamed the culture of informality and its emotions for the problems of Cuban society and politics. Cultural pessimism (or what can be called, in a more positive turn of phrase, "therapeutic critique," following Habermas) has an old genealogy in Cuban intellectual history. The initiator of this current was a theologian, Father Félix Varela, who contrasted what was with what ought to be. Varela admonished Cubans for their lack of civic interest. He claimed that only money and personal fulfillment motivated them. The tradition he initiated is imbued with a moral tone. It critically highlights those qualities of Cuban culture and *cubanidad* that undermine the normative aspirations the society seeks. Not all Cuban intellectuals, however, have defended the cultural pessimism argument. If the nation is narration, the narrative of Cuban historians is predominantly one of love and happiness tempered by the suffering of those who forged the national epic.[6]

It is hardly possible to separate emotion from nation as nationalism relies on the affective to create community. Scholars, particularly historians, helped to craft the sense of Cuba as a community of sentiment (using Weber's phrase); its history is deeply emotional. Cuban historians acted as nation builders, a self-conscious and self-appointed role that they share with many of their professional colleagues elsewhere. All the traditional historians begin their texts with exalted love for the motherland accompanied by the nostalgia of dreams deferred and the burdensome sorrow of a painful national experience. Given the internal and external difficulties associated with the construction of a nation-state, their passion and interest in fostering a shared feeling of nationalism were warranted. Factionalism, international interventions, economic dependence, and racial conflict threatened to fracture the nation and compromise the state.

Two standard texts of Cuban history reflect the emotional connection between nation and history. In the introduction to *Historia de la nación cubana* (History of the Cuban Nation), Ramiro Guerra y Sánchez and his coauthors narrate the epic of the island's devastating war of independence against Spain. In somber tones they write that the aftermath was so terrible that it "could not but move the strongest of souls and impress the human being of the most hardened heart."[7] Their prelude to the national saga is almost a ballad, a sad love song that turns gay later in the text with the advent of prosperity and electoral democracy by the 1940s. According to Guerra y Sánchez and his colleagues, Cuban history is the synthesis of "the anguish[,] . . . the sweat[,] . . . tears, [and] valor" of the Cuban people.[8] The historians were, in their own words, "motivated by imperious duty, intimately tied to a fervent desire" not only to recount the past but also to construct the future nation through "spiritual values that determine the constitutive essence of a fully defined nationality."[9]

In contrast to the influential group of cultural pessimists who wrote during the Republic, Cuban historians, regardless of ideological proclivity, celebrated the exceptionalism of the nation. Such was the case of Herminio Portell Vilá, who introduced his *Historia de Cuba* (History of Cuba) with the same heroic tone as Guerra y Sánchez et al., if more optimistic and *machista*: "[The Cubans are] a virile people . . . enamored of perfection . . . due to which at times they despair and criticize bitterly what are growing pains."[10] According to Portell Vilá, "The history of Cuba is dignified, stimulating, full of exemplary lessons and sufficient to build the future of a country admirably endowed to be happy, rich, free, and respectable." [11] The rhetorical inflation of Cuban nationalism was intensely romantic as it portrayed nationals defying the odds, conquering nature and external imposition (namely, colonialism and neocolonialism).

Although the romantic idealism of Cuban historians was tempered by the reality of a less than perfect national life, the lens that colored their view of the national experience was rosy. No other historian synthesized the teleology of Cuba as Portell Vilá did, but he was the first to acknowledge one of the darkly passionate undersides of *cubanidad*: the incidence of suicide throughout the island's political history. Recent historians, even those writing from revisionist and neo-Marxist perspectives, have continued to underscore the emotional underpinnings of Cuban history. Through their discourse the notion of nation as emotion and the vision of politics as passion have been transmitted to and reproduced (literally) in generations of Cubans whose views of the motherland it affected.

As a counterpoint, cultural pessimism has been articulated by the foremost intellectuals of the island, including Varela, Fernando Ortiz, and Mañach. While upholding an ideal view of what the nation should be, they criticized the failures of the national community rather than blindly singing its praises. After independence the pessimistic current was expressed from the first decades of the Republic through the 1940s and 1950s by a host of intellectuals representing a spectrum of political persuasions. Even an optimistic Catholic nationalist like Cintio Vitier concluded that one of the distinctive qualities of *cubanidad* was its impossibility, "Cuba como imposible" (Cuba as impossible). [12] Their portrayal of Cuba's social political landscape and the features of Cuban culture they highlighted have not lost their relevance, even though their attachment to modernist presumptions should not go unchallenged. Fidel Castro, the perennial optimist, has fallen in step with the cultural pessimists as time after time he has called on Cubans to transform their cultural habits, to develop *conciencia* (consciousness), to leave *chapucería* (shoddiness) and *blandenguería* (wimpiness) behind. Neither he nor the revolutionary state, in spite of the dramatic changes in public life and the vast mechanisms of co-optation and coercion, has been successful in transforming some of the cultural patterns of the people. Within the institutions of the state and the Communist Party one finds the traits that official pronouncements have attempted to eradicate. The state itself is not immune to culture. After all, what is the state if not a group of individuals who share a culture? The state is a product of Cuban culture—liberal, corporatist, and informal. It is the latter that presents the greatest challenge to law and order in society and to many of the tasks of the state. It is also in the informal where one finds the emotional codes of Cuban political culture.

The critical current paralleled sociopolitical crises on the island, specifically from 1902 to the advent of the revolution in 1959. It gave voice to widespread disillusionment, not with modernist ideals per se, but with the society that was unable to reach them. The unattainable ideals—national sovereignty, a virtuous republic, democracy, civility in public life, honest leaders, strong organizations, the rule of law—were not at fault, the people and their culture were. The initial discussions on the culture of *lo informal*, particularly during the first decades of the Republic, were directly connected to "the emotional character" of the Cuban people and their inability to form a modern polity. In the second decade of the Republic a social observer established a logical connection between indiscipline, political passion, and the absence of solidarity for common social projects: "The impulsive, exalted man who is dominated by passion is common in undisciplined countries, or at least it is in those countries where he finds the favorable medium to impose himself." Born out of "pessimism and inconformity," social indiscipline reflects the lack of solidarity among members of society, which leads to the failure of joint efforts.[13] The writer, influenced by modernity's rejection of the emotional, saw the affective as opposed to the rational; the irrational character of Cuban culture contributed to the demise of the nation-state.

In a similar vein, in 1914 Enrique José Varona, a noted Cuban scholar influenced by positivism, argued that the cause of "our" indiscipline was the exceptionalism exhibited by particular groups—what I call the politics of affection—and the mistrust of public authority: "Wherever, and for whatever reason, a part of the community grants itself superior rights, or even different ones, to those of the rest, there is no real and permanent solidarity there."[14] Six years later another observer highlighted the "vile passions of selfishness and pride and the able use of the masses for private ends" as one of the principal causes of "decay" of public life in Cuba. Officials would use "any type of weapon, regardless of how immoral it was," to achieve their own personal interest, usually profit. "Idealism disappears from public life. Vulgar materialism . . . is the guiding light of all public and private initiative."[15]

In 1940 Rafael Estenger, one among a group of remarkably talented and insightful intellectuals writing during the Republic in a series of *revistas* (journals), published an essay entitled "Cubanidad y derrotismo" (Cubanity and Failure). The essay encapsulated many of the ideas these scholars shared regarding the political culture of the island and its affective dimensions. In his essay Estenger posited that Cubans were more emotional than conceptual, accepting the traditional opposition between emotion and reason: "We give supreme value to the spontaneity of the affective. To be likable is magical among us, to the point of moving even the most hidden springs of public life. The sentiments, free of ancestral formulisms or deep convictions, represent for us the coordinating element of conduct, they direct and govern life." [16] Disrespect for institutional norms resulted in unbridled individualism ("every Cuban is an island") [17] and in the inability to form associations beyond those of the family and friends. Estenger argued that "the spirit of association cannot subsist when ideas in common and mutual goals are missing." He concluded, typical of political modernists, "Sentiments are anarchic by nature, if not tyrannical." [18]

According to Estenger, Cuban society lacked an ideology, a set of core beliefs that would guide the nation and shape the institutionalized norms that would regulate public life. Lack of national consensus and its institutionalization undermined civic spirit. The situation bred three social ills: *tuteo* (the informality implied in addressing someone you do not know well by the second-person singular *tú*, instead of the formal and more distant and respectful *usted*), *embullo* (eruptions of enthusiasm, short-lived pangs of interest, followed by disinterest), and *choteo*. These three forces corroded social life. Estenger concluded that "it is difficult to govern people who are set in the triple convergence of these anarchic factors." [19] The only solution to the predicament was to find directives for civic conduct.[20] As time would show, this was easier said than done.

Estenger was not the only social observer of the times whose arguments about social informality can be linked to the politics of passion and affection. Mario Guiral Moreno, writing in 1941, complained about the "undiscipline[,] . . . *el choteo*[,] . . . the informality, the sensualism[,] . . . the lack of civic values" that permeated Cuban society in the Republic.[21] As early as 1914 the same author had analyzed the problems confronting the young Republic and called for improved public behavior. He pointed to *el furor* (like *embullo*, it is a quickly dissipating burst of enthusiasm) that pushed Cubans to rush in support of any cause or fad just to see their short-lived enthusiasm end in pessimism, doubt, and pain as reality proved to be much less satisfying than expected.[22]

Years later Guiral Moreno admonished the destructive way in which Cuban political and cultural elites engaged in polemics. His description of this aspect of Cuban political culture resonates with the tenets of the politics of passion and affection: "Simple divergence in criteria about political or literary topics resulted in the opposing parties labeling each other with the harshest of epithets. . . . [F]requently personal matters surfaced between the polemicists, who in search of victory for their opinions, relied on weapons of last resort in the field of honor." [23] Intolerance for opposing points of view and the dishonor of the opposition became synonymous with Cuban politics. The notion of honor, which modern theorists expected to be replaced by the concept of merit, lends itself to "taking politics personally," instead of the depersonalization that allegedly characterizes modern polities.

Not all passionate exchange in public life was circumscribed to petty personal rivalries. On the contrary, issues of "honor" were associated with intractable social dilemmas usually imbued with moral overtones. Cuban politics was, on the one hand, a crusade for moral ends for the nation and, on the other, a campaign for personal aggrandizement, profit, and prestige. In the 1940s and early 1950s Eduardo R. Chibás, founder of the Orthodox Party who influenced many Cubans of his generation and younger leaders such as Fidel Castro, represented the first type of crusader. His emotionally charged attacks were moral judgments on the corruption that plagued public authority. Chibás's pursuit of absolute moral ends as an imperative to save the nation typifies the Cuban version of the politics of passion. His political style had long roots in Cuban history, most important in José Martí, and would continue well into the future.

The Codes of Passion

José Martí was not only the father of the Cuban nation but also the father of the politics of passion. He portrayed and embodied a vision of politics that is one of the intellectual sources of the problems that democratic practice has encountered on the island. Martí's political idealism, if not romanticism, which emphasized morality and unity above all—a remnant of corporatism— became an ill-suited basis on which to construct a liberal democratic form of government in which compromise among divergent interests and second-best solutions are unavoidable. The rhetorical inflation of what the nation should and would be laid the autochthonous intellectual roots of politics as passion. Martí's personal example of *numancia* (sacrifice through death) as he rode off to the battleground in an encounter with Spanish troops in 1895 reinforced the role model for future Cuban heroes.

The passionate bases of Cuban politics after 1902 were a product of the pervasive violations of the normative frameworks on which the Republic was supposed to stand. Leaders and citizens reacted emotionally, that is, with judgmental intensity, because they perceived the sociopolitical situation as "immoral." Politics came to be perceived as a crusade to save the nation. While society at large aspired to a higher level of moral political order, in its daily practice social actors undermined their lofty collective aspirations. The particular "Cuban" way of relating to politics as a crusade rested on what can be labeled "the codes of passion." These codes are a set of cultural motifs running throughout Cuban political history. Based on a moral imperative for a better, if not utopic, political community, the codes of passion are essentially romantic norms of conduct, influenced by the Spanish cultural legacy, that carry an intense emotional and moral charge.

Nelson Valdés has uncovered four important codes in Cuban political culture that fall into the category of what I label "the codes of passion."[24] The first is the generational theme in Cuban political history. Younger generations have been perceived as the embodiment of courage, idealism, and purity of heart. As such they were expected to regenerate the island's political system, shedding the vices of the past. The young would save the nation; they would construct the moral community Martí envisioned.

The second code is a complex moralism-idealism syndrome in which politics are perceived as a matter of honor, duty, and dignity. Aristocratic norms of behavior are the basis of political behavior. Pragmatism seems crass; compromise is understood as unmanly weakness. In pursuit of righteousness one cannot be satisfied with anything less than total victory. From this perspective, to be uncompromising is a sign of one's superior conviction and strength of character.

Third is the concept of betrayal that has played a decisive role in Cuban history and culture. Betrayal implies that loyalty and truth are absolute and admit no deviation, notions that are central to the politics of passion. Any opposition is disloyal. The integrity of the group and its aims must be absolute. These standards lead to extremism, polarization, and the unacceptability of compromise, resulting in the fourth code of passion: the politicization of Thanatos. The willingness to die for political ideals is understood as the highest manifestation of altruism and moral conviction. This helps to explain not only political violence in moments of crises but also the frequency of suicide as politics by other means.[25]

These codes underscore a political culture characterized, on the one hand, by high personal affectivity and, on the other, by a moral imperative, two competing logics meshed uncomfortably. The scope of the two diverge. The first, the politics of affection, focuses on the level of the individual, the local, and the micro, whereas the second, the politics of passion, is universal, metacosmic, and macrocosmic. Moral projects for the community at large co-exist with a logic of instrumental means at the personal level—the province of the informal and the affective—that undermines the tenets of the collective pursuits. The conflict between the logics and the paradigms they represent—the normativity and rationalization of modernity, the corporatist emphasis on order, and the "everything goes" instrumentality of informal personal rela-tions—leads to loss of faith in the big projects of the modern state and results in national flagellation and anomie.

The pursuit of lofty goals in an emotionally charged crusade is the im-perative of the politics of passion. The instrumental logic of the informal where anything goes is the wherewithal of the politics of affection. Although they seem to run counter to each other, in fact they also are codependent: one needs the other. The more the informal undermines ideals, the more press-ing is the moral imperative for absolute ends, the greater the likelihood that those engaged in the politics of passion will also resort to the logic of infor-mality and the networks of the politics of affection to achieve their ends, in the process tarnishing their collective moral quest. Cubans tend to resort to instruments of everyday life associated with the politics of affection to pursue the moral goals of the nation. Their social and political practice combines a moral quest with an instrumental logic in which the ends justify the means. Such a combination will always result in less than ideal outcomes as one has to compromise standards to achieve the ultimate goals.

The Emotional in Context

The cultural tendency toward informality and affectivity is not per se the only reason that Cubans behave in a manner in which emotions, affection (and dis-affection), and passion loom large in the island's politics. Throughout Cuban history, local, national, and international politics and economics have had an immediate impact at the personal level and have propelled the politics of emo-tions. Politics have been relevant in daily matters as well as in foundational ways. Whether the nation had sovereignty or not, whether roads and hospitals were built or the money from the treasury disappeared into the pockets of the politicians in power, whether political manifestation ended with the death of a loved one, politics hit close to home. You could feel politics because they re-volved around day-to-day issues of material import as well as matters of iden-tity. The immediacy of these issues is characteristic of societies in the midst of defining political community as well as those dealing with the growing pains of state building and economic modernization.

Issues of immediacy lend themselves to the politics of affection—who you know and who cares about you can help to satisfy your material and non-material needs. In a similar manner, when confronting foundational issues people resort to affective attachments (and hyperattachments) to national ideals. If those ideals prove unattainable, as they have in Cuba frequently, individuals and groups will express moral indignation through their emotions. Emotional reactions are understandable when people face such vital questions, especially if the desired (and moral) outcome is derailed. As the next chapter explains, in Cuba's case the disorientation associated with constructing the national political community and its ruling authority was exacerbated, on the one hand, by the lack of consensus on core ideas as to whether the nation should be annexed to the United States, autonomous from (but still linked to) Spain, or independent; and, on the other, by the weakness of instrumental-functional ways of implementing those alternatives. The plantation economy, with its hierarchical and inequitable class structure, seasonal employment, and foreign control (until the 1940s), posed an additional obstacle to the creation of political consensus and community. Rapid economic growth in the 1920s and in other periods, rather than ease social tension, accentuated them by making socioeconomic cleavages more pronounced.

International factors contributed both to the politics of passion and to the politics of affection. Spanish colonialism (until 1898) and U.S. neocolonialism in the form of U.S. tutelage rendered Cuban sovereignty a chimera for years. The United States represented and presented a "moral" model that, try as it may, Cuba could not copy.[26] The politics of passion were fueled by the frustration of sovereignty and the inability to establish a virtuous republic. The politics of affection were in part a response to the imposition of regulations by both imperial powers and, later, the national state. The next chapter examines in detail the structural context in which the politics of passion and affection unfolded and the interrelationship among the affective, the political, and the economic throughout the twentieth century.

Conclusion

Cuban political culture is a mix of divergent paradigms, each with its own standards, its own powerful logic, and its own pull and each in contradiction to the others. Political-cultural eclecticism is not the exception in Cuban culture; it is the rule. Eclecticism is typical of Cuban art and architecture, partly because the island was a crucible in which many crosscurrents and ethnicities converged, more or less forcefully. The logical tension among liberalism, corporatism, and *lo informal* leads to untenable theoretical and practical dilemmas. Lofty goals of modernity prove unreachable, not only because of their intrinsic idealism, but because they convey patterns of conduct and values that go against those prescribed by the other paradigms.

Collectivities and individuals respond emotionally as the gap between what should be and what is widens, as the Cuban case shows. The emotionally and morally charged crusade to redress the gap fuels the politics of passion. The irony is that the Cuban people, although disenchanted, do not abandon totally their aspirations for a new and improved polity and yet continue to act in everyday life in ways detrimental to the normative models they so desire. While seeking in the informal sphere and through the informal practices of the politics of affection satisfaction for immediate needs and wants, they also pursue the utopia implied in the politics of passion. The crusade for state sovereignty, democracy (or socialism), and civil society combined, all modern goals, has coexisted with the struggle for such corporatist values as order, regulation, harmony, and a moral community. Leaders and followers pursue both modern liberal and corporatist ideals that resonate with the collective goals, but at the social level of everyday life individuals and groups act in informal ways that subvert both sets of ideals.

The Cuban people have been caught in the tug-of-war of competing ontologies and epistemologies. Part of the problem is the inherent weakness of the model of modernity devoid of affect, not a shortcoming of society per se. What is perceived as "ineptitude" at political maturation is really alternative norms in which the emotional is valued in part because it is instrumental. By refusing to accept the distance between the public and the private, by making the public familiar, and by personalizing the seemingly impersonal, the informal and the politics of passion and affection challenge modern notions of rationalization of social life. The operative and normative standards of the emotional dimension of political culture are at odds with the modern logic of reason, cost-benefit analysis, and the rationalization of life.

Cultural and material factors have given Cuban politics a strong emotional foundation over time regardless of governments and regimes. The politics of affection and passion have been played out at both the elite and the social levels. They have coexisted with an attempt to regularize and institutionalize the political system of a modern nation-state. But democracy and civil society have been elusive quests, partly due to the impact that the politics of emotions have had on state-society relations. Although *lo informal* has undermined modern aspirations, it is a valued social epistemology and ontology, one in which affection and passion are not only accepted but cherished as well. Modern aspirations have not been able to dissipate the emotional, and they will be unable to do so for a number of reasons. First, individuals need "enchantment" in their lives, not only institutional-rational and instrumental mechanisms. Second, even modern notions such as nation contain an emotional subtext. In social life one cannot escape from the affective. And third, affection and passion are ways of judging the world and bases for decisions and choices, probably as good as any other standard.

Informality and the political culture of emotions have had multiple impacts on modern projects in Cuba—be they liberal democracy or socialism— as the next chapters show. The politics of emotions helped to mold order and disorder on the island since colonial times. The relationship between emotions and politics is intimate; its results are paradoxical. Yet the emotional and the political can never be divorced.

3

EMOTIONAL POLITICAL HISTORY

Cuba in the
Twentieth Century

This chapter offers a rereading of Cuban politics from the independence movement in the nineteenth century to the 1990s with emotions considered in an attempt to uncover the heart of Cuban politics. To understand Cuba's political history, particularly from the perspective of the protagonists, one should feel it. In the following account I attempt to do just that by imbuing the past with the passion and affection of the principal and supporting actors. To that end I rely on documents that reveal the general political climate as it relates particularly to the politics of passion and affection in specific historical contexts. This is not an exhaustive historical retelling. Instead I provide chronological highlights of the interplay of politics, society, economics, and culture with feeling now.

From the establishment of the Republic in 1902 to the end of the twentieth century, politics in Cuba reveal the repetitive point and counterpoint of the politics of passion and affection: the collective pursuit of absolute moral ends and the persistence of an instrumental logic that justified the satisfaction of personal wants through networks of affection at the everyday level of social life. National aspirations have remained rather constant over time. They have been, and continue to be, primarily modern ones: sovereignty, democracy (with order, honesty, justice, and a level of equity for all), economic growth through industrialization, and social welfare; in short, modernization. Informality and the politics of affection as a way of behaving socially continued to manifest themselves while assuming different modalities over time.

The politics of passion and affection are not innate, natural predisposi-
tions. Rather they have been culturally constructed and reproduced over time
by Cubans of all social strata—from top leaders to scholars, from journalists
to housewives. They intersect with structural factors, economic and political, national and international; in the process, the material and the ideational
helped to constitute each other. The structural challenges the country faced
fueled both the politics of passion and the politics of affection. And the norms
of passion and affection framed the issues, served as lenses through which
Cubans interpreted their reality, and provided tools to address it. Passion and
affection help to explain why certain choices were made and certain strategies
were adopted, as well as their consequences.

The politics of passion and affection undermined the institutional procedures that prescribed how the modern state should function and the civility
that should characterize social relations in the public sphere. Combined they
have contributed to the leitmotiv of Cuban history: frustration. But the politics of passion and affection have also energized groups in Cuban society that
sought a new Cuba. The passion behind Cuban politics is to be found in the
normative constructs of modernity, in the utopianism of corporatism, in the
romantic codes of the political culture, and in the urgency of issues confronted
in the process of nation and state creation. Politics came to be perceived as
a crusade to create and, later, save the nation, materially and spiritually. The
structural factors that limited the attainment of such lofty goals heightened
the passion of the pursuit at the same time that they pushed individuals to
seek informal ways to satisfy material needs. Passion was not divorced from
interest, though. More often than not competing passions merely indicated
competing interests. The intensity of the objectives pursued reflected the significance of the ends sought. These were deeply political and moral questions
relating to the nature of the national community: power and authority, meaning and identity, inclusion and exclusion, and distribution of benefits. In short,
what was just? The networks of affection provided the initial infrastructure
for those would-be agents of change (who in turn tended to resort to the cultural codes of passion and affection characteristic of the past). Change and
continuity played out simultaneously as reflected in the variegated modalities
of the politics of passion and affection.

The Passion for Independence

The politics of passion and affection had their initial expression under Spanish colonialism and during the separatist effort after the mid-nineteenth cen-

tury. The quest for Cuba Libre (Free Cuba) became a quasi-religious crusade in which the ends justified the means. Colonized by Spain in 1493, Cuba remained under the Spanish Crown until 1898. That year, as the result of the Spanish-American War, the island became a protectorate of the United States. Twice in the nineteenth century Cuban nationalists attempted to gain freedom from the mother country. Although on both occasions the Cubans failed in their objective, the two independence wars (1868–1878; 1895–1898) were the most destructive in Latin American history. The scorched earth policy adopted by the insurgents, the Spanish policy of *reconcentración* (relocation of villagers to controlled areas), and the intransigence of both sides were harbingers of the extremist tendency that would characterize much of the island's politics in the years to come. The most laudable end (self-government) justified the most sinister means (economic devastation and total war). The codes of passion and the logic of their corresponding politics played out during the independence struggles. Yet on both occasions the costly efforts ended in frustration for the rebels. Not all Cubans, however, were unhappy with the outcome.

The islanders were divided into three main tendencies: those who supported independence, the reformers (or autonomists) who proposed greater autonomy vis-à-vis Spain short of formal separation, and those who advocated annexation to the United States. The autonomists achieved their goal after 1878, but it proved to be short-lived. The annexationists (generally wealthy sugar estate owners) were not displeased with the failure of the anticolonial struggle or with the tepid results of *autonomía* (autonomy), for they preferred to replace Spain with the United States rather than see Cuba independent. Some annexationists were democratic populists who saw union with the United States as a means to achieve progress and democracy.

By the 1890s *autonomía* was discredited as the Spanish Crown did not grant the islanders much room to conduct their own affairs. In 1895 a second armed insurrection erupted. The outcome of the second independence war was particularly bitter as U.S. military intervention turned the tide at the last moment. Washington had declared war against Madrid when the president and Congress blamed Spain for the explosion of the *Maine,* the ship sent to the Havana harbor to protect U.S. interests and display U.S. power. U.S. intervention not only foreclosed the possibility of a Cuban victory over Spanish forces but also shut the door, at least temporarily, on sovereignty. Several Cuban generals were so disillusioned with the situation that they opposed laying down arms and unsuccessfully proposed to turn them against the U.S. occupying forces.

The anticolonial struggle, whether through the peaceful means of *autonomía* or through the violent ones of the battlefield, was the first taste of disenchantment that Cubans were to experience, not the last. To the chagrin of many, the national epic ended in bitter anticlimax. Louis Pérez captures the sacrifices the rebels made, their commitment, and their ensuing disappointment: "Dedication to Cuba Libre was more than a duty to a cause, it was a devotion to a faith. And to the faithful, no loss was too much. . . . The ranks of *independentismo* were crowded with Cubans who had sacrificed personal fortunes, lost private property, and abandoned professional practices to make Cuba free."[1] The politics of passion were compelling Cubans to give their all in the hope of a better tomorrow in a moral community: "All expected independence to produce a new society: land would be restored, property returned, and economic opportunity assured. Instead, they discovered that during their toil for independence, the control over resources, property, production, and the professions had passed irretrievably into the hands of others."[2] The affective intensity of the political quest for nationhood demanded material investment and carried with it economic aspirations for the future. The imperative behind independence was both moral and economic, or, to phrase it differently, carried its own sense of moral economy. Passion and interest—or better still, passion/interest—went hand in hand even as personal fortunes were lost along the way.

Passion and Affection in the Republic (1902–1959)

Although the U.S. protectorate lasted until 1902, after a convention ratified a republican constitution for the island nation, Cuba did not become formally sovereign until three decades later. The U.S.-imposed Platt Amendment, attached to the 1902 Constitution, allowed Washington to intervene in Cuban domestic affairs whenever it deemed necessary. Formal sovereignty had to wait until 1934 when the Platt Amendment was abrogated. Statehood was not the only modern project that did not match expectations. Nationhood met a similar fate. From 1902 to 1959 the life of the Republic was tumultuous, culminating in revolution. Republican democracy fell prey to disenchantment as the politics of affection and passion undermined the pillars of democratic governance. Paradoxically, through the politics of passion an alternative vision for the political community was articulated that compelled Cubans to revolution.

While passion provided the overarching vision for the "independent" Republic, the politics of affection exerted their influence in informal everyday life, subverting the normative democratic project. The Republic was inaugurated by a joyous civic march from Oriente to Havana led by the first elected president of the new Cuba, Don Tomás Estrada Palma (1902–1906). In Marifeli Pérez-Stable's words, the march "constituted a truly national and foundational performance, which signaled not only the 'alegría inefable de tanto sacrificio, tanta sangre derramada, tantos hogares divididos' [ineffable happiness of so much sacrifice, so much bloodshed, so many homes divided], but also the essentially modern challenges the young republic faced."[3] Thousands of Cubans of all socioeconomic strata met the president along the route, cheering "Viva la República."

The impact of the politics of affection came early on in republican life. In 1906 Estrada Palma, supported by a coterie of friends and associates—the network of the politics of affection—sought reelection even though the official party opposed his candidacy. Confronted with opposition, Estrada Palma created a personal political machine, reinforcing a tradition in Cuban republican politics in which parties and other associations of political and civil society constituted instruments for the pursuit of personal objectives. The turmoil Estrada Palma's actions caused, including his request to Washington to send in the Marines, ended with a second U.S. intervention (1906–1909).

From the initial years of the Republic, a peculiar mix of the politics of passion and affection became symptomatic. Relations between political leaders were characterized by mistrust.[4] Loyal opposition was absent. While the state was based on general liberal democratic norms and pursued economic and political modernization, much of everyday politics was defined by personal aspirations rather than programmatic agendas in support of collective goals. Cliques dominated political parties and state institutions, such as the armed forces. Electoral campaigns meshed the politics of passion and the politics of affection as they became battles between men in which the winner took all the spoils. Several years of republican life led an observer to conclude,

The party man is a dangerous man: for he resorts to lies, injustice, violence, fanaticism and any tool available, regardless of how immoral it may be, as long as he wins. . . . The forms of struggle provoked by the spirit of partisanship engender mutual antipathy and reciprocal hate between the participants. The battle between parties, instead of being about ideas and opinions, is transformed in a purely personal conflict, in which one hurts and usurps the power of the opponent, his position and his honor. . . . And a deathly particularism emerges, a deep separation of the national body . . . ; important national ventures die, frequently, due to the corrosive effect of disaggregation.[5]

The nation's problems were perceived as stemming from politics, with their personalistic and passionate characteristics destructive of social harmony, democracy, and progress. More than one observer agreed that passionate personalism undermined the Republic: "Political passions impeded an accord regarding the person who should assume the reins of the government. . . . The Republic had failed due to the intransigence of its own sons."[6] The nation needed moral order.

U.S. occupation did not resolve the deep-seated problems of the Cuban polity or placate the emotionally charged politics. On the contrary, it exacerbated the challenges associated with nation and state building by handicapping leadership formation and national institutions, accentuating cleavages, and fostering a mentality of dependence. During the first decades of the Republic, and after the withdrawal of the U.S. military in 1909, the distinguishing features of public life were electoral fraud, corruption, personal aggrandizement, and a fractious and uncivil political and civil society incapable of either producing a loyal opposition or making leaders accountable for the honest conduct of the public sphere. Concern for the honest conduct of public life never succumbed to the grim reality though. The moral imperative became urgent.

In a 1913 analysis of the causes and effects of the pessimism that enveloped public life, José Sixto de Sola argued that the notion of the colonial factory continued to operate under the Republic. According to him, after independence the state continued to be perceived as a source of extraction of goods, this time for individuals at the top of the political and economic ladder, as it once was for the Crown: "Social and political pessimism is a weed that grows with extraordinary abundance, at times surprisingly so, in our national soil. . . . [M]ost commonly, pessimism is produced by fatigue; those who have fought for many years in search of an ideal, when it seems to be near, notice the defects of the work. . . . [T]hey lose hope, and they fall into pessimism."[7] But Sola reminded his fellow Cubans that the Republic's achievements were not insignificant; a better future could be erected on them. Confronted with pessimism, Sola responded with passionate optimism.[8]

The opportunistic, materialistic, and instrumental dimensions of Cuban politics, part and parcel of the politics of affection, were encapsulated in a 1916 book, *Manual del perfecto fulanista* (Handbook of the Perfect Opportunist), by José Antonio Ramos. Echoing Varela, the author chastised the lack of civic responsibility of businessmen, political leaders, and Cubans in general. Presidents had no clear agenda; the public only desired material gain. In their pursuit of personal gain and power, Cubans were more passionate than logical, Ramos concluded, falling into the traditional dichotomy typical of most social observers of the times. He proposed to save the Republic by sustaining politics on reason, not on emotions.[9] Much to the chagrin of Ramos and others, emotions continued to move Cuban politics in destructive and constructive directions. The more elusive the moral Republic that José Antonio Saco, one of the founding fathers, and Martí dreamed of, the more pressing the quest became. Younger generations, intellectuals, and assorted groups (e.g., the Veterans of the Independence Wars) hurled the banners of morality and emotional/moral judgments. What could be conceptualized as a social movement rallied around the politics of passion throughout the republican years.

The politics of affection did not disappear. On the contrary, they became quite functional, expressing their own affective rationality that must be understood within the material context of the young Republic. Harsh economic reality was a fertile ground for the politics of affection to flourish, and with them a host of consequences. For middle-sector Cubans, the state and access to it represented a source of economic security in a volatile environment in which foreign capital had acquired the upper hand. Political power came to be equated with economic power: "Means became ends."[10] The struggle over government was instrumentally carried out through the networks of the politics of affection. The effects were not exclusively pernicious, as the process facilitated the creation of a middle class and capital accumulation.[11] Graft, an integral part of the informal and the politics of affection, was widespread. *La botella* (the bottle) was Cuban slang for the "chronic evil" that plagued the Republic[12] as hundreds of friends or friends of friends of those in power received public salaries without working for the state. *La botella* was not the only informal deal that relied on networks of associates to defraud the public. *Los chivos* (the goats), another colloquialism typical of the lexicon of the informal, referring to underhanded business dealings using state funds, enriched many.

The economic boom generated by sugar in the 1920s not only supplied the necessary funds for bribes and graft, it also financed a growing industrial sector, unmatched in the rest of the region. Economic growth produced a sizable elite, a relatively strong middle class, a magnificent capital city, and many other achievements that enhanced the image of Cuban exceptionalism. By Latin American, and even world, standards Cuba's economic development was among the top ranks well into the twentieth century. The Cuban state became a siphon for public moneys to pass into private hands. Administration after administration was accused of corruption, which is not unusual in the course of modernization. Corruption was a source of capital accumulation that contributed to economic growth.[13] Despite its logic and potential benefit, these practices came with a social cost. In the minds and hearts of many Cubans, most politicians were *unos ladrones y unos descarados* (an unprincipled bunch of thieves). Moral leadership was needed.

Material attainment was insufficient to appease the Cuban people. Development, uneven as it was, did not translate into political modernization or social peace. Racial inequality combined with economic inequity continued to be a source of potential and real conflict, as the 1912 armed rebellion by blacks showed. Honesty, morality, and social equity mattered.

The instrumental base of Cuban politics did not always mesh well with the ideals behind a better Cuba. Intellectuals and veterans led the attacks against the condition of public life on the island. Fernando Ortiz, a reformist intellectual who assumed the leadership of the Junta Cubana de Renovación Nacional (Cuban Coalition for National Renewal), was among those sounding an alarm regarding the economic and political ills that afflicted republican society. In defense of the critical posture he adopted in the 1924 essay, "La decadencia cubana" (Cuban Decadence), he claimed that "it is not antipatriotic to recognize the weaknesses of our national life" as he condemned the "public consciousness of impunity" characteristic of political leaders in the country.[14] Universal rule of law did not exist; the powerful were exempt from punishment. Congress would periodically pass amnesty laws to absolve members who committed legal misdeeds. The fatherland was in crisis, Ortiz wrote. The result was "an evident and fatal weakening of popular faith in republican institutions."[15] In another essay Ortiz argued that the "foolishness [of political leaders] is our civil death . . . which we punish with the most implacable arm: *el choteo,* without thinking that this is a double-edged sword typical of countries that lack other more noble, more civilized, and more dignified arms."[16] Intellectuals, students, and army veterans assumed the vanguard in a struggle in which moral renovation became a form of nationalism. U.S. official involvement in Cuban politics was perceived to be proportionate to Cuban political malfeasance; honest government at home would keep the United States at bay.[17]

By the early 1920s politics were perceived as an ill in need of a cure, specifically after the embarrassingly corrupt administration of Alfredo Zayas (1920–1924). President Gerardo Machado (1925–1933), a reformist nationalist, claimed he had the solution to the problem. After a successful first term in office, he inaugurated a dictatorship under the aegis of *cooperativismo.* The strong support he enjoyed from followers who "deified him" facilitated Machado's 1928 decision to abolish the organized opposition to his regime and undo the Constitution, another example of the politics of affection and passion combined.[18] *Cooperativismo* echoed corporatism in more ways than mere alliteration. Machado sought a formula that would incorporate new social actors emerging in a developing Cuba at a time when the Great Depression was hitting the island that would allow him to remain in power indefinitely. *Cooperativismo* was the answer. Machado co-opted a broad reformist social movement of workers and various sectors of the middle class who were becoming increasingly active, but he was unable to silence the opposition and resorted to force. As state violence increased, so did resistance to the regime.

The movement to oust Machado, although driven by the desire for a virtuous Cuba, revealed many of the problems of public life on the island: fragmentation of groups, violence, political gangsterism, and the mingling of the armed forces in politics. Cliques, led by a leader or two and composed of armed followers, were not uncommon and would continue to exercise their influence well into the last years of the Republic. Such networks were the modus operandi of the politics of affection while pursuing the politics of passion. The lack of consensus, the incivility, and the inability of political society to forge and comply with acceptable democratic rules of the game had become chronic.

The Machadato ended with what has been called the revolution of 1933. The dictatorship collapsed under the combined force of economic crisis, popular pressure, and increasing state violence. But ultimately it was a group of sergeants, Fulgencio Batista among them, in association with civilian politicians and students, that forced Machado from power. After the dictator's fall, a process of political and economic reforms led by civilians ensued with the purpose of forging a "new Cuba," democratic and sovereign. Reforms were greeted with popular approval, but U.S. opposition thwarted the process. The alliance between Washington and segments of the military determined the course of events, forestalling the movement for social change. The "revolution of 1933" was not without success though. Significant portions of the economy passed into Cuban hands as a result of legislative action, and relations with Washington were redefined in principle (not necessarily in practice) as the Platt Amendment was abrogated.

In spite of its considerable achievements, the revolution of 1933 became known as the aborted or frustrated revolution because it did not fulfill the aspirations of either reformers (middle-class nationalists) or radicals (socialists and communists). The post-1933 Republic soon fell prey to the same incivility, personalism, corruption, and fragmentation of the past. The politics of affection once again undermined expectations of what Cuban political and civil society would bring. The politics of passion continued to exert their influence, especially among a new generation of leaders that would erupt onto the national scene in the years to come. Joven Cuba (Young Cuba) was emblematic in this regard. Formed by younger Cubans who had rejected electoral politics, Joven Cuba endorsed armed struggle against the "old Cuba" to create the new one. Their dream of revolution would have to wait two decades.

The revolution of 1933 eventually produced one of the few moments of national consensus on the island: the Convention that drafted the Constitution of 1940. The document was, and in some quarters still is, widely acclaimed as the epitome of national ideals. The Constitution drew its support from the fact that it promised "everything"—material and nonmaterial—to "everyone." Its strength was also its weakness. Each social sector and political tendency was awarded something. The combination of foundational text with a legislated wish list (regarding salaries, vacation time, and maternity leave, among many other items) was precariously fragile. The more specific the Constitution was, the greater the likelihood that it would be treated like any other piece of legislation and eventually challenged. The devil was in the details. Moreover, the Cuban state, like the socialist one years later, was setting itself up for failure by making promises—usually of an economic nature—that it could not keep, due in part to the structural limitations that dependence on sugar places on the Cuban economy.[19]

In the final analysis the Constitution of 1940 was typically Cuban. It reflected both the impossibility of bringing the political community together without distributing material and sectoral privileges—much in line with corporatism and the instrumental logic of the politics of affection—and the idealism/moralism characteristic of much of Cuban politics. While the Constitution of 1940 is cherished for its normativity and its inclusiveness, the less well known *intrahistoria* (inner history) of rivalries, acrimony, and divisions behind the scenes of the Constitutional Assembly reflected aspects of the island's political culture and was indicative of what was to come after the euphoria of 1940 subsided.[20]

Elected freely and under the beloved Constitution of 1940, President Ramón Grau San Martín (1944–1948), who had served temporarily after Machado's ouster, more than any other head of government up to that point embodied the desire for honesty and social responsibility in the conduct of public affairs. Cubans soon were disappointed. Grau San Martín proved not to be the man who would deliver a moral political nation. In spite of the period's highly charged nationalism, corruption continued to undermine public trust in government. The Grau San Martín and later the Prío Socarrás (1948–1952) administrations did not break the tradition of graft. Failure (or unwillingness) to rid public institutions of *amiguismo* and fraud left the Republic morally bankrupt. *Gangsterismo* in the university and throughout civil society undermined democratic practice and civility. Once again the expectations of most Cubans were dashed as the passion for Cuban republican virtue, undermined by the politics of affection, was more an illusion than a reality.

Economic growth during the Republic was not unrelated to the politics of affection and to extensive informality in Cuban society. The norms of *lo informal* were conducive to the formation of small family businesses and to a thriving entrepreneurial spirit that relied on flexibility, personal connections and charm, and instrumental logic to maximize profits. Informality and its networks, while detrimental to the conduct of state regulations, fostered qualities supportive of capitalism. Although the island's economy grew, the same cannot be said about the Cubans' ability to run their government in an efficient, "rational," and "modern" manner. Cubans were caught between competing paradigms. They wanted a leadership and a state that would supply the modern moral norms that society at large did not live by and subverted in practice.

Disillusionment with republican politics was one of the major themes in the work of Cuban intellectuals. Jorge Mañach, one of the leading progressive intellectuals of the times, in his essay "La crisis de la ilusión" (The Crisis of Illusion) claimed that Cubans had lost their illusions about what independence and republican life would bring. Hope was replaced by lack of faith in heroic gestures. The notion of fatherland was emptied of idealism, and, as a result, a "nothing-is-worth-it" attitude plagued public life.[21] Pessimism, cynicism, and opportunism flourished. Honest and sensitive men left the political arena to immoral and self-serving ones. The politics of affection seemed to overcome the politics of passion.

Mañach's attacks against the negative traits of Cuban civic life were unbridled. He voiced the hope of many who wanted an improved Cuba: "If there is something which has characterized in general our public life it is precisely the total absence of norms of public morals. This has always been a show, more or less turbulent and *descarado* [brazen], of minor instincts and of passions."[22] In his works passion was construed as corrosive of morality, not as an element that could contribute to moral social order. Three interrelated causes explained the lack of civic commitment among Cubans, particularly the youth: the crisis of the economy, the crisis of culture, and the crisis of illusion.[23] Claiming that people wanted fulfillment of spiritual and affective needs, not merely monetary ones, he argued that if those personal needs were not satisfied, they would lead to boredom, resignation, indifference, and a high incidence of suicide among Cubans. While Mañach's diagnosis of Cuban social qualities was on target, his prognosis was not. Cubans did not abandon their moral imperative for the nation. On the contrary, the crisis of illusion served to underscore the need for a moral crusade that was not far away.

The failures of the government and the limitations of economic dependence and its reliance on a monoculture did not go unnoticed by younger leaders, who vented their anger at the sorry state of affairs. Eduardo Chibás mustered the greatest clout precisely because of his emotionally charged attacks against corruption. Chibás broke from a morally discredited party, the Auténticos, to form his own reformist one, the Ortodoxos. Chibás's crusade is a prime example of how emotions can be understood as moral judgments. His banner, "Verguenza contra dinero" (Honor against Money) encapsulated his political message by pitting morality against money, the principal poles of Cuban politics and of politics in the modern age in general. In an open letter to President Prío, Chibás identified the reasons for his passionate pursuit: "The Prio government, which is as bad and demoralized as Batista's, lacks moral authority."[24] In Chibás's last public speech in his weekly radio program, his moral indignation reached an emotional high: "I could not present the physical evidence that they were stealing the money of the national treasury, but I continue repeating, firm in my moral conviction: They steal it! They steal it!" At the same time that he condemned the depravity of the regime, he praised the Cuban people for the fact that corrupt governments "[had] not been able to desensitize [their] moral sensibility."[25] Chibás committed suicide as the radio program came to an end.

Chibás's suicide resonates with the codes of passion of Cuban politics, that strand of political culture that revolves around issues of personal honor and absolute moral goals for the society at large and the politicization of Thanatos. Within these parameters compromise is impossible; martyrdom is necessary. Chibás's suicide symbolized the death of the republic of virtue that Cubans had dreamed of. Chibás the martyr became the moral inspiration for a new generation of leaders, including Fidel Castro, who, despite significant differences, pursued politics as a march against "evil." But in the pursuit of the utopia, instrumental logic expressed in informal practices continued to undermine what ought to be. Both logics continued to be meshed, leading to unsavory outcomes, loss of faith in the normative frames of reference, and renewed calls for morality in public life.

The final blow to republican democracy came in 1952 at the hands of General Fulgencio Batista and his associates. The armed forces, never immune to factionalism based on the politics of affection, staged a coup that interrupted electoral regularity. Following the suicide of Chibás in 1951, the coup generated more apathy and cynicism than popular opposition. With the doors closed on reform, several groups opted for armed struggle, including the July 26th Movement organized by a member of the Orthodox Party, Fidel Castro. After years of growing civil strife in the cities and in the countryside, on January 1, 1959, Batista opted to seek exile. A popular revolution had triumphed.

Despite its middle-class, nationalistic, reformist, and democratic origins, the revolutionary process became radicalized after 1959 because of a number of domestic and foreign factors, as well as a fair share of happenstance. Initially the movement pledged to reinstate the Constitution of 1940, but in 1961 Fidel Castro declared a government based on Marxism-Leninism, taking the revolution, with crowds cheering behind him, in a new, unexpected and uncharted direction. Most Cubans enthusiastically followed a leader who spoke like Martí and Chibás, who vowed to rescue the nation from degradation and promised a new Cuba. The politics of passion and affection came together to sustain the revolution under the charismatic leadership of Fidel Castro. They would leave their mark in the process. The long-awaited moral day of the nation was dawning. At last the Cuba that ought to be would be. Or so it seemed.[26]

An Affair of the Heart

Revolutions are affairs of the heart, Fouad Ajami has said. And the Cuban revolution was no exception. As the next chapter shows, the revolutionary politics in the first several years had a strong emotional and passionate foundation that helps to explain the type of regime that was established. Revolution was made possible not only by the bankruptcy of liberal democracy *a la cubana* and the armed movement that ousted Batista, or exclusively by rational calculation based on material self-interest, but by the emotional infrastructure that accompanied it. Popular disenchantment with politics-as-usual in combination with deep-running emotional streams (anti-Americanism, hate of the Batista regime, frustration over the lost opportunities of the past, and the bitter side of sugar—*el tiempo muerto* [the dead season], the cyclical booms and bust of the economy, and the thousands of poor workers in the countryside) fanned the fires of radical social change. If emotions contributed to the downfall of the Batista dictatorship, emotions—in the form of the politics of passion and affection—also helped to construct the foundation on which the revolution would stand.

Like in the Machadato and the Batistiato, opponents of the revolution were silenced readily. Nonconformists were purged from the ranks, and interest groups were eliminated or incorporated into state-led mass organizations. Crowds rejoiced as firing squads aimed at Batista's cronies and later as the property of the rich was appropriated and churches were closed. The traditional fragmentation of Cuban civic life, the weakness of legal institutions, and pent-up feelings facilitated the excesses of the regime and the centralization of power. The tendency toward incivility assumed a new look—this time guided by quasi-religious zeal to set all wrongs right. Revolutionary passion, with its myriad accompanying feelings (joy, hate, resentment, hope, fear, adoration), consumed almost everyone. The passion born of indignation eventually would trample moral values dear to many. In the euphoria of the moment, *el embullo y la novelería* (the surge of enthusiasm and the tendency to partake of novelty), two common features of Cuban popular culture, resurfaced. Revolutionary violence and radical social change were sustained by the political-cultural proclivity to regard opponents with the mistrust reserved for enemies and by the notion that in politics the winner takes all. The expectations of a better future that would deliver material progress and moral renewal for a sovereign nation justified any and all actions. As a new beginning dawned, the specter of the past was also rising in a new political landscape.

Nowhere are the emotions of the revolution better captured than in the photographs and newspaper accounts of the time. *Diario de la Marina,* a conservative, pro-business and Catholic newspaper, *Bohemia,* the most popular magazine on the island, and international publications such as *Life* portrayed the revolution as a momentous happening, part fiesta, part communion—affection and passion combined. The desire of the majority of Cubans was graphically captured in a host of documents ranging from the sublime to the improbable. Tropical Brewery's advertisement in *Diario de la Marina* congratulating the interim president of the Republic, Manuel Urrutia, and the leader of the Rebel Army, Fidel Castro, was both sublime and improbable: "Let us struggle without respite and with the same faith and enthusiasm that gave the Cuban people the triumph, so that the hoped-for economic recovery completes the historic cycle from which a new Cuba, free, honest, prosperous, and happy, will emerge."[27]

Photographs of early 1959 show bearded young men wearing olive green uniforms and toting rifles, hardly menacing in their postures. They all seem like brothers, comfortably at ease, if a bit starstruck, proud of what they have achieved and of the adoration of the folk surrounding them. The pictures tell the story of the optimism and spontaneity typical of youth. They reveal the personal, intimate, and emotional dimension of the social revolution and its agents. These are friends or friends of friends who joined the ranks of the Rebel Army. This is a social movement in which people knew each other or felt they knew their leader, Fidel Castro. The politics of affection and the politics of passion became one during this effusive moment. Politics were intensely personal, collective, informal, instrumental, and utopian at the same time.

Idealism and informality were the two hallmarks of the revolution in the early times. Romantic idealism, verging on utopianism, permeated the editorials of the period and the speeches of the Comandante en Jefe (Commander in Chief). Through Fidel the aspirations of hundreds of thousands of citizens were articulated. Newspaper editorials painted with epic strokes the heroics of the young rebels who were "willing to give it all, including life, embracing an ideal and a flag." [28] Rhetorical inflation, not an unusual characteristic of Cuban political discourse, was the literary and linguistic style of the moment. It captured stylistically the grand hopes, long dashed, for a future when Cuba would become the nation that José Martí dreamed of: " 'Tomorrow!' —that word is almost a magical message, decorated with the colors of the dawn, carried on the wings of hope by those who believe, awaited by those who desire it, commended to God by those who without passion and malice place the community above the individual and above it the fatherland of all." [29] Tomorrow would bring the long-sought "sun of the moral life." [30] The roots of the crusade ran deep in Cuban history, as far back as the first founding fathers, Varela and Martí, and from them to Chibás and Castro, among others. The moral charge demanded passion, understood as intensely meaningful judgments, that in turn reflected the urgency of building an ethical community. But passion carried the seeds of the possible destruction of a moral community. To think that passion had been set aside, as the quote above suggests, was either wishful thinking or a naive misunderstanding of the emotional force behind rapid social change. To see the revolution as a "rational" phenomenon misses the heart of the matter.

Passion alone did not sustain the revolutionary regime though. Idealism found expression in concrete public policies such as the attempt to create the New Man, to implement far-reaching social reforms in the areas of education, housing, medicine, land tenancy, among others, and to replace material incentives with moral ones. The new government immediately moved to distribute goods, securing with material benefits the goodwill of the people. Health, education, housing, and land reform benefited millions. Equity and social justice would now become reality.

Like idealism and passion, informality and affection have a long history in the revolution. Through the years the revolution has oscillated between informality and formality. The organizational genesis of the armed struggle (a core group of friends and acquaintances), the guerrilla tactics employed, and the programs implemented throughout the 1960s relied on "informal institutions" (mobilizations, volunteerism, the armed people, a personalistic leadership style) rather than on formal institutional procedures. Ernesto "Ché" Guevara, one of the protagonists of the revolution, was the standard-bearer of anti-institutionalism, favoring spontaneity. The dilemma of reconciling revolutionary spontaneity and statist institutionalization was a pivotal one, which revolved around the age-old question, how much should a dynamic social process be formalized without risking popular support and thwarting creative energy? The antibureaucratic bias of the early years has continued to coexist in tension with the opposite tendency advocated by individuals who, due to either personal idiosyncrasy or ideology, preferred the discipline of forms and institutions.

Since 1959 Cuban socialism has been like a seesaw moving between the extremes of formality and informality. The Cuban revolution could be called the informal revolution in spite of its trappings of institutionalization after 1970. Throughout its four decades Cuban socialism has been identified with experimentation, doing and undoing, and ample discretion for the top leadership to make decisions, despite structural constraints. Widespread everyday resistance at the grassroots, particularly in the 1980s and 1990s, is another manifestation of the informality of Cuban politics since 1959. Domestic and international pressures (principally from the Soviet Union, the main benefactor of the regime) came to bear on the leadership to adopt measures of formal institutionalization. By the end of the 1970s the regime had acquired a marked Soviet style, but for a number of reasons Cuba never quite fit the mold of the typical Soviet satellite. As in the rest of the socialist world, informality never disappeared. On the contrary, it increased in response to the state's attempt at greater regulation and penetration of society and the economy of scarcity, eventually posing a long-term challenge to the regime.

Since the late 1980s Cuba's political system and the nation have been facing their most serious crisis. The collapse of the Soviet Union, an unparalleled economic tailspin starting in the mid-1980s, and the erosion of the political formula by which the country had been governed since 1959 strained state-society relations, plunged the nation into a desperate economic situation, and dealt a blow to the idealism of the revolution.[31] The factors that brought the regime to power and sustained it—the charisma of Fidel Castro, the unity of the revolutionary forces in one party and in mass institutions, social equity, nationalism, anti-Americanism, and the not small dosage of coercion—became increasingly difficult to maintain in light of new social, political, and economic forces nationally and internationally.[32]

Since 1959 the Cuban revolution has promised far more material and nonmaterial goods than it could deliver. As the expectations of Cubans were raised, the state had an increasingly difficult time fulfilling them. The many benefits provided (education, health care, guaranteed employment, basic nutrition) came with a political price: conformity to official dogma and, at least for several decades, a level of economic dependence on the Soviet Union. Over time, fewer Cubans, especially the younger ones, found the cost acceptable. The religious passion the revolution inspired in its initial years faded as the gap between rhetoric and practice became insurmountable. The politics of affection became increasingly significant when socialism entered a period of crisis starting in the 1980s.

By the mid-1990s economic necessity pushed the Cuban state to adopt a series of reforms. Although the process of economic rectification was announced initially in 1986 as the Campaign to Rectify Errors and Negative Tendencies (and five years later became the Special Period in Times of Peace), in practice this was an austerity program. Confronted with an unparalleled economic crisis, the government had to reduce social programs dramatically. As it backtracked in many areas (e.g., guaranteed employment, distribution of a minimum food ration, and health and education) the legitimacy of the regime suffered. Modest economic reforms (e.g., joint ventures and self-employment) failed to resolve deep-seated policy and structural deficiencies. Socioeconomic differences were accentuated as some Cubans had access to dollars (legalized in 1993) and others did not. Throughout the 1990s the economy teetered on the edge of bankruptcy as it declined about 45 percent since the late 1980s. Imports decreased about 70 percent. Sugar production reached its lowest output since 1959. Life became very hard.[33]

The socialist safety net was in tatters. Unemployment soared as the state laid off excess workers and closed unproductive plants that did not have the necessary inputs to continue operating. Securing daily portions of food became the number one priority of Cuban households as the government could no longer import or produce as it once did. Increasingly people resorted to the informal sphere, outside the control of the state, to *sobrevivir* (survive). Inequality reappeared with a vengeance. So did prostitution, as the regime sought to attract foreign exchange through tourism. A culture of illegality, ever present but submerged, flourished; most, if not all, Cubans saw the need to steal from the state or operate in the black market to *resolver* (make do, survive).

As the crisis worsened and broadened, the networks of affection became most important; they became the channels through which to satisfy affective and material needs, replacing many of the state's functions. Cubans' physical and spiritual quality of life suffered, as novels of the times, such as *La nada cotidiana* by Zoe Valdés, reflect.[34] *Lo informal*, with its politics of affection, threatened the basis of Cuban socialism. Popular discontent became manifest in a new desperate wave of migration (on this occasion in makeshift rafts), and, for the first time in decades, a riot erupted in Old Havana in 1994, revealing an emotional social infrastructure that could undermine the regime. Yet the *líder máximo* (maximum leader), always the believer, has not abandoned the discourse of passion: "Socialismo o muerte! Venceremos!" (Socialism or death! We shall overcome!).

Conclusion

Throughout Cuban political history the pursuit of a moral absolute for the nation as a whole has coexisted with instrumental logic based on personal exceptionalism and opportunism in day-to-day social life. The two tendencies seem to be contradictory but in practice have supported and co-constituted each other over time in diverse ways, depending on specific political and economic contexts. Leaders within the moral imperative current—those motivated by the politics of passion—have criticized the informal aspects of Cuban culture but have also relied on informal networks of friends to pursue their goals. The politics-of-passion crusaders have depended on an instrumental logic in which the ends justify the means, similar to the logic of the politics of affection. Affection has also helped to consolidate the politics of passion as leaders were deified and supported by groups of friends and fervent followers. Eventually the politics of affection tend to undermine passion as well as the bureaucratic norms and institutions of the state. Yet the politics of affection are highly functional, constructive, and modern in the sense that they manifest interests, alternatives, and identities. The politics of affection and their networks are instrumental, not merely sentimental, carrying their own affective rationality. They have contributed to the emergence of a specific type of economic enterprise that relies on personal connections—small family firms—and activities—corruption and the black market—during the Republic and during the socialist regime.

Throughout the twentieth century, in both the republican and socialist regimes, modern political aspirations coexisted with corporatist ones as well as with informal practices. Modern projects for the collectivity at large were undermined from within as well as from without (i.e., U.S. neocolonialism). Although the politics of passion and affection have been present in Cuban politics over time, their intensity depends on political and economic factors. At moments of political crisis the politics of passion energize groups to carry forward the moral pursuit of a new and improved national community. In periods of economic opportunity the politics of affection siphoned resources from the public to private, elite, or middle-class hands. During periods of economic scarcity the politics of affection served as alternative distribution mechanisms in the black market at the grassroots for survival needs. The politics of affection play more than a mere economic role. They have also given Cubans space to articulate meaning and identity. The rise of the politics of affection in the informal sphere in post-1980 Cuba has challenged the material and ideological bases of Cuban socialism and the operations of the Cuban state. As the politics of passion faded, the politics of affection flared.

The next chapters focus on how the politics of passion and affection were manifested during different periods in Cuban "revolutionary" history and analyze their impact on and interrelationship with the political system. Passion and affection laid the basis for the new regime in 1959, but by the 1980s a new emotional infrastructure could be detected at the grassroots level that has mounted an indirect challenge to the established order.

AN AFFAIR
OF THE HEART

Passion, Affection,
and Revolution

The Cuban revolution of 1959, like other revolutions, was an affair of the heart. To understand its origins one must locate the passion and affection in it. The moral imperative for a new Cuba brought the rebels and the population together. The networks of affection made revolutionary organization possible in its formative stage, and affection also cemented the bonds between leaders and followers. The Cuban revolution demonstrates the constructive dimension of the emotional in the political. Since modern times, passion has been considered detrimental to politics insofar as it threatens the social order. Yet emotions in general can help to erect political regimes. Revolutions, radical social transformations usually initiated through armed struggles, cannot be explained thoroughly, or from the point of view of those involved, if emotions are not taken into account. Otherwise we would be at a loss to understand why individuals risk their lives in an enterprise that entails great suffering in the present for the promise of a better future. An emotional infrastructure (of resentment, frustration, indignation, and aggression but also of fraternity, camaraderie, solidarity, and hope) provides the basis for a political campaign for revolutionary change.

The Cuban experience shows that a revolutionary movement requires an emotional infrastructure. Without it the movement will not find the necessary support to carry out the armed struggle or to implement an agenda of rapid social transformation. The emotional connection is made possible when situations are understood/felt/judged in similar ways by groups of individuals. Emotions are crucial in the beginning of the revolutionary campaign and in its consolidation. Once institutionalized, however, the reproduction of the sentimental basis of support is one of the biggest challenges the new system will have to confront.

Affection and passion played central roles in the advent and consolidation of the revolution in Cuba, in the leadership of Fidel Castro, in the discourse of the period, and in the strategies pursued. The politics of affection sowed the seeds for group formation and bonded the leaders to the followers. The politics of passion construed the revolutionary process as a crusade against the evils that had plagued Cuban politics; the passion that drove the revolutionaries was the quest for a moral community, sovereign, honest, and socially progressive. The personal and the affective were as important as, if not more important than, the structural in determining the immediate origin, the support for, and even the initial course of the revolutionary process from the early 1950s to the early 1960s, when radical social policies were implemented. A revolutionary movement is rarely motivated merely by material factors. More often than not, the desire for moral, spiritual, and sentimental redress compels the collective struggle, as the Cuban case demonstrates. Economic issues, vital as they are, are shrouded with the veil of intense affective symbology, quasi-religious in nature, and vested with appealing moral force that acts as a catalyst for mobilization and ultimately constitutes a source of power.

The triumph of the rebels against Batista's dictatorship and the trajectory of the revolution, with its unanticipated twists and turns, have been explained from a number of angles. Most accounts are based on institutional-structural factors (i.e., breakdowns of democratic governance, class structure, dependence on the United States, and U.S. hegemony); historical teleology (the frustrated national mission to fulfill Martí's vision of Cuba); ideological explanations (Fidel Castro's communist dogma); or the great man thesis of history (Fidel's desire for power and his superlative skills as a political leader).[1] I offer a different, and complementary, interpretation. I examine the political culture of emotions and the role affection and passion played in bringing individuals together to fight the dictator, in consolidating Fidel Castro's leadership, in the emergence of a political religion that facilitated centralization and mobilization, and in shaping the principal features of the regime. The time frame is the first two years of the new regime (1959–1961), a defining period in terms of the consolidation of the revolution that marked state-society relations.

I analyze the charismatic bases of authority and authority's affective dimension from the perspective of the religious feelings the maximum leader generated in different sectors of the Cuban population.[2] Affection and passion brought individuals to join forces in a common struggle. The moral imperative of "saving Cuba" rendered politics passionate and made many of the followers believers and many of the believers fanatics who resorted to any means possible to achieve higher ends. The politics of affection provided the organizational glue necessary for the Rebel Army and other groups to form and launch the struggle against the Batista dictatorship. In the process of social revolution, modern, corporatist, and informal paradigms coexisted and collided.

"The Incomparable Happiness that Cubans Feel Today"

December 31, 1958: On the last day of the year, General Fulgencio Batista, facing mounting civic and armed resistance at home and pressure from abroad, leaves the island. The regime collapses as the old year ends.

January 1, 1959: The New Year brings the promise of a new Cuba: the triumph of the revolutionary movement led by, among others, Fidel Castro Ruz, his July 26th Movement, and the Rebel Army. From one end to the other, the island is immersed in celebration, in the streets of cities, towns, and villages. *La nueva Cuba* (the new Cuba), that most modern of notions—newness, nation-state, and revolution all packaged in one phrase—is being born. Euphoria takes hold as old frustrations give way to hope. With the exception of small sectors of the society, the population greets the revolutionaries and their leaders with enthusiasm and devotion. As the young bearded men in olive green uniforms come down from the mountains where they had fought the Batista forces, they are greeted with cheers, food, flowers, and amulets. Women give them rosaries, medallions engraved with the figures of patron saints, hugs, and kisses.

The veneration with which the rebels were received was the first sign of the feelings they sparked in their compatriots. The relationship that was being established between the people and the leaders (and between the incipient state and the society) must be seen as based on attachments akin to those inspired by religious feelings: rapture, faith, hope, elation, devotion, and love. The connection between leaders and followers was powerfully affective and constituted the basis of a charismatic authority. It pointed the way to the specific type of regime and governing strategy that would eventually be established—a centralized state with a maximum leader and a maximalist social agenda and popular mobilization in a one-party system.

People flocked to see, hear, and touch the young hero, Fidel. From one day to the next he became the savior of the Cuban nation and was treated as such: "The crowd applauded jubilantly at every comment he made and every so often interrupted him, yelling '¡Viva Castro!' And Castro now has Cuba at his feet."[3] The island rejoiced in "the incomparable happiness that all Cubans feel today."[4] *Bohemia*, the most popular magazine of the time, reported the "apotheosis" in Havana as Fidel and the Rebel Army marched in from the mountains.[5] In Pinar del Río, the westernmost province of the island, "the people [took] to the streets . . . ; wave[d] the flags in the air; they scream[ed], embrace[d] and even cr[ied]. It is the emotion of the populace that overflows when what has been desired year after year becomes reality: the end of the dictatorship, the dawning of liberty."[6]

The religious feelings the *barbudos* (the bearded ones, as the rebels were commonly called) inspired were reflected in the media and in the discourse of the revolutionary leaders, which in turn fueled the zeal of the populace. The discourse is better understood as the language of passion that gave form to a political religion, not an ideology narrowly defined. Charisma, popular religiosity, and political religion, all within the realm of the informal, are keys to understanding the emotional force of the revolution in its early years and the issues of legitimacy, authority, political strategies, and violence. The revolution evoked feelings and also relied on those feelings to muster support and, in no small measure, to survive in power. The strong affective reactions stemmed from a moral sense of justice expressed as radical nationalism, based on judgments about Cuba's past and future. Morality permeated the political religion that was crafted on the island. The traditional codes of passion of Cuban political culture resonated in the rhetoric and in the lived experience of making revolution. Politics became passion.

Passion and Political Religion

To understand how and why the politics of passion thrived during the first years of the revolution, one must analyze the social and economic context of the times. The politics of passion found a fertile terrain not only in the unfulfilled hopes of millions but also in the weak official institutional landscape, particularly with regard to religion. The most striking aspect of religious life in Cuba was its informality. Although the institutional presence of the Catholic Church paled in comparison to its counterparts elsewhere in the region, the Cuban people were deeply religious. According to one estimate, approximately 80 percent of the population considered itself Catholic, but only 24 percent attended mass regularly.[7] Other estimates put the number of practicing Catholics at between 4 and 6 percent.[8] Protestants constituted 6 percent of the population.[9] Anticlerical sentiments were widespread, the result of the intellectual repercussions of the French Revolution and the Catholic Church's support of Spain during Cuba's independence wars. There were few priests, and most of them were Spaniards, concentrated in urban areas. Nevertheless, a 1954 survey revealed that 96.5 percent of those Cubans polled believed in the existence of God while only 17 percent attended church services regularly.[10]

Catholicism was the dominant religion in name only. In practice popular religiosity was the primary form of religious expression. Popular religiosity was a multilayered mixture of Christianity in its many variants (Catholicism, Protestantism), Afro-Cuban religions, *espiritismo* (spiritism, a form of animism) and *brujería* (witchcraft). Cubans manifested in their culture a preoccupation with the spiritual and the transcendental: the meaning of life and death, the difference between good and evil. For the majority of Cubans religion was not an institutional phenomenon but a personal one. Popular religious practice was eclectic rather than purist, informal rather than formal. Unlike other religious dogmas, popular religiosity provided a flexible and open framework of beliefs in which seemingly incompatible codes could coexist to deal with issues of daily life as well as with transcendental ones.

Informal religiosity contributed to the consolidation of the revolution in several ways. First, it helped to counter the institutional power of the Catholic Church when the ecclesiastical hierarchy turned against the revolutionary regime and to neutralize the organized Church—a potential power contender, or at the very least the potential rallying point for opponents of the new government. Second, and more important, it provided a receptive cultural backdrop against which revolutionary symbols, myths, and values would resonate. Popular religiosity became one of the pillars on which the support for the revolution and the charismatic authority of its leader would stand. It provided the affective (and effective) material for the political religion the leaders, followers, and cultural elites tailored.

David E. Apter defines political religion as a special type of ideological position "put forward by government that identifies the individual with the state." He continues,

> Modern political leaders come to recognize quickly . . . that no ordinary ideology can prevail for long in the face of obvious discrepancies between theory and practice. A more powerful symbolic force, less rational, although it may include rational ends, seems necessary to them. This force is what I call political religion. It feeds its own categorical imperatives into authoritarian political structure on the one hand. On the other . . . it affects the most fundamental needs of individuals by speci-

fying through the state religion the permissible definitions of individual continuity, meaning, and identity.[11]

Political religion is an affective discourse. It is produced as a conscious decision by top leaders and through cultural interaction with and by the people. Political religion touches people directly as it deals with issues of immediacy couched in moral language and with the big issues of life and death: Who are we? Where are we going? How should we get there? Its references are the culture and the experience of national life. The symbols and myths of political religion make sense contextually as they resonate with long-held beliefs, aspirations, desires, and collective goals. Political religion is close to the heart. It resurrects intense feelings because it responds to a moral concern for the national project in crisis. Moreover, for the millions of Cubans living through the uncertain times of the revolution, political religion provided a measure of comfort by making sense of a world that was rapidly changing around them. Fidel and the revolution relied on traditional symbols, themes, and myths of the past as guideposts for the future and as the means for radical transformation. They rendered "otherwise incomprehensible social functions meaningful, to so construe them as to make it possible to act purposefully within them." [12]

The worldview of the revolution was based on a series of layers of beliefs: (1) the informal traditional beliefs of the Cuban people; (2) modern values associated with liberal democracy, nationalism, and, later, socialism; (3) the corporatist legacy of the colonial period with its proclivity for order, centralization of power, and chartered-group participation; and (4) the personal ideology of Fidel Castro—Castroism—defined by Andrés Suárez as anti-Americanism, social change through revolution, militarization of society, centralization of power in the maximum leader, mass participation in controlled organizations, and nationalism.[13] All these beliefs and values, seemingly incompatible, were meshed into an eclectic "framework," serving different purposes and different constituencies at the same time. The result is a powerful, affective, and authentic worldview, a Cuban political religion. In the Cuban context, the language of the politics of passion referred to recurrent themes of Cuban history (including the relationship with the United States, social equity, economic diversification, honest democratic conduct of public affairs) and to the aspirations for a moral sovereign political community with greater economic opportunity and equity for all. As such it was an autochthonous cultural expression, meaningful to the Cuban people.

Through political religion the leadership catalyzed mobilization and exerted social control. The leaders, the revolution, and its emblems (later the state and the party) became the sacred source of politics, of morality, of meaning and identity. The private and public spheres became politicized and their borders blurred; the individual and the collectivity were inseparable in the quest for a better nation. Politics became an ethical phenomenon, a crusade against imperialism, economic dependence, counterrevolutions, corruption, laziness, illiteracy, exploitation, and selfishness. The revolution would create a new society and a New Man. Accepting those goals demanded faith in the leader and in the ability to reach them; it required assuming, or presuming, the perfectibility of Cuban society in particular and of human nature in general. Cuban exceptionalism propelled revolutionary optimism.

As in most crusades, unity was paramount; deviation was treason. Mass mobilization in revolutionary organizations would guarantee harmony of purpose and the order to achieve it. To that end an umbrella organization of revolutionary associations was formed in 1961, the Organizaciones Revolucionarias Integradas (Integrated Revolutionary Organizations; ORI), a sort of *partido único* (sole party), precursor of the Communist Party of Cuba (PCC). Mobilization was supposed to bring a host of associations together in support of the revolution. In mass organizations Cubans would find not only venues of representation and participation but also solidarity and fraternity in an atmosphere of *pachanga* (festivity). Through these institutions affection and passion would be generated and regenerated, in the process defining the limits of participation and expression.

Operating under the logic of political religion, in the months after the triumph of the Rebel Army its high priests and millions of acolytes closed churches, banned clergy and other antirevolutionary nonconformists, and defined the social space in terms of support for the revolution. Batistianos (cronies of Batista) were executed, exiled, combated, imprisoned, or silenced. By 1961 the major organized critics, such as the Catholic Church, were eliminated or crippled, although guerrillas continued to fight the government until 1965. An external enemy, the United States, served to heighten the need for unity and unanimity in the name of national security. The politics of passion and its political religion supplied what the Catholic Church or any other ideology had been unable to do in the past: a sense of the nation united in the quest for a moral absolute.

Political religion had to coexist with Marxism-Leninism, the official ideology of the state after 1961. As the revolution became institutionalized (particularly after 1970) and embraced the Soviet Union (especially after 1968), Marxism slowly displaced some aspects of Cuban revolutionary political religion, but not all. While political religion was the informal ideology of the regime, Marxism-Leninism was the official one. As in other aspects of Cuban social life, for the majority of people the informal was more significant than the formal. In practice and in theory the regime and its official ideology sustained key aspects of political religion, including charismatic authority and notions of unity and harmony for high moral ends. Marxism lends itself to political religion, by advocating the notion of the unity of the working class in a one-party state, offering a teleological view of history, and setting forth a spiritual optimistic view of human beings and their possible emancipation. Marxism, like political religion, promised heaven on earth.

Political religion seemed to be successful where Marxism-Leninism was not: it provided a culturally authentic worldview by addressing issues, earthly and otherwise, in a language that made sense to Cubans. Without political religion, the state would have encountered greater opposition to the adoption of Marxism-Leninism. The people followed their leader as he implemented state socialism not because they supported the radicalization of the revolution per se (although there is evidence that some segments of the population favored that course for economic reasons) but because they believed in him and in the political religion he preached: "Si Fidel es Comunista, yo también" (If Fidel is a Communist, I am also one). But faith also rested on the material benefits that the revolutionary government distributed.

The institutionalization of the late 1960s and 1970s was supposed to encapsulate revolutionary feelings and give them an organized form. The regime, however, was unable in the long run to reconcile the tension between feelings and institutions, between spontaneous revolutionary fervor and the requisites of a modern state, between utopianism and performance, and between the material and moral dimensions of revolutionary politics. The result was periodic oscillation between both poles and less than hoped for results in the reproduction of passion, as the next chapter shows.

Affection, Passion, and Charisma:
"Because God has sent them to bring good fortune"

Political religion was effective in relation to Fidel Castro's brand of leadership. Affection, passion, political religion, and charisma mutually reinforced each other, shaping revolutionary politics in tandem with material and international policies. The maximum leader of the revolution provided the direction that made political religion possible by conforming to what Weber labeled charismatic authority. According to Weber, charismatic figures appear, usually in premodern societies or even in modern societies in crisis, to deliver the people from doom. Unlike in traditional or legal-rational leadership, the charismatic leader defies great odds and conquers them with brio. Followers perceive such leaders as superhuman, otherworldly, far superior to the rest. Individuals who are perceived to have charisma, the gift of grace, attract a strong following. The basis of the charismatic bond is fervent affection for the leader. It is an emotional response to the presence of what one feels to be providential. People *feel* someone is charismatic. Therefore, charisma, like beauty, is always in the eye or heart of the beholder. Charismatic leaders tend to emerge at times of crisis, when institutional breakdowns occur, especially in places where formal institutions are weak or illegitimate. Ironically the failure of modern institutions opened the way for charismatic leadership. Cuba's institutional impasse after the demise of the Constitution of 1940 combined with the weakness of the Catholic Church, the fragmentation of civil society, and Cuban political culture were conducive to charismatic authority. The codes of passion and informal popular religiosity contributed to the development and sustenance of charismatic authority. The "Fidel phenomenon" should not be understood only as the sign of a big man in history but also, and fundamentally, as a product of Cuban culture.

The bond between leader and masses and the governing strategies employed by the revolutionary government must be seen in the light of political culture with the affective dimension included. Cubans perceived Fidel and the revolution as a moral struggle for "the revision and the reconstruction of the Cuban process, for a different fatherland, in line with the principles of the apostle [José Martí], negating its sinful adulteration."[14] The symbols, myths, values, and feelings associated with the maximum leader, the advent of the revolution, and the discourse of the times (particularly that of Fidel, Ché Guevara, and Camilo Cienfuegos, another revolutionary leader) were permeated by religiosity. Cultural codes such as the virtue of personal sacrifice and death (even *numancia*, which is sacrificial death as the ultimate heroic gesture) on behalf of the nation predated 1959 and can be traced at least back to Martí and Catholic dogma. By feeding into this moral current in Cuban intellectual history, the revolution embodied the unfulfilled aspirations of the founding fathers. Massive popular support for the rebel leaders and the process of radical social change stemmed both from the redistribution of income during the first eighteen months and from the moral quest that inspired the rebellion from its onset. Material benefits cemented support by proving that this time promises would be kept; long-standing nationalist reformist goals would be finally realized.

Religious motifs appeared in the discourse of the revolutionary leaders early on. Castro's first national message to the Cuban nation (after he was captured by Batista's army when the July 26th Movement attacked the Moncada barracks in 1953), "History Will Absolve Me," inaugurated the use of biblical metaphors in the political discourse of the revolution. In that speech Castro portrayed himself as a man with a mission entrusted to him by history. He was the heir to Cuba's founding fathers, searching for a higher moral order for the nation. He spoke frequently and forcefully of setting wrongs right, quoting Jesus on national television: "My kingdom is not of this world." As he initiated the transformation of the Cuban nation, he called on Cuban society "to purify itself." [15] This was a man motivated by the politics of passion.

The spin doctors of the revolution, associates and the press—supporters all—harped on the divine aura of the national hero and his epic. Carlos Franqui, a close collaborator, wrote a book titled *Cuba: El libro de los doce* about the twelve followers of Fidel who survived the landing of the *Granma,* the boat that brought Fidel and his supporters to Cuba from exile in Mexico to resume armed struggle against the dictatorship. "Los doce" is a barely veiled reference to the Twelve Apostles, although the veracity of the account is in doubt.[16] In early 1959 *Bohemia* portrayed Fidel in the likeness of Christ, bearded and mystical, on its cover. This was the man who would take Cuba, as the magazine had put it in an earlier edition, "from darkness into the light." [17]

Even the conservative *Diario de la Marina* contributed to the creation of the religious aura surrounding Castro. In an early January 1959 column the *comandante* and his guerrillas were compared to the Three Kings who visited Baby Jesus in Bethlehem. The 1959 celebration of Three Kings Day (January 6) coincided with the march of the Rebel Army from the Sierra Maestra into Havana. The *Diario*'s columnist wrote that, as in the past, the Three Kings "came from Oriente [the easternmost province of the island where most of the fighting had taken place and a reference to the biblical Wise Men of the Orient] and had beards." But in 1959 the Three Kings were "uniformed in olive green, bearing the arms that gave us victory, wearing around their necks a number of rosaries, medallions, crosses, *detentes* [amulets] and *escapularios* [scapulars]—their most precious gems and their best credentials.... They are the Three Kings of this year ... [b]ecause God has sent them to return good fortune to this island." [18]

Reality contributed to the religious interpretation of the *comandante* Fidel Castro and the revolution. On January 8, 1959, as he delivered his first nationally televised speech after the Rebel Army took Havana, a white dove (one of many that had been let loose during the event) perched on Fidel's shoulder, two others on the podium. Heaven seemed to be sending another sign to the people of Cuba.

Diverse religious perceptions on the island converged in 1959 to create a single perception of Fidel. He was seen by all as the emissary of a higher power sent to deliver the Cuban nation from evil. Although no group was monolithic in its support and not all members saw the developments of the times in exactly the same light, ample evidence suggests that a large portion of the population considered Fidel providential. Surveys of the times and other data confirm that a majority perceived the revolutionary leader as a demi-god. Discredited political institutions of the past, the low educational level (particularly in the countryside), the prevalent *machismo* and personalism, the socioeconomic reforms that helped millions, and the codes of Cuban political culture help to explain why Castro elicited such strong feelings of admiration among the population.

In January 1959 the archbishop of Santiago, Enrique Pérez-Serantes, who years earlier had interceded with General Batista to spare the life of the rebel leader and release him from prison to exile in Mexico, wrote a pastoral letter titled "Vida nueva" (New Life). In it he claimed, "The commitment of a man of exceptional qualities, backed enthusiastically by almost all of his coprovincials and a considerable portion of the Cuban people, and supported by the unwavering effort of his courageous followers, . . . are the letters with which Divine Providence has written on Cuba's sky the word TRIUMPH." [19]

Although the Catholic hierarchy was divided in its appreciation of the revolutionary movement, an influential current in it, particularly the younger and most progressive clergy, not only supported the agenda of the July 26th Movement—a nationalist reformist democratic program that resonated with the recommendations of the papal encyclicals "Rerum Novarum" and "Quadragesimo Año" advocating social change—but also contributed to the emerging image of Fidel as the incarnation of goodness. Their support for the leader and the movement also rested on the illegality of the Batista regime, the atrocities it had committed, and on the fact that several Catholic organizations (among them the Juventud de Acción Católica [Catholic Action Youth] and the Acción Católica Universitaria [University Catholic Action]) and scores of Cuban Catholics had participated in the struggle against the dictatorship. Fidel himself had studied in the prestigious Belén Jesuit school in Havana. Several priests joined the rebels in the Sierra Maestra and years later defended Fidel against charges of being a communist.

Among the Catholic public the revolution stirred great enthusiasm accompanied by high moral and material expectations. Priests, nuns, and lay

Catholics rushed to meet Fidel when he marched from the Sierra on his way to Havana.[20] The outpouring was such that a Catholic leader claimed at the time that "it is possible that in Latin America there is no other case of such collaboration of Catholics with a revolutionary movement."[21] Support for Fidel and for socioeconomic reform was strong among Catholics of all classes, except those at the very top of the economic pyramid. Fidel was deified by most rank-and-file Catholics. Pérez-Serantes's "New Life" was only one of several ways in which Catholic officials established a direct link between God and Fidel. *La Quincena*, the Catholic magazine with the largest circulation on the island, depicted both Castro and Cienfuegos, who was Protestant, as Jesuslike. The March 6, 1959, cover of the magazine was a close-up photograph of Cienfuegos in which he bore a striking resemblance to Jesus Christ.[22] The magazine portrayed the revolutionary struggle as the Cuban expression of the conflict between good and evil. In this version, good would triumph to redeem the Cuban people.

Key Protestant leaders also perceived Fidel Castro as heaven-sent. In July 1960 Rafael Cepeda, president of the Cuban Evangelical Council, assessed Castro in *Bohemia* in no uncertain terms: "It is my conviction, which I share here with full responsibility, that Fidel Castro is an instrument in the hands of God to establish His Kingdom among men."[23]

Believers in Afro-Cuban religions, commonly referred to as *santeros*, were more important than Protestants in terms of numbers and influence and constituted a strong base of support for the revolution, especially blacks, who, traditionally underprivileged, stood to gain the most from the economic reforms. Their religion is a superimposition of African deities and rituals on Catholic saints and practices. In their pantheon, for example, Oshún, the goddess of pleasure and fertility, is represented by the Virgin of Charity, the patron saint of Cuba. The syncretic nature of Afro-Cuban religions lent itself to the syncretization of revolutionary symbols with *santería* beliefs. In celebration of the New Year high priests organized the *gran ewo* of 1959 in honor of Fidel Castro. During the *ewo* the priests read the oracle for the coming year. On that occasion the *santeros* interceded with their gods to prevent further bloodshed and to guarantee Fidel's triumph.[24] Key symbols of the July 26th Movement could be interpreted as *santería* codes.[25] Afro-Cuban believers, therefore, could understand signs that to others were unintelligible or meaningless as an indication that the revolutionary struggle and its principal leader were connected to the supernatural. Black and red, the colors of the July 26th Movement flag, represents Changó, the god of war. That the bulk of the armed struggle occurred in Oriente, the region where *santería* was most prevalent, also seemed to point to its affinity with Afro-Cuban beliefs. Many of the rebels wore a medallion of Santa Barbara, Yemayá in the Afro-Cuban pantheon, the patron saint of warriors, during the revolutionary campaign.

With the triumph of the revolution, Fidel had become known as *el caballo* (the horse). While for many Cubans this image referred only to his power, for certain Afro-Cuban sects the horse is the medium through which the spirits communicate with the people. The syncretism between spiritism, *fidelismo*, and revolutionary zeal is captured in the title of a 1961 booklet: *The Supreme Revelation, Preceded by an Ode to the Revolution, a Liminal Note and the Seven Rules of the Perfect Spiritist, with Fidel Facing Mankind.*[26]

The religious background of the Cuban people was not the only factor that contributed to the deification of Fidel Castro and the religious sentiments he inspired. Material interests underscored the support of Afro-Cuban religious believers in particular and poorer Cubans in general, most of whom lived in rural areas and worked seasonally in the cane fields. Not only did they expect their religion to be recognized on the same footing with Christianity, but they hoped that their economic situation would improve as a result of the revolution; the reforms of 1959 and the early 1960s made many of their expectations reality, securing goodwill for the revolutionary government.

Support for the revolution was not limited to one class or one group. Fidel and the revolution generated intense positive feelings throughout Cuban society. A 1960 survey revealed that 43 percent of the population surveyed were fervent supporters, bordering "on the fanatic in their expression of fervor."[27] A Cuban housewife commented, "Fidel has the same ideas as Jesus Christ, our protector and guide."[28] Fervent supporters were significantly higher among those with only an elementary-school education or no schooling and among those living outside Havana and members of lower socioeconomic groups, the bulk of the population.[29] Although he was perceived as extraordinary, Fidel was not the type of leader who was distant from the people. On the contrary, the affection that comes from proximity had a real, immediate, and direct role in forging the connection between the leader and the followers. Not only did Fidel articulate the hopes and desires of the people, he was also accessible to them. He toured the island and visited with people in schools, in workplaces, in sports arenas. He conducted politics with a personal touch. He was informal in his language and his behavior, and yet he was revered. Although people called him by his first name, they still saw him as superhuman, godly. Cubans placed posters of revolutionary heroes in their homes accompanied by stickers proclaiming "Fidel, esta es tu casa" (Fidel, this is your home). The portraits and slogans reveal the love and familiarity the leaders of the revolution inspired. The public persona of the leader was accepted as one would a relative; the rebels, and Fidel especially, were brought into the homes and into one's family as if they were fathers, sons, brothers, friends, lovers.

The relationship between leaders and followers even acquired a gendered and sexual undertone. For his fellow men, Fidel and the *barbudos* epitomized manliness in a society that valued *machismo*. For women, the revolutionaries incited romantic feelings. Young women would kiss the new idols and have their pictures taken arm in arm with them. A photograph in *Bohemia* typifies the sexualized dimension of the politics of the times. It shows a young smiling woman clad in a tight top and pants, her arm intertwined with that of a rebel. The caption reads: "Beauty and the *barbudo*: A *barbudo*, armed to the teeth, smiles saintlike due to the admiration he inspires in this pretty young woman."[30]

The distance between the public and the private, the leaders and the followers, the state and the society, and the political and the affective was blurred and intertwined. The politics of passion and affection came together during the early years of the revolution. The combination was both a construction of and an aid in constructing revolutionary politics. At the same time it undermined aspects of civility and democracy, marking the course of social change with a dark underside.

The Politics of Passion: Emotions, Morality, and Paradigms in Conflict

The emotional outpouring of the people in the early days of the revolution and the effusive welcome they gave the revolutionaries reveal a moral subtext. Cubans hoped that what should be would be spurred; their emotions mirrored this normative judgment. Fidel's speeches are emblematic of the indignation that had been brewing in society for decades as its leaders trampled national ideals time after time. In his discourse he offered the vision of a utopia. He found a receptive audience who felt the same way he did. Emotional/moral synchronicity secured the affective bond between the charismatic leader and his followers. Fidel touched a moral nerve as he repudiated the old order and ushered in a new one.

The emotions at the heart of Fidel's discourse and those the revolutionary process inspired had their basis in liberal frameworks: democracy, nationalism, sovereignty, and material progress. Emotions and corporatist normativity also contributed to the contours of the emerging regime. Mass mobilization became the governing strategy of choice during the first years of the revolution. The political religion of the times mandated mobilization and militarization of society. Cubans were to be a unified army, combating the ills of the past and the threats of the present en route to a bright *mañana* (tomorrow). The moral crusade, born out of past frustrations and expectations of an honest autonomous political community, charged revolutionary politics with passion. Affection for the leader imbued revolutionary politics with the personal exceptionalism, instrumentality, and affective rationality that justified actions that otherwise would be unacceptable.

From the politics of passion and affection to incivility was one short step. Manichaeism reduced politics to a metastruggle between right and wrong, good and evil, for the revolution or against it, for or against Cuba. Opponents, and even positive skeptics and enlightened critics, a minority in the first two years, were singled out as traitors, counterrevolutionaries, *gusanos* (worms), and *anti-cubanos* (anti-Cubans). They were dealt with severely, setting a precedent for how to treat "deviants" in the future. Everything and anything could be, and was, justified by the higher end aspired to and by the affective attachment to the leader. Batista cronies were executed after "popular" trials, even though these courts did not conform to the legal procedures of the much-hailed Constitution of 1940. But many, including the Catholic Church, turned a blind eye. Claiming that it did not condone the executions, the Catholic hierarchy justified them. Eventually the Church would suffer from the same excess of revolutionary passion and affection. By 1961 the Catholic Church was a crippled institution, having lost schools, property, access to media, and most of its priests and followers.

The revolutionary experience of the first years was not only characterized by affection and passion toward the leaders and the revolution but also by petty (and not so petty) disaffection and hatred that motivated many to engage in reprehensible acts against enemies. The contrast between the moral crusade with its carnivalesque frenzy, on the one hand, and the ends-justifies-the-means logic that unleashed retribution against opponents, on the other, is graphically captured in the pages of *Bohemia*. In one instance, juxtaposed photographs depict two attractive and smartly dressed couples smiling, waving the Cuban flag through the windows of their shiny black car; below is the photograph of the bloody, almost naked corpse of a Batista "chivato" (snitch). Page after page of the January 11, 1959, special edition of the magazine contrasts the festive effervescence of the young with displays of bodies, bruised, stripped, eyes half closed, dead.

Showcasing the corpses of Batistianos required no justification: it was understood that this was revolutionary justice; they got what they deserved. That *Bohemia* did not consider the photographs offensive to the sensibilities of its readers hints at the continuation of a pattern of incivility in Cuban politics. Overriding passion for one's ideals warranted any step taken; the affective rationality, the instrumentality and personal exceptionalism of the politics of affection, could, and did, justify any and all actions. This sort of incivility is not atypical in revolutionary situations. The polarization inherent in civil war usually leads to the dehumanization of the opponent; Cuba was not an exception. Not all societies, however, extricate themselves from such situations in the same way. That the Cuban government never abandoned political religion, because it served the purposes of the elite and because people supported it, helps to explain the endurance of revolutionary incivility. At a deeper level, the conflicting paradigms at the heart of Cuban political culture lend themselves to this type of behavior as well. The resulting incivility is based on the culture of the people, making it quite resilient, particularly if alternative legitimate institutions are not created to control or change it.

The governing style during the first years accentuated informality rather than institutions. Personalism, spontaneity, and experimentation rather than what is usually described as rational calculation or standard operating procedures were the main features of decision making and governance; emotions play a larger role in the latter than in the former. Fidel and Ché epitomized the tendency to rule against established institutional formulas, partly because there were no self-evident standards at that time that applied to the new context, but also because this type of behavior was idiosyncratic and culturally based. Decisions that would have a significant long-term impact were made at the spur of the moment but reflected deep-seated concerns. This was the case during the preparations for Fidel Castro's first visit to the United States. His advisers, many of whom later sought exile, encouraged Fidel not to beg for aid from Washington, revealing their anti-U.S. feelings and their romantic notion of safeguarding Cuba's honor.[31] What has been interpreted commonly as a rebuff by Washington officials—not to provide assistance to the new government—had a much more mundane and heartfelt cause.

Desire and Disenchantment: The Fall from Grace of Political Religion

Economic reforms, part and parcel of the moral crusade, increased the expectations of the Cuban masses. Land, urban, educational, and health reforms made accessible material goods to a greater number of Cubans. Swiftly undertaken in the first year and a half, the measures garnered greater popularity for the leadership and the process, dramatically changing the face of Cuban society. From early on people expected the state to provide goods either free or at low cost (a revised version of the old notion of the paternalistic state as provider of goods and limits). Fidel himself fueled the bonfire of expectations from his first day in power by promising both sweeping reforms and simple symbolic redistributive acts. In early January 1959, in front of a cheering crowd, he recounted the promise he had made himself when he was fighting in the Sierra: "One day I told myself during a bombardment: Those planes will return here and will drop gifts. And I will deliver on that promise! . . . To bomb the Sierra Maestra with toys for the kids." [32] Promises of material and spiritual well-being were not scarce during the initial years of the revolution.

So many promises would not be easily realized or sustained, especially on a relatively poor island. The remarkable accomplishments in the areas of health, education, sports, and social equity not only came at a cost but also, ironically, set the stage for increased demands from and higher expectations of from the state. The next generations would want more material and nonmaterial goods and less state limitations. As early as 1959 an astute observer forewarned Fidel about such a possibility. Under the title "Fidel: Do Not Fail Us," the *Bohemia* writer expressed his plea, his hope, that the past would not repeat itself. "But, beware!" he cautioned. "In this romantic euphoria the revolution runs greater risks than those in the military fields. What the tanks of the dictator could not crush, or his bombings exterminate, can be ruined by that rhetorical exuberance to which we are so prone in the tropics. No long declarations. . . . [N]o utopic promises. No demagoguery." [33]

The rhetorical inflation of the times, characteristic of much of Cuban politics, would lead, contrary to what the author hoped for, to utopianism and, by the early 1980s, to disappointment. No state could sustain in the long term all that the revolutionary leaders promised. How, then, would passion and affection be reproduced over time? What would undergird popular support, governability, and legitimacy? The state and its leaders continuously demanded that the society reinvent itself along the lines of greater *conciencia* (revolutionary conscience) to work harder, to produce more, to be better revolutionaries, to sacrifice more. In turn, the people expected more and more from the state. The two contending demands distanced the state and the people, as neither could satisfy the other. The passion and affection behind charismatic leadership, mobilization, socialism, and revolution were in trouble, and so was the soft basis of the regime, its emotional infrastructure.

By the early 1980s many of the problems of Cuba's past had resurfaced under socialism (witness the *actos de repudio* [acts of repudiation] during the *Mariel* boatlift in 1980 and thereafter; dependence on sugar and tourism; corruption; inequity; abuse of power; intolerance). These were exacerbated by the economic crisis after the demise of communism in the USSR. The gap between theory and practice, promise and delivery, has cost the regime legitimacy and support. For many the revolution has become a failed utopia. Another modern project that came to naught. The principal response has been disenchantment with public life, resulting in a retreat to the personal, to the informal, or to alternative sources of hope, such as religion. Affection and passion for the leaders and a revolution no longer revolutionary have faded in most quarters. What remains is the passion of the few and the disappointment of the many, a new variant of social polarization. The greatest disenchantment perhaps was not the material one caused by the breakup of the Soviet Union but the moral one, because the revolution was supposed to be, above all, a spiritual renovation of the nation. Since 1959 when Fidel pledged "Never in my life will I tolerate consciously any immorality," [34] the notion of Cuban political society as a moral community has suffered greatly.

Contrary to what Apter argued, political religion does not fare better than other ideologies in bridging the gap between theory and practice. The failure of political religion in Cuba has been a failure of prophecy. Political religion failed in the long run to deliver the material and spiritual promises it had made. The feelings of devotion for the maximum leader and the affection connecting the state and the people have been eroding, to be replaced by sentiments that separate the people from the leadership and the society from the state. Disenchantment with political religion, clearly manifested in 1980 when more than one hundred thousand Cubans left the island in a massive boatlift and in the *balsero* (rafter) exodus of the early 1990s, opened the doors to a renaissance of traditional religions and alternative worldviews. At a time when the institutions of the regime are atrophied, a proto-civil society outside the ideological territoriality of the state is emerging as a way of expressing diverse passions and interests (see Chapter 7). Moreover, as the state fulfilled some promises, new demands emerged from an educated society with high expectations.

The regime's legitimacy comes into question as people look for alternative beliefs and practices outside those of the state. Traditional religions, with their own cosmographies of life and death, right and wrong, experience a resurgence as a result. This is precisely what has occurred in Cuba after the 1980s. During the previous decades, institutional religions suffered, and less institutionalized, more personal and "informal" ones such as *santería* prospered. The reason for this was that while the state eliminated or co-opted institutional challengers, the informal arena became the realm of resistance and alternative expression. Those religions that could be practiced in the privacy of one's own home and did not require a physical infrastructure (such as churches and bureaucracies) were able to thrive, especially because participation in the more formal religions carried steep social costs as believers were deemed unrevolutionary until the early 1990s.

The state did not have the way, in spite of its maximalist will, to provide all. As the politics of passion wilted, the informal and its networks of affection started to provide what the state could not: satisfaction for personal, spiritual, and even material needs through the flourishing black market. By the 1990s Cuban socialism was confronting ideological challenges from several quarters, from erstwhile followers who had stopped believing in the regime and now flocked to Christian and Afro-Cuban religions to human rights activists who advocated multiparty elections. Even PCC members proposed economic and political means to revise, and revive, Cuban socialism. International events conspired against political religion as well. The breakup of the Soviet Union and the transition to capitalism throughout Eastern Europe underscored the ideological predicament of the Cuban state.

Conclusion

The politics of passion and affection helped to shape the unexpected course of the revolution of 1959 and the distinguishing features of the regime. Passion for the moral struggle and affection for the charismatic leader energized the radicalization of the process. By the wayside went the Constitution of 1940, elections, a competitive party system, and liberal democracy, the initial nationalist reformist agenda. A new modern utopia—Marxism-Leninism— guided by a nonmodern political religion and its charismatic authority took its place. In the same way that feelings provided the fire for the destruction of the old, the emotional infrastructure of passion and affection laid the foundation for the new revolutionary regime.

Passion stemmed from moral value judgments regarding the ideals the political community should strive for. But that moral compass undid its own axis by not applying moral directives to all citizens alike, including enemies or "outsiders." Rhetorical inflation and utopianism, characteristic of the politics of passion, and the opportunistic and particularistic logic of the politics of affection contributed to disappointment. The state had to deliver material and spiritual goods that put it in an untenable situation in the long run. Moreover, the state was continuously challenged by informality through Cuban society (see Chapters 6 and 7).

From the beginning, continuity in the political culture set the stage for internal conflict and, in the final analysis, contributed to the less than stellar results of the revolutionary process. Moral codes combined with instrumental logic, on the one hand, and high expectations that would not materialize, on the other, scripted what was to come. The new order was not totally new. The revolution did not create a society from scratch; the mixture was already there. Society turned out to be the biggest obstacle to the state, because the state was incapable of molding society as it had envisioned. Society persisted in acting in ways that resisted, challenged, and subverted, as well as supported, state policies.

The affection, passion, utopianism, and informality of the initial years would come to haunt the regime and eventually conspire slowly against it. Confronted with a state that could not satisfy all needs as it promised, society resorted to familiar venues in the informal to deal with daily and transcendental needs that a secular state with its fading early political religious light could not illuminate. The notion of revolution became suspect, as did the modern ideology of Marxism-Leninism. Disenchantment increased over time as the promises of heaven on earth did not materialize fully at a time when younger Cubans were demanding more. By the 1980s the socialist revolutionary project *a la cubana* was in crisis, for material, ideological, spiritual, and affective reasons. As the gap between promise and delivery widened, the old leaders and the state, try as they may, could not rekindle the fire of passion. No better mirror of the difficulty of that task has there been than the experience of state-youth relations since the 1960s.

5

LOSING THAT LOVING FEELING

The Regeneration
of Passion
and Affection

From the 1960s to the 1990s the affective and passionate foundation of Cuban politics changed. Nowhere is the transformation better reflected than in young people's feelings about the political system. The interaction between *los jóvenes* (youth) and the government mirrors the general dynamics of state-society relations over the past four decades: erosion of the politics of passion, fading affection for charismatic leadership, and loss of attachment to the status quo. As a result the reproduction of the institutions of the socialist regime is in question. In contrast to the initial years of the revolution, by the late 1990s the predominant sentiment among the young is detachment.[1]

The politics of youth bring forth the difficulty of reproducing an emotional bond between the people and a revolution once it has been institutionalized. For the young of the 1980s and 1990s, the 1959 epic reads like ancient history; it is not their story. Political affection and passion, even if retransmitted through socialization, seem to be insufficient to guarantee the support of succeeding generations. Simply put, love was not enough; feelings about the regime came to rest on standards other than sentimental ones, namely, the congruence between the theory and the practice of the state. With time, delivery rather than promise assumed greater significance in sustaining popular support. When a regime fails to act according to its own criteria and make good on the promises made, the emotional and moral glue that helped to consolidate it will not hold. At that point the survival of the regime over the long haul is in doubt.

That point in Cuba came in the early 1980s when generational, material, and ideological factors coincided to undermine the regime. By 1980 the generation of Cubans who had been born after 1959 or had grown up under the new system, now in their teens, twenties, and thirties, expressed discontent and skepticism. Younger Cubans did not feel the same about their government as their parents did in 1959. Time and experience had distanced them from the revolutionary struggle. Their daily experience had become routinized and institutionalized. The political had lost its spontaneous celebratory quality, falling into repetitive ritualism, into what young Cubans call *teque* (official harangue). But the ritualization of politics was not the principal reason for the shift in young people's feelings. What explains the growing tension between the state and youth was the realization of the dissonance between theory and practice in Cuban socialism, the failure of the utopia. As a result the emotional ties that bound the state, the leader, and the revolution to the people, *los jóvenes* specifically, frayed.

Over time affection and passion for the system revolved less around charisma and political religion and increasingly around four issues that all political systems must contend with: (1) efficiency and inefficiency; (2) efficacy and inefficacy; (3) participation and control; and (4) conflict and consensus.[2] These issues speak to the legitimacy of the system as well as to long-term governability and the prospect for change. By analyzing them, one can find fault lines in state-society relations and uncover how individuals perceive and feel about their government.

These issues are not calculated exclusively in strict and traditionally defined rational terms; they are interpreted subjectively and emotionally, reflecting the affective (and disaffective) side of modern politics. What individuals voice when asked about political issues is not exclusively based on a mathematical cost-benefit formula but on an affective mixture of hopes and despair, illusion and disillusion, what ought to be as opposed to what is. These four key areas illustrate to what extent expectations match reality. Lack of fit between normative frameworks and day-to-day life in *socialismo real* (real socialism) hurts the affection and passion youth (and older Cubans as well) once felt for the revolution, its *líder máximo*, political religion, and official ideology. Youth are particularly sensitive to the gap between ideals and reality because it is precisely during these years that individuals tend to measure the codes handed to them against actual practice.

By the 1990s the signs were clear that the Cuban regime had been unable to reproduce the necessary emotional infrastructure to guarantee legitimacy and governability. On the contrary, feelings of alienation, exhaustion, skepticism, and anger had flourished, coexisting with aspirations for the ideals of the revolution: equity, liberty, progress, and the quest for a moral nation. Here resides the greatest challenge for the Cuban government and the regime. The problem is a difficult one: How does a state regenerate its emotional capital, especially when that sentimental base rested on charisma, political religion, and the epic of the armed struggle and when the material base was inadequate to provide the goods promised? The inability to sustain the delivery of economic benefits coupled with political religion's failure of prophecy put the Cuban state in a predicament. While nationalism continues to generate affective attachment and the maximum leader still commands a level of support, the emotional revolution has been unable to secure among the young the required affective wherewithal to replicate itself. Whereas the state demanded institutionalization and rationalization, the revolution required passion and affection. The stage for contradiction, tension, and change was set from the beginning of the new regime. To complicate matters, the revolutionary government in 1959 and in the early 1960s unwisely raised expectations by promising far more than the material base could produce. The demise of the beneficial trade and aid regime with the communist bloc in the early 1990s produced an economic crisis that undermined the politics of passion, accelerating the rupture between the young and the state.

The dilemma for the construction of modern nation-states is inescapable. While affection is required to bring a collectivity together, it is not enough to ensure legitimacy and governability in the long run. The very institutionalization necessary to improve regime performance tends to undermine affection and passion for the political system. Who loves bureaucracy? Efficiency per se is an inadequate basis for legitimacy. States require a measure of emotional capital and affective magnetism to guarantee support and imbue citizens with a measure of identity and meaning. The modern state is caught in the conundrum of too much or too little affection; the logic of modernity does not resolve it.

Cuban Youth

Defining "youth" is not an uncomplicated task. The first difficulty is that it is suspect, if not simplistic, to speak about hundreds of thousands of individuals as a monolithic group. Although I use the term "youth," I do not pretend to include all young people at all times. Rather the focus is on patterns of behavior, attitudes, and feelings within that group. The second definitional challenge is how to demarcate the category "youth." While some Cuban sociologists argue that youth covers the period between sixteen and thirty years of age, others mark the start of youth at age thirteen. There is no consensus as to when youth ends either. For instance, the upper age limit for membership in the Unión de Juventud Comunista (Union of Communist Youth; UJC), the youth arm of the Communist Party of Cuba, from which many of the PCC cadres are recruited, is the mid-thirties.[3] Moreover, any definition of youth is problematic because the boundary between childhood, youth, and adulthood is blurry. Strict age limits do not conform to individual and contextual differences that influence the passage from childhood to youth and later to adulthood. Yet an age-based definition serves the purpose of demographic identification. Approximately 40 percent of the Cuban population is under the age of thirty. Their numbers, however, are not the only source of their political and social importance. Because of their high educational level (which in turn has increased their expectations), one would expect Cuban youth to show considerable political activism. Throughout Cuban history *los jóvenes,* particularly university students, have indeed played a leading role in ushering in sociopolitical change, as was the case in the 1930s and 1950s.

Youth's pivotal political and social position, according to Karl Mannheim, stems from the "uncertainty and doubt" that results when "one's questions outrun the scope of one's inherited answers."[4] When prescribed formulas do not stand the test of time, questions regarding the validity of theory and practice come to the fore, challenging cosmographies and institutions. According to Weber, the young are caught between two divergent ethics: the pure ethics of absolute ends characteristic of adolescence and the ethic of responsibility of adulthood. Precisely due to the former, the politics of passion might be attractive to *los jóvenes.* The two competing perspectives make the young measure ideals transmitted to them by families and society in general with the reality they experience firsthand. The young everywhere face the gap between what ought to be and what is. The larger the gap, the more traumatic its discovery and the more dramatic the possible consequences.[5] In the Cuban case, in which the political culture combines conflicting paradigms of romantic idealism and the instrumental, particularistic "everything goes" logic of the informal, the encounter is potentially explosive and helps to explain why the younger generations have been the catalyst for change and the standard-bearers for moral renovation time after time in Cuban political history.

Socialization, Desocialization, and the Reproduction of Passion

The reproduction of affection and revolutionary passion for the regime hinges on the issue of socialization and desocialization of youth. Political socialization is traditionally defined as the "acquisition of *prevailing* norms and modes of behavior. In this sense the 'socialized' person is one who has successfully internalized the prevailing norms of behavior modes."[6] This definition represents the behavioral school of political socialization. The other principal school of thought, the psychological, stresses the acquisition and maintenance of values and patterns of thought. Neither explicitly addresses the emotional link to the system through the affective base of behavior or the emotional dimension of psychology. In everyday life the lines between behavior, thoughts, values, and feelings are more diffused than is assumed in socialization theory. I approach the topic from both the behavioral and the psychological perspectives, adding to them the emotional factor: the maintenance or breakdown of affective attachment to the political system. This inclusive definition is useful because the Cuban state, like most others, has attempted to shape not only the behavior and attitudes of the people but also their sentimental bond with it, its leaders, and the nation.

Over time collective feelings regarding the political system depend on one main issue: whether the promises of the state become reality. Such promises are not merely material in nature. Perhaps more important is the normative dimension. Where the gap between theory and practice is wide, people will not only stop believing in the government and eventually in the regime, they will not feel attached to it. Desocialization is the by-product of this lack of faith and sentimental loss. It involves rejection of the dominant values of the state and a loss of affective identification with the status quo.

In the Cuban case, the informal sphere of everyday life in which the politics of affection play a key role attracts those who are disenchanted with the state, its official ideology, its actual moral code, and the institutional spaces controlled by the party and the bureaucracy. The informal includes expanding the margins of the permissible within official institutions, subverting the prescribed codes of conduct, and allowing alternative norms, behaviors, and identities to manifest themselves. Young artists have been engaged in this process since 1959. In the informal, among friends, in the politics of affection between families and *socios* (buddies), youth find the real, sincere, and immediate values that the official social arena has lost.

When youth experience irreconcilable contradictions between norms handed down to them—what ought to be—and praxis—what is—oversocialization may occur. Oversocialization is "the realization by a socialized individual of the gap between reality and ideals and a consequent refusal to regard reality as acceptable."[7] Oversocialization may result in desocialization and eventually in resocialization. Oversocialization and desocialization may take place in every type of political system, especially in moments of crisis (such as the Vietnam War in the United States). However, maximalist states, those that assign themselves a pervasive and dominant socioeconomic, political, and moral role in society, are particularly prone to the oversocialization and desocialization of individuals. The more the state promises and the higher the expectations of the citizens, the greater the likelihood that those expectations will not materialize, resulting in a performance gap that leads to oversocialization and desocialization.

Political, economic, and moral factors compound to undermine socialization. An economy of scarcity, combined with high expectations, for instance, foments discontent with and questioning of the political system. For Cuban youth reduced socioeconomic opportunities and continued sacrifice in daily life throughout the 1980s and 1990s have put to the test the performance vis-à-vis the promise of the socialist system. But economic scarcity is not the sole cause of desocialization, only a contributing factor. The root cause is deeper. It relates to the normative frameworks of the regime in theory and its instrumental procedures in practice and the clash between both. Youth, due to their own existential sorting of ends and means, idealism and pragmatism, as well as their personal struggle for identity and meaning, find the dissonance repulsive and difficult to accept. The tendency is to reject the *doble moral* (dual moral code: one for the public arena and another for the private), which in turn loosens the bonds of affection and passion required by charisma, political religion, and Marxism-Leninism.

The feelings expressed by Cuban youth in regard to their society and the political system refer to this normative clash as well as to the material difficulties that render daily life burdensome. Two developments, one national and the other international, underscore the confrontation between theory and practice that affected youth's perception of their government. The first was the 1980 Mariel boatlift. The boatlift had a serious impact on young people and the population at large for several reasons. The underlying cause of the massive emigration was the realization that Cubans who had sought exile earlier had done quite well for themselves in the United States while those who stayed on the island had fewer economic options. Moreover, during the exodus the Committees for the Defense of the Revolution, neighborhood watchdog organizations, orchestrated *actos de repudio* against those who wanted to leave. Neighbors threw stones and eggs at them. Others were assaulted. Obscenities were hurled and scribbled on the walls of their homes. Attack dogs were unleashed. Whole families were under siege by furious crowds that threatened them night and day outside their houses. For many Cubans the spectacle of the Mariel boatlift was a breaking point. They could not accept living under a system that encouraged that kind of behavior; basic moral norms were transgressed in a system that portrayed itself as highly moral.

The second development that represented a watershed in terms of youth-state relations on the island was the process of reforms in the Soviet Union post-1986. Glasnost and perestroika awoke interest and hope among Cubans who expected a similar course of reforms at home, but their expectations were dashed. Cuban socialism would not engage in restructuring and liberalization along the lines of its former allies. Instead the leadership opted for *socialismo o muerte* (socialism or death), at most gingerly tinkering with reforms. The cost to the regime in terms of support was considerable, especially among *los jóvenes*, who increasingly felt that there was no way out for them, except to leave the island. In the early 1990s thousands took to the seas in makeshift rafts.

The situation was aggravated by the fact that, despite attempts since the mid-1980s to rejuvenate the party and the state, the top positions in the political and administrative apparatus remained the domain of older Cubans. The latter, while not having the glowing academic or professional credentials of their younger compatriots, could count on personal connections, seniority, the moral capital associated with the revolutionary experience, and the politics of affection that the former do not have. Feeling left out is an important political motivation for the young in Cuba as elsewhere. After considerable research on youth and social order, Frank Musgrove concluded that "the youth will provide an impetus toward social experimentation and change not when they are given power but when they are denied it."[8]

The Ideals of Political Socialization

Every state and its institutions socialize individuals in ways supportive of the system and the status quo. Soon after the advent of the revolution the state undertook several major campaigns to socialize individuals according to revolutionary norms. A host of programs, such as the literacy campaign of 1961 and educational reforms, were launched to transmit the values of the new society; they constituted the nuts and bolts, the hardware, with which to reproduce the politics of passion. Socialization was revolutionary in that it attempted to transform the culture of the nation in ways supportive of the immediate and long-term goals of social change. Values such as collective spirit, *conciencia,* egalitarianism, self-sacrifice, patriotism, internationalism, and loyalty to Fidel Castro and the symbols of the revolution would be functional to the state and the society under construction. All these values required, and presumed, an emotional infrastructure: particular feelings (such as solidarity, love for the nation, affection for the leader and others, optimism, respect for authority, trust) that would displace the old society's emotional base (selfishness, aggression, frustration, mistrust). The new values and sentiments would be the clay with which to form the New Man, that being of glowing qualities of mind, body, and soul. The future generations would be cast in this mold, as the leaders (and the official ideology, Marxism) viewed them as being malleable. The older generations, more set in their ways, and partly responsible for Cuba's past downfall, were not as easily molded.

The Cuban state from 1959 has had superlative expectations of Cuban youth. They were expected to embody the ideals of the revolution, to put their best foot forward and model their behavior on the guidelines set forth by the *lider máximo* and state agencies. To this end, the state established a series of institutions and drafted a code of conduct to socialize (and control) the young. The objectives were twofold: to foster the revolutionary personality and to develop a labor force, which was considered of great importance to Cuba's development. In Fidel Castro's words:

> In the conditions under which we live, because of the problems that our country is facing, we must inculcate our youth with the spirit of discipline, of struggle, of work. In my opinion, everything that tends to promote in our youth the strongest possible spirit, activities related in some way with the defense of the country, such as sports, must be promoted.[9]

Communist youth were expected to be selfless, martyrs for the cause: "Being a Communist youth will not entail privilege at all, on the contrary: being a Communist youth will entail sacrifice, will entail 'renunciamiento,' will entail abnegation. . . . [T]he Communist youth . . . will have to be willing to give his life for the Revolution and for his fatherland without vacillation. This is the essential condition of every Communist youth."[10] These ideal types would have to be consumed by the passion for the nation, the revolution, and communism and could not entertain other emotions that were not useful to the regime. The expectation rested on a fundamental contradiction: the archetypical communist youth would have the capacity for great sensibility (necessary to be in touch with the needs of others), yet he or she had to be in some basic way numbed to his or her own needs, wants, desires, and individuality. As the state educated these youngsters, not only was socialization occurring, but, at the same time, education, unwittingly, provided tools for questioning the tenets of the regime and the roles and rules it established.

There are four channels by which Cuban youth are socialized: family, schools, state-controlled mass organizations, and the informal sphere. The messages these channels transmit are not always congruent; contradiction is common. While in the family and in the informal sector personal exceptional-ism, particularism, and affection form the basis of personal relations, schools and mass organizations attempt to foster affection for the regime, the nation, and the collectivity above all. The informal sector, the non-state-controlled arena of daily life, has manifested resistance to state policies; behavior, atti-tudes, and feelings that challenge those prescribed by socialist ethics predomi-nate in it. The politics of passion clashed with the politics of affection in *lo informal*, creating a dissonance between public official discourse and practice in everyday life.

The Cuban government has emphasized the role of education in the de-velopment of society and individual personality. Schools are one of the two principal venues of state-controlled socialization. Schooling starts with the *Círculos infantiles* (day care centers). After day care, all elementary-school-aged children are to join the Pioneros (Pioneers) and wear distinctive red ban-danas. High school, university, and technical/vocational students have their own mass organizations. The Federación Estundiantil Universitaria (Federa-tion of University Students; FEU) is one such organization, but the most im-portant is the UJC. In the early 1990s the UJC had almost 1.5 million members, approximately 25 percent of Cuban youth.

Cuban youth are expected to participate in a host of other mass organi-zations, such as the Committees for the Defense of the Revolution (CDRs) and the Ejército Juvenil del Trabajo (Youth Labor Army; EJT), whose purpose is to assist in production in key sectors of the economy. All these institutions try to mold the youngsters according to the ideals of a perfect communist. The emphasis is on respect, obedience, hard work, and collective over individual satisfaction. The expectation was that as a result of this socialization process the New Man and New Woman would emerge. Socialism would produce the perfect human being in a perfect Cuban society.

The process of socialization and the institutions in charge of it have had one main purpose: to inculcate values, patterns of conduct, and emotions sup-portive of the regime. The dynamics of socialization, however, have not been smooth or unilinear, or without unexpected consequences and shifts in gear. On the contrary, the story is one of mixed results, of accommodation and resistance, and of unfulfilled expectations. One of the consequences of state socialization is that in the spaces provided young people form networks of friends that generate horizontal solidarity, below and outside the state's pur-view, and not infrequently engage in activities contrary to state dogma. The result is a subversion of the state's purpose. Through those networks of friends emerge alternative practices, identities, and feelings that challenge official at-tempts at socialization.

The agencies of state socialization also serve as a check on reality in the sense that *los jóvenes* are able to judge whether those organizations live up to their mandates. Their goals and actual accomplishments may not coincide, contributing to the realization of dissonance. For example, *las escuelas al campo* (schools in the countryside) are supposed to help students value agricultural work by having them work in the fields. Participants provide an alternative account. According to them, *la escuela al campo* is *un relajo, un choteo* (a disorder, a joke), where the young do the least possible amount of work and the most partying possible. Inefficiency is rampant, and disrespect for farm work is common. What students learn is how to get around state mandates, how to resist informally. One of the lessons of *la escuela al campo* is that the state does not achieve its stated purpose while exerting formal control over the students. Such lessons slowly erode legitimacy and create feelings of disdain for the state. Young people stop believing in the official discourse as they see that reality teaches them otherwise.

Losing the Feeling: State-Youth Relations since the 1960s

Official expectations of young people have turned out to be elusive. In spite of the resources invested, the Cuban state has been unable to shape the behavior, attitudes, and feelings of Cuban youth as it had hoped, particularly after the 1980s. The pattern of state-youth relations has been characterized by coercion, not only consensus, and resistance, not only accommodation. It has become clear that increasingly young people have been losing that loving feeling for the revolution.

In 1962 the first youth congress, sponsored by the Asociación de Jóvenes Rebeldes (Association of Rebel Youth), the predecessor of the UJC, set optimistic standards for young Cubans and sky-high expectations of what the state would supply. *Los jóvenes* were praised as the embodiment of the future of the revolution, a romantic notion underscoring the politics of passion and traditional Cuban codes of passion. If youth failed to achieve their potential, so would the revolutionary process. The congress promised that young Cubans would eventually "live in the bounty of socialism." They would construct the socialist society, the new utopia, because they lacked "the vices, the limitations, and the unenlightenedness of the past."[11] This unblemished view soon gave way to a less appealing perspective, as young people proved to be human and Cuban after all, reproducing some of the cultural traits of the past.

By 1972, when the second youth congress was held, the UJC and the state admitted the difficulties they encountered in attracting youth to study and work. State socialization was not uniformly successful. The *desvinculados,* unconnected teenagers, appeared. They were dropouts, sixteen or younger, who exhibited behavioral and attitudinal problems. The state was unsure of how to deal with them. A greater dosage of ideology mixed with repression and work was the (ineffectual) solution provided at the time. The mounting problems with youth, ranging from unsatisfactory educational performance to academic fraud, from the adoption of capitalist lifestyles to ideological formalism, were some of the issues presented at the third congress, held in 1977. By that time the government admitted its limited ability to shape society in general and youth in particular: "The analysis of our tasks demonstrates that we have not generated successful initiatives that mobilize thousands of youngsters. . . . We are on the defensive." [12] Cuban youth were manifesting themselves in ways unpalatable to the regime. They expressed alternative norms of conduct informally, at times accommodating formally but rejecting in practice the state's codes; the *doble moral* became endemic.

Since the 1960s the struggle for the hearts and minds of Cuban youth has been expressed in semiotic and material ways: in discourse, in fashion, in hairstyle, in music, in lifestyle. The manifestation of individuality, and the feelings implied by it, ran counter to the official values of collectivism and egalitarianism. Those who challenged the state through their "extravagant" and decadent behavior had to pay dearly: expulsion from schools, harassment, even incarceration. But those nonconformists at the margins were not the only ones who failed to live up to the high standards expected and imposed on them. Fidel Castro even criticized UJC cadres who displayed *blandenguería* and *chapucería* in their conduct.[13]

By the early 1980s several developments pointed to the checkered results of the socialization of Cuban youth, many of whom were failing to meet the standards of the state. Of the 125,000 Cubans who left the island through the Mariel boatlift, 41 percent were under the age of twenty-seven. The would-be New Man and New Woman were abandoning the revolution. The same pattern would be apparent during the rafters' exodus in the early to mid-1990s. Juvenile crime was on the rise, as were unemployment and dropout rates. Rock and roll, long hair, and Western capitalist fashion attracted young people (or distracted them, according to the government).

In 1987 the fifth congress of the UJC tried to tackle the problem head-on by facing the source of the desocialization: the formalism that had befallen the revolution. The revolution was no longer a matter of affection for the leader or passion for the moral and material reconstruction of the nation. It was a bureaucratized and formulaic phenomenon that failed to ignite the hearts of the younger generations. This is the principal noxious consequence of the rationalization and routinization of power: individuals tend to lose the affective attachment to the system. Thus states and nations need emotionally charged symbols and discourses to arouse feelings of support and sustain order in the collectivity. Periodically those emotions must be recharged to reproduce the status quo. Furthermore, the state is especially vulnerable to the loss of affective bonds with the population if it does not fulfill its technocractic functions efficiently.

For the young, the revolution had fallen prey to *el teque* by the 1980s. Young people rejected *el teque* not only because of its litany-like nature, but principally because it did not ring true. In response to their concerns, the fifth congress of the UJC adopted "Sin Formalismos" (Without Formalism) as its slogan. The precept was that formalism had robbed socialism of its authenticity, immediacy, and vitality, leading to alienation and distance between the young and the state. Young people wanted to inject Cuban socialism with real meaning, not with empty phrases. The leadership of the party and the state seemed to agree that a reanimated and rejuvenated socialism was needed to bring youth into the fold.

Sin Formalismo was an attempt to inject meaning into the staid political system. It worked—partially. The UJC and the media catering to young people underwent a period of self-analysis that eventually redesigned programs that were found "lacking in significance for the cadres."[14] Minor changes in style ensued. The UJC, under the leadership of Roberto Robaina (who later became foreign minister) embraced rock music as a way to attract the young. The youth media started to cover issues of significance to the daily life of teenagers, topics once considered taboo. But cosmetic makeover was not enough to deal with the problems of *los jóvenes,* particularly those relating to antisocial behavior and economic dissatisfaction. Unemployment, crime, dropout rates, and other social ills were reaching unprecedented levels.

Young people found themselves with less opportunity for advancement in the workplace and limited access to prestigious university careers, both of which created tension in a sector that had been taught to believe that the revolution would provide ever-growing opportunities. The coming-of-age of these youngsters, the future of the nation, met the harsh reality of a declining economy and a virtual economic collapse after 1989. By late 1989 young people represented a scant 2.6 percent of all economic managers, although one-third of those who occupied those positions did not meet the necessary educational requirements.[15] The profile has not improved significantly in the 1990s.[16]

The process of rejuvenating the UJC (and Cuban socialism by extension) was launched at the same time that the Rectification Campaign was in full swing. While the rejuvenation attempted to reenergize the organization, give it a "hip" look, and promote an affirmative action program on behalf of younger cadres, the Rectification Campaign called for an expanded role for ideology (in daily life and in economic management) and inaugurated an austerity program that undid many of the economic reforms of past years. As Cuban socialism started to respond to the concerns of the young, economic and political opportunities were being foreclosed simultaneously, as the regime had to confront the greatest economic and political crisis of the past three decades.

In the end Rectification and the Special Period in Times of Peace overtook rejuvenation. Both alienated youth even more. The government's periodic reversals in economic policy toward greater centralization created uncertainty and the impression of incompetence. The economic tailspin of the late 1980s and early 1990s shook what goodwill the regime still enjoyed among the young as the hopes and expectations for a better tomorrow were truncated by the harsh reality of today. Tomorrow was far away. The order of the day was to make ends meet, to *resolver*. Even those who had played by the rules of the game now found that their sacrifices had come to naught. Their hopes wilted as promises crumbled.

The sixth youth congress in 1992 addressed the domestic and international challenges by focusing on *sobrevivencia* and *supervivencia*—resistance in order to survive. The top priority was to convince *los jóvenes* that the Cuban leadership had chosen the correct road. Cuban socialism was fighting for its life. The UJC, less preoccupied at that point with behavior, led a campaign to change the perceptions of the young. Subjective appreciation of the cause of the debacle was the most pressing concern for the leadership because the young blamed the administration and its leadership, not exogenous factors far removed from Cuban shores. The result, according to the government, was "the mirage [among youth] that everything can be fixed if the administrative apparatus is improved." [17]

The sixth congress candidly revealed the feelings of the young regarding the political system, its leaders, and the juncture at which Cuban socialism found itself. The young, according to the report of the congress, were "wavering, they simply have stopped believing in the Revolution or consider that it is impossible to resist and triumph. . . . They are the ones who criticize all. . . . They are the super-revolutionaries. . . . One hears them say that everything is going wrong, that they are tired, . . . that we have spent 30 years saying that we are in the worst moment." [18] From 1959 to 1992 the political system, its leaders, and the young had lost their bond of affection and passion.

After 1992 the split between young people and the state seemed irreparable as the regime adopted policies that undermined the principles on which socialism had stood. This was the case with the overture to international tourism. Tourists who visited the island had access to hotels, beaches, discotheques, restaurants, stores, and commodities not available to ordinary Cubans. The practice was labeled informally "tourism apartheid" and generated anger among Cubans. Even before its legalization in summer 1993, the U.S. dollar had become the currency of choice in the internal economy. But not all Cubans had access to it, only those who worked in the tourist sector or those who had generous relatives abroad—another modality of the politics of affection. As the economic crisis took its toll, the socialist safety net, on which most Cubans relied for basic needs, was sharply reduced. The standard of living of Cubans, including the young, declined.[19]

The emotions of the young at this point must be understood not only as a personal reaction to the dire conditions of daily life but also as a reaction or judgment against the political formula that was not meeting expectations and that was in contradiction with its own normativity. The crisis of belief had been etched deep. With it, political religion and charisma eroded, as did legitimacy and, to a lesser extent, governability. The sentimental ties between the population and the system, so important in its origin, failed. The reproduction of the system was unsure.

From Passion to Performance

The conflict between the state and the young from the 1980s on (if not earlier) has revolved around four issues of governmental performance. The government's inability to address those areas of concern to the satisfaction of *los jóvenes* has generated in them negative feelings toward the political system.

Efficiency and Inefficiency

One of the major issues for Cuban youth and for state-society relations in general is the bureaucratization of the Cuban political system. Bureaucratic formalism is contrary to the spontaneity, the experimentation, and the effervescence of the early revolutionary years, which led to massive support and were indicative of the politics of passion and affection. Red tape and inefficiency result in the rejection of the public arena dominated by the state and a turn to private and informal spaces.

Governmental efficiency is related to legitimacy and governability. The less efficient the system, the less legitimacy it will summon and the less likely it will be to sustain governability. Cuban youth, entering adulthood with lofty aspirations, confront time and time again the inability of the system to deliver the goods and benefits promised. Part of the problem with delivery, admits a government official, is "the plethora of controls and paperwork. . . . This is part of our whole system of formalism, whose weight is felt on how the people's government functions." A young construction worker agreed: "There is no end to the red tape and hassle at the municipal level." [20] Young people on the island condemn the pervasive inefficiency, ranging from the food rationing system to public transportation and education. The entire political system is indicted indirectly.

Efficacy and Inefficacy

Efficacy, the sense that representatives and ordinary citizens have the ability to deal effectively with political problems, makes individuals feel that the government is legitimate. The discourse of the Cuban government and the official ideology have emphasized the common person's access to the organs of power. While the rhetoric increased expectations, the system has failed to deliver on its promise. Since the 1980s young people increasingly have felt that their representatives and the institutions of government do not command the necessary autonomy to exercise authority in a decisive manner. A *Bohemia* poll revealed that more than 40 percent of those questioned did not have confidence in their representatives and said that the elected officials were "errand boys." Of those polled, 48 percent believed that "the representative does not have sufficient authority to solve problems in his district." The author of the article in which the poll was reported concluded that "the lack of power to find solutions to many problems tends to break down voters' faith in their representative." [21] Cuban youth express those feelings readily. Interviews with former UJC members, both in exile and on the island, conducted from the 1980s to the 1990s, indicate that the sense of powerlessness and frustration prevalent in other sectors of the society is also common among the young.

Participation and Control

In Cuba the young are not only highly educated but also mobilized, which results in greater pressure for participation. Official participation is conditional on "revolutionary credentials" and conformity with the principles of Marxism- Leninism. Mass organizations foster participation with control, but given the lack of efficacy of these institutions, *los jóvenes* are increasingly attracted to participate in unofficial arenas, limited as those spaces are and as risky as such involvement might be. The young are channeling their political and social participation into the informal through the politics of affection. Involvement in the informal indicates that the official venues are less and less binding and attractive, that the bonds of affection between the institutions of the state and youth are loosening, and that socialization is less and less successful. Furthermore, the young want participation in a manner that respects and acknowledges the diversity of Cuban society and the freedom to express alternatives. The monolithic nature of the early years of the revolution, so much a part of the crusade for a new Cuba, is no longer a reality. During this stage of their lives, *los jóvenes* want to express their individuality.

Conflict and Consensus

Although the political religion of yesteryear is hardly convincing, the young still hold on to nationalism and to other revolutionary values (such as basic equity). At the same time they have found and have crafted alternative modes of expression, new interests, alternative identities, and multiple attachments. The young are well aware of the diversity of Cuban society and the atomization behind the facade of unity of mass organizations. The greater the pressure exerted on them to conform through coercion, the less likely it is that the system will garner the support of younger Cubans. Religion and Western pop culture — music, fashion, television, and ideas — are attracting more and more Cuban youth. The grandson of Ché Guevara, Canek, dreams not of being a revolutionary but a rock star. Postmodernism, with its challenge to traditional notions, has also influenced the young intelligentsia, making them question many of the inherited meanings. The young public is generally less likely than their parents were in 1950 and 1960 to accept the official discourse at face value. *Somos Jóvenes* (We Are the Young), a principal publication for youth on the island, captured these attitudes succinctly. In one illustration, the magazine juxtaposed a drawing of an orangutan with a photograph of the controversial Irish singer Sinead O'Connor. The caption below read *Que remedio, hay que evolucionar* (There is no remedy but to evolve).[22] *Somos Jóvenes*, signaling the existential position of the youth, quoted Diderot in another issue: "It is as risky to believe everything as to believe nothing."[23]

Informal Resistance and Disenchantment

The young both accommodate to and resist governmental demands. They evade agricultural work, voluntary service, meetings of the CDRs. They skip school, drop out, dodge the draft. Crime, alcoholism, and prostitution have increased among the young, particularly during the economic crisis of the 1990s. In the poorer neighborhoods the situation is critical. A study showed that 54 percent of thirty-one minors interviewed had behavioral problems and 38 percent had attended a reeducation center.[24] Dissimulation is another, more benign and widespread, form of resistance, leading to the dual morality that espouses one set of codes in public and another in private. Over time the young have increasingly challenged official norms by asserting their personal beliefs in public.

The dissatisfaction of the young has an emotional foundation with repercussions for their commitment to the regime and their economic productivity. A young textile worker interviewed by *Somos Jóvenes* explained why production at the Bellotex factory had not met targets: "We don't even deliver half what we could because we lack love and desire to do so. But that is not only our fault. In the end, he who won't change will be crushed by the wheel of time."[25] The feelings of the young spring from the disenchantment they have experienced. The result is the retreat to the private after the exhaustion of political activism. In the Cuban case, that "retreat" entails informalization and the revamping of many of the traditional aspects of Cuban political culture: *choteo*, incivility, the politics of affection. Part and parcel of the process is a loss of hope in many of the projects of modernity: social engineering, revolution, socialism. Disenchantment and disbelief, however, are not the exclusive province of Cuban youth. They are common to youth elsewhere who share some of the basic experiences of late modernity.

Conclusion

Can the socialist regime reproduce itself with the current emotional infrastructure prevalent among youth? It is unlikely, because the symbols and myths of the past have lost their original emotional charge, their ability to compel the politics of passion. Disenchantment envelops Cuban youth in the 1990s. Many UJC members seek ways out of their political compromises, abandoning political activism for domesticity, private commitments, or alternative engagements. The young intelligentsia, once the interlocutors of the politics of affection and passion, are exiting the island for temporary or permanent positions abroad in a silent brain drain. Others who stay find in nihilism and neoexistentialism their response to the crisis of Cuban socialism and Cuban society as evidenced by a crop of new writers.[26] Young writers and artists have painted a portrait of an entire generation whose principal features are ennui and angst.

The younger generation's attempts to push the limits of expression and to put on the table critical issues have had partial results at best. Within the Unión Nacional de Escritores y Artistas de Cuba (National Union of Writers and Artists of Cuba; UNEAC), the umbrella organization for intellectuals and artists, as in the UJC, members periodically raise their voices in an attempt to challenge meaningless repetition of *el teque*. They long for an authentic discourse and for greater autonomy. Young technocrats also share the same frustration over the direction of the economy and public policy. Although they conform, many break the codes of conduct in a variety of informal ways. Many are left with the despair of those who have something to say but no one to listen. Others seek far more literal departures from reality. More than 75 percent of the latest wave of emigrants, the *balseros* who left the island in the early 1990s in makeshift rafts, were under the age of thirty-nine.[27] Many died at sea.

Relations between the state and the young in Cuba have been marked by lofty expectations followed by mutual disappointment. The leaders and the state expected the young to behave in ways different from those characteristic of past generations. *Los jóvenes* were to become the New Men and New Women of the new Cuba. The affection and passion of the revolutionary struggle and the early years of the revolution would be transmitted to and reproduced in them indefinitely. That affective attachment to the political system and its leaders and to the passionate pursuit of the revolutionary order would guarantee the continuation of the regime forever. The standards by which Cuban *jóvenes* judge socialism show that states are confronted by two different but related demands: affective and technocratic. Modern states must satisfy both, or experience alienation between the state and society. These two standards, traditionally identified with emotion and interest, are not contrary or divorced from each other. Quite the opposite: they are intimately connected and each co-constitutes the other.

To warrant that affection and that passion, the Cuban regime promised material and nonmaterial benefits for the young. Although it delivered on many of its promises, by the 1980s the state was caught in the inescapable logic of modernity, the process of social change created new desires and higher expectations. Confronted with a younger generation that listened to rock and roll, adopted capitalist cultural styles, embraced ideas of diversity and postmodernity, and judged the political system not mainly on promise but on performance, the state's ability to reproduce itself was in doubt. The young have had expectations that the state did not find acceptable and could not meet. The internal contradiction between ideology and praxis, coupled with a downward-spiraling economy since the mid-1980s, led to unsatisfied hopes and a growing chasm between the state and the young. The government has realized the alienation of the youth and in the 1990s has attempted to address it by partial rejuvenation of party and state structures.

Both the state and the young have accommodated and resisted each other. Even a maximalist state such as Cuba has faced limits in making individuals act in prescribed ways at all times. The normative paradigms that the leaders espoused, with their idealistic view of the perfectibility of human nature and the possibility of social engineering to craft a utopia, are the root causes of the disappointment, as once it confronts reality, the dream proves impossible to realize. The attempt to reproduce the feelings of passion and the intimate bonds of affection between leaders and followers was also futile, because with the passing of time the life experiences of the young are increasingly removed from 1959. The bureaucratization of the state after the 1970s and the routinization of power worked against the politics of passion, while the failure of prophecy subverted political religion. Consequently the young find it impossible to reconcile the theory and practice of the regime. Within this context, the cultural patterns of Cuba have continued to manifest themselves in spite of the state's attempts to eradicate the old. The revolutionary imperative for absolute ends typified by the politics of passion has coexisted with the less savory dimensions of Cuban political culture. Where the state failed in socializing the young, traditional Cuban culture (carried forth by families and in the informal practices of daily life) succeeded. The young have found in the informal a space to satisfy some of their needs, both economic and affective. We now turn to the informal and the challenges it presents to Cuban socialism and to Cuban politics in the future.

6

WHERE DID OUR LOVE GO?

Emotions and
the Politics
of *lo informal*

As the politics of passion failed to sustain collective politics over time, the politics of affection became the main expression of social interaction on the island. In the politics of affection Cubans found a way of dealing with material and affective needs that were not satisfied in the state-controlled arenas of public life. Economic decline, government's inability to enact reforms, bureaucratic inefficiency, officially imposed limits on self-expression, and pervasive mistrust contributed to the proliferation and predominance of informal spaces and practices in which affection and its politics played a leading role. Precisely in *lo informal* the socialist state has encountered one of its most formidable adversaries.

In all political systems the chasm between theory and practice is reflected in the divergence between the formal aspects of the regime and the informal dimensions of daily life. The greater the gap, the more likely that challenges to the status quo will be expressed through everyday practices in arenas outside the purview of the state. Especially in maximalist regimes, where dissent is penalized and the economy is centrally planned, liminal spaces and day-to-day behavior provide a mirror of the feelings of individuals. *Lo informal* captures those emotions, needs, identities, and alternatives that motivate people to behave in ways that do not conform to the norms of the state.

In the informal a silent, corrosive, long-term challenge to maximalist states brews.[1] That challenge has its own emotional and operational infrastructure manifested as judgments individuals make regarding their sociopolitical and economic condition among networks of family, friends, and acquaintances. These networks provide individuals with greater room for expression of interest and identity. Through them economic needs can be met. In contrast to state structures, the informal and its politics of affection are flexible and can respond more quickly to individual necessities. They are functional and efficacious (if not optimal) alternatives to official procedures and institutions; the power of individuals is augmented in the informal. As the state's ability to deliver declines, the informal rises. This has been the case not only in Cuba but also throughout Latin America. As structural adjustment during the 1980s and 1990s narrowed the scope of the social safety net, people resorted to reciprocal networks of exchange and to the informal economy. Although the Cuban government has not adopted neoliberalism, it has enacted structural adjustment that met with a similar response at the grassroots.[2]

The crisis of Cuban socialism in the 1980s and 1990s has been accompanied by pervasive informality at the level of *la calle* (the street). Informality in turn exacerbates economic and political difficulties by chipping away at the tenets of the system and its effectiveness. Informality is, therefore, both a cause and a consequence of the problems facing the country since the 1980s. The expansion of informality resulted from two main and interrelated sources: the economy of scarcity and widespread social disaffection with the material and nonmaterial conditions of daily life. The shaky normative framework of the regime is an additional contributing factor to the rise of *lo informal*. As Cubans express their feelings about the status quo and secure material survival through the informal sphere, their practices present long-term negative consequences for socialism.

Cuban socialism is not exceptional in terms of the presence of informality. All societies have a measure of informal social relations. Several factors, however, make informality particularly relevant in the case of Cuba: the island's political culture (in which informality — *choteo, tuteo,* anti-institutionalism — has played a commanding role since colonial times), the type of regime in power since 1959 (a maximalist state that has attempted to regulate and penetrate not only public but private relations as well), and the economic and political situation of the post-1980 period.

The most daunting task confronting the Cuban state has been the attempt to formalize through official norms the culture of informality. The two sets of standards — the official and the unofficial — have coexisted, resisting and accommodating each other. To understand politics in a broad sense, the relationship between the formal and the informal, the institutions of the state and the informal institutions of daily life, must be explained, for it reveals what constitutes the political at the grassroots. Such an approach helps to un-cover the limits of the state, the cleavages in state-society relations, the dy-namics of continuity and change, and the articulation of alternative interests, sentiments, and identities that are the building blocks of civil society. When the formal and the informal are at odds for extended periods, the credibility and legitimacy of the regime are in question, as is long-term governability. Be-fore examining the impact of *lo informal* on the course of Cuban revolutionary politics, a discussion of formality and informality is in order.

Approaching the Informal

How does one study something that is informal? Political scientists are not trained to do so, partly because it requires close-up observation of ordinary people in daily life, the province of sociologists and anthropologists. To study the politics of the informal one must go to the people and, as the sociolo-gist Susan Eckstein has written, "bring the people back in." [3] The work of Barrington Moore on injustice and domination, James C. Scott on informal resistance, and Joel S. Migdal on the limits of state power is helpful in ap-proaching the topic of informality and its impact on state-society relations for a number of reasons. The three, to some degree or another, have brought the people back in. But their contributions do not interpret informality fully be-cause they miss the emotional/normative frameworks of social informality. If one is to bring the people back in to the study of politics, one must usher the emotions to their rightful place, that is, as a source of norms and judgments on social reality. [4]

Moore sees the relationship between those who govern and the governed as a liminal phenomenon. According to him, the rules of what is politically permissible are never crystal clear. Therefore, "what takes place . . . is a con-tinuing probing on the part of the rulers and the subjects to find out what they can get away with, to test and discover the limits of obedience and dis-obedience." [5] At the margins, issues and authority are contested and defined. In a one-party state it is in the informal sphere and in informal practices that people's desires and disappointments are readily expressed. Through infor-mality ordinary men and women resist and accommodate to what is allowed and what is not.

In a similar approach to the relationship between superiors and sub-ordinates that focuses on liminal spaces and practices, Scott has argued that the relatively powerless have their own particular arsenal against the power-ful. He identified the weapons of the weak as a host of everyday forms of resistance "short of collective outright defiance" that include "foot dragging, dissimulation, false compliance, pilfering, feigned ignorance, slander, arson, sabotage and so forth." These activities "multiplied many thousandfold . . . may in the end make an utter shambles of the policies dreamed up by 'would-be superiors.'"[6] These "pedestrian" actions constitute, in Scott's words, the wherewithal of "the infrapolitics of subordinate groups."

An emotional and normative infrastructure upholds these modes of everyday resistance. When the right to subsistence is threatened, the perception of injustice justifies "illegal" actions and revolt. The term "moral economy" captures the normative dimension of economic life that legitimizes individual actions that, from an outsider's or an official's point of view, might seem inappropriate.[7] Infringing on a peasant's right to subsistence—one of the pillars of his moral economy—may compel him to stand up to the landlord or attack the tax collector. Before open revolt erupts, though, a hidden transcript capturing the feelings of the weak is elaborated between friends and family members, in small groups, outside the purview of the representatives of the state.[8] The hidden transcript is scripted in the informal; it relies on the politics of affection and its networks to be expressed. Its subtext is emotional and moral. For example, anger at the rulers is a value judgment on how they transgress notions of what is just. This argument regarding the emotional aspect of broken normative "compacts" is not explicit in Scott but flows from his analysis, close to the surface.

Whereas Scott's focus is infrapolitics, Migdal offers a macro perspective on the relationship between the seemingly powerful state and the relatively powerless society. He has argued that, contrary to what one would expect, in most Third World countries societies have been stronger than states. The weakness of states arises from their inability to make people "in even the most remote villages behave as state leaders want." The capabilities of states to "*penetrate* society, *regulate* social relationships, *extract* resources, and *appropriate* or use resources in determined ways" have been minimal. Migdal writes that "the failure is also a result of unrealistic standards for state behavior" and that such a weakness "affects the very coherence and character of the states themselves."[9] This is precisely what has occurred in Cuba, slowly over time, although, ironically, Migdal did not reach this conclusion.

Migdal places states in two main categories: strong and weak. Strong states are those with high capabilities to penetrate society, regulate social life, and extract and appropriate resources. Weak states are those with low capabilities to accomplish these tasks. These categories, however, oversimplify what is a nuanced phenomenon. In practice strength and weakness are a continuum and are relative to the context and the task to be performed. Not all the characteristics associated with strength necessarily come together. Although some states are strong in appropriating resources (as in the case of Cuba, by and large), they might be weak in regulating social relations.

Migdal refers to the Cuban state as strong. Compared to other states, particularly those in Africa, Cuba seems like a true leviathan. This portrayal is the predominant one in the literature, but it neglects two important considerations. First, the Cuban state has not consistently performed all tasks in an effective manner, nor has it been able to implement its agenda thoroughly or with the desired results. And second, despite state strength, the Cuban people have not been easily malleable objects of politics. Throughout the past four decades official mandates have been met with informal resistance, ranging from absenteeism and low labor productivity to noncompliance with the tax code, from tuning in to U.S. radio stations to diverting resources from the state to the black market.

The Cuban state, particularly since the 1980s, has been ineffective in making Cubans feel and act in officially preferred ways, especially in the informal sphere of daily life. The desocialization of youth is a case in point. The clash between official norms and the norms of the informal and its politics of affection has resulted in rampant dissimulation, as Cubans opt for *la doble moral*. The contradiction between the two normative frameworks—the public and the private—slowly undermines the system's credibility and its operation in specific material ways. The emotional infrastructure of the informal sphere challenges the political order insofar as it is the initial necessary (but not sufficient) step to make people question and confront authority, to develop hidden transcripts, and to resist informally, undoing in the process the legitimacy of the government and its ability to govern effectively.

Formality and Informality in Cuban Socialism

Cuban socialist politics can be conceptualized as a conflict—or a seeming paradox—between formality and informality. Formality refers to the apparatus of the state, official decision making, and governmental regulation and penetration of social relations. In the economy, the formal is state-managed production and distribution and the executive planning of it. The informal is the non-state regulated, which usually runs against the officially prescribed norms and is embodied in the daily experience of people. The economic dimension of the informal is also known as the second, parallel, or unofficial economy, or the black market.

The formal is also the expression of the official ideal—what should be according to the dictates of the state. The informal is "the real" insofar as it is life at the grassroots. The tension between the formal and the informal stems from the imposition of procedures on a society that has alternative norms that are expressed in divergent ways of conducting social and economic relations. But the formal and the informal also coincide and complement each other; they relate in ways not necessarily or exclusively oppositional. For instance, state policies contribute to the expansion or contraction of informal practices, depending on how they define what is or is not permissible in society. The distance between the state (i.e., the formal) and the society's culture and way of life (i.e., the informal) is not as great as one would imagine, for the state is composed of individuals who share national patterns of behavior and attitudes. As a result the regime assumes distinctive features of the predominant cultural values of the society. Informal religious beliefs, as explained in Chapter 4, helped to consolidate the leadership of Fidel Castro.

The interrelationship of the formal and the informal has been part and parcel of Cuban politics since colonial times. It has been clearly manifested on a number of levels since 1959. The personalism of charismatic authority coexisted with institutionalized Marxism, its large bureaucracy, and its strong military; the modern and the premodern blurred into each other, forging one another in original ways. Nationalism, that most sentimental notion, for example, was fused in the state's official ideology, Marxism-Leninism, a supposedly scientific analysis of the world. The theoretically and practically conflictual relationship between formality and informality has been unresolved in Cuban socialism. From the beginning of the revolutionary state the leadership debated two alternatives regarding fundamental aspects of the regime. Each revolved around one pole or another in the spectrum of formality and informality: a people's army versus a professional armed force; moral versus material incentives; a charismatic authority versus an institutionalized party bureaucracy. Such contradictions have escaped easy resolution. The Rectification Campaign of 1986 was the official response not only to the economic difficulties the country was beginning to encounter but also, at least in rhetoric, to the formalism that permeated Cuban politics. Instead of deformalizing the system, the Campaign did the opposite. It attempted to revamp ideological control over the society and put some of the mass organizations (e.g., the CDRs) in the hands of military officers. Militarization, one of the principles of Castroism and one of the distinctive features of the political system, is anathema to informality. Yet both formality and informality have thrived on the island, revealing the resilience of old tendencies in Cuban political culture.

Informal Politics and Daily Life

Five main factors contribute to the pervasiveness of informality in Cuba: (1) individuals make personal connections based on interests and affection, resulting in networks outside the purview of the state; (2) the institutions of the state do not work smoothly, efficiently, or, at times, justly; (3) the economy of scarcity and the material constraints of daily life make individuals resort to networks of family members, friends, and others in an effort to make ends meet or *resolver;* (4) the limited space available for deviants and nonconformists in society pushes them to the margins where they seek a life space; and (5) the national culture of informality tends to reproduce itself over time.

Informal politics is the stuff of everyday life. Informality coexists with formal state procedures and institutions of the state. It cannot be otherwise unless society is composed of unsentimental robots preprogrammed with standard operating procedures devoid of affect. Social informality is not only part of the cultural way of relating to the world but also a very functional manner of dealing with needs, especially in a situation of scarcity and frustration. Expressions of informality can be categorized into two, not completely separable, types: economic and sociopolitical. In practice they are intertwined; both require, at the very least, some measure of personal affective attachments, an "emotional hardware." To satisfy economic needs in a situation of scarcity, affective personal networks are instrumental (what in the Soviet Union was called *blat,* or good connections).[10] They are the "ropes" of the informal economy.

"Informal economy" is a broad term for a variety of practices associated with the black market, or underground economy, outside the control and legal provisions of the state economy. Although it has always related symbiotically to the official economy, the second economy mushroomed in the 1980s as the result of the economic crisis. The less the state was able to deliver, the more people had to resort to their own devices, their families and friends, to survive. The informal economy is not a faceless entity, anonymous and impersonal. On the contrary, it is embodied in people. Who you know is as important as your material resources.

Personal relations are a resource, a form of capital — network capital [11] — for they can provide access to different goods and services. Individuals can serve as intermediaries to others who might provide the necessary product or service, including protection from the authorities. "El que tiene un amigo tiene un peso en el bolsillo" (He who has a friend has a dollar in his pocket) is an old Cuban saying that rings true in Cuban socialism, where the limits of the state-planned economy render personal connections much more vital.

So much so that socialism is popularly referred to on the island as *sociolismo* (cronyism or buddyism). The maxim suggests the politics and economy of affection as it equates friendship with monetary value. This is especially indicative of a context in which economic survival depends on personal bonds due to structural limitations, institutional weaknesses, and alternative norms in which the affective is "valued" not only over the material but largely because of it; the affective safeguards the financial. Once again, emotion and reason, passion and interest, are complementary. Together they constitute an affective realism and an affective rationality.

Not all transactions in the informal economy are based on affection, although affection loosely defined can facilitate and guarantee exchange. Whereas family members and friends are united by the bonds of affection as well as of interest, associates are linked by instrumental considerations and by trust and reciprocity. Many of the transactions in the informal sphere are at least as utilitarian as those in capitalism in the sense that no protection is offered to the buyer or to those who provide the service because it is mostly an unregulated economy; trust, honesty, and affection play regulatory roles in the informal economy.

Although the politics of affection are pivotal in the expansion of the informal economy by creating networks, they are not limited to economic transactions. The politics of affection are integral components of practices and social spaces through which individuals express alternative sentiments, perceptions, interests, and ways of being contrary to the ideals of the state. The politics of affection permeate social life in all of its dimensions.

The Spaces, the Language, and the Norms of
the Informal in Cuban Socialism

Where does one locate informality? Everywhere. Its spaces are the home, the streets, the parks, but also the locales of state agencies, anywhere that individuals come together and form personal bonds that carry with them the cultural codes of *lo informal*. Informality is to be found in the markets, where the baker takes home some of the flour that was supposed to be distributed through the rationing system and sells it in the black market through his networks of *socios;* in the neighborhood Committee for the Defense of the Revolution, whose director might act as an intermediary selling cheese, meat, or soap to neighbors; in government offices, where co-workers share foreign newspaper articles critical of the regime; in the use of a state vehicle as personal taxi; or in the museum and galleries that exhibit the work of an artist (on

the government's payroll) who uses her paintings to criticize metaphorically
the situation the country is in. The informal politics of affection are found
also in groups of friends who dare to reveal to each other their rejection of
the party and among the small circle of human rights activists who rely on
personal trust to pursue their work.

As Chapter 2 argued, the informal has its own language and its particular norms. Both stand in opposition to *el teque* and the official. The keywords
of informality in contemporary Cuban socialism are *inventársela* (to "invent"
or find solutions), *resolver* (to make do, to find solutions to problems), *buis-
near* (to do business), *socio, fula* (dollar), and the expression *no es fácil* (it is
not easy), among many other phrases and neologisms. Together this vocabulary forms a parallel language, developed as a response to the socioeconomic
process of socialism and its crisis.[12] The new language attempts to hide from
the authorities the practices that are at the margins of legality; it reveals as
much as it conceals. It indicates the limits of state socialization and the power
of the society to resist governmental norms. It is a colloquial language that
points, on the one hand, to the leveling of Cuban society as everyone adopts
the vox populi of the grassroots and, on the other, to the vitality of folk culture
in generating discourse.

The lexicon of the informal is the vernacular of the lower segments of the
population, verging on the vulgar and desocialized. It is an authentic expression of daily needs and everyday practices in an economy of scarcity within
the confines of an authoritarian political system. It provides an alternative to
the officialese that, due to repetition and formalism, has become meaningless.
Like *el choteo*, the language of *lo informal* is a great equalizer, but like *el choteo*
it also serves to demarcate group membership: it keeps others out as it cre-
ates an in-group with a grammar not taught in schools. With its vocabulary,
rules, participants, and customs, the informal is a set of rules and networks—
a society of sorts—that coexists with the formal ones of the modern state,
challenging state socialization, governability, and legitimacy.

The Impact of Informality on Legitimacy and Governability

Informality implies resisting and accommodating to the forms of Cuban socialism. The two codes of conduct—the informal and the official—clash. Informality propagates relationships and practices between friends and associates to subvert the forms of rational-legal society. It also acts as an obstacle to
state penetration of society. For example, family doctors sign bogus disability
papers for young men who do not want to be drafted. In the informal not

everyone is equal, as individuals differ in terms of their network capital and in their ability to gain access to resources. In short, the tenets of Marxism-Leninism are not upheld in the transactions of *lo informal*, and the state has a harder time accomplishing its tasks as a result.

Given the benefits of appearing to comply with the government and the high costs associated with noncompliance, the informal is an arena in which "the truth" can be spoken (although important debates and differences of opinion are also aired in official spheres). In the informal the hidden transcript is developed. Alternatives are articulated and feelings are vented among small groups of kin, friends, and associates. Weariness, for example, not the optimism of official propaganda, is one of the principal emotions expressed in the informal. Opposition to the ways things are and the stress associated with survival on a day-to-day basis is expressed freely among close-knit friends. But *lo informal* is also the arena of *choteo*, gossip, and humor, all alternatives to official rituals, news, and state socialization. Informality allows people to relax; one of its messages is *no cojas lucha* (take it easy, don't worry, relax), as opposed to the government's call for *sacrificio* (sacrifice).

In the informal one finds *sociolismo*, not *socialismo*. *Sociolismo* is the system of access to goods and social standing based on who you know and who you love, on *amiguismo* and cronyism. If you have a connection with a *mayimbe* (a top leader), employment opportunities might be forthcoming or you might not be convicted of selling stolen goods. The *maceta* (a big-time black market operator) will get you the television set or the pork you wanted (usually with payment). At times of crisis such networking provides greater access to goods than do the institutions of the state. The politics of affection also grease the wheels of the bureaucracy and cut the red tape. They substitute or bypass standard operating procedures to get something (an apartment, a visa) for a friend, a *socio*, or a family member. The procedures of the informal are like a shadow state that operates with an alternative set of codes not based exclusively on interest but on interest *and* affection.

In *sociolismo* your personal qualities and your personal connections, not your political rectitude or your professional credentials, are your greatest resource, for they make survival possible. Women in neighborhoods, for instance, have established long chains of friends, friends of friends, and extended family members to supply the basic necessities of life. These networks expand from family to friends, from neighbor to neighbor and to distant acquaintances, branching out throughout the neighborhood to *municipios* (towns) and well into other provinces. Complex webs of distribution through bartering, monetary exchange, and the economy of affection have emerged outside the official bureaucracy of the state and the official economy. They supply goods and services that the state and the planned economy do not.

Informal networks operate through mutual interdependence, reciprocity, and trust. Their relations are flexible and fluid, especially the further removed the connections are from the individual's blood relations. The greater the personal distance, the greater the potential of distrust and the less power the logic of affection has. In Cuba transactions in the informal carry a level of stress, fear, and vulnerability vis-à-vis the unknown other, because participants are well aware of the extensive security apparatus and the risks involved in conducting illegal transactions. Who is to say that your new *socio* or *socia* is not an undercover security agent? The resulting condition seems paradoxical, but it is real: social collaboration in small groups, atomization of the individual, and mobilization in controlled mass organizations.

Although the informal can be perceived as the arena of "positive" sentiments—honor, honesty, affection—among loved ones, in practice the informal also carries a host of "negative" feelings: mistrust, anxiety, incivility. Mistrust is as much a part of the realm of the informal as is trust. Mistrust is prevalent outside small circles of relatives and *amigos*. Insecurity and fear are as much a part of the informal as are security and affection. These feelings are the result of the vulnerability experienced by those who break the law. Consider the following example. A clerk at a state bakery agreed with her supervisor to reduce the amount of flour used to bake the loaves of bread Cubans are entitled to buy with their ration cards. The flour they saved was used to make smaller rolls for sale in the black market. Profits were shared equally by the two. Although the women trusted each other to a point, each felt uneasy about the risks involved and the other's power over her.[13] Such a relationship fosters solidarity and empathy but at the same time a measure of insecurity. The coexistence of two opposing codes of conduct, the official and the unofficial, renders social life very complex as individuals must adapt their behavior to accommodate both. In such contexts individual charm and a person's moral capital gain in importance because they represent resources to safeguard one's well-being.

Informality and the politics of affection are the backbone of the culture of "illegality." The culture of the informal justifies breaking the law to satisfy personal and family needs. It is not that the informal is immoral or amoral but that it stands on another moral and affective logic that is highly instrumental as well. Two other examples demonstrate how informal networks operate and the social, economic, and political implications of economic informality (which the government labels "economic criminality"). The first is the case of Manolito Café who was accused of heading a group that sold coffee stolen from the state. Manolito was "living high on the hog due to enrichment from that activity" and had started to organize a gambling operation when he was caught.[14]

Several important aspects of the case merit analysis. First, the diversion of resources from the state to private hands and into the informal economy undermined the ability of the state to plan and distribute goods. Multiplied over time and in other sectors, this makes the state less efficient and, as a result, exacerbates discontent. Second, "class" differences and inequality have risen dramatically since the 1980s, as some individuals enriched themselves through the informal economy and displayed their wealth in a poor society. In private conversations and in official publications Cubans manifest great resentment of the *macetas* and the state's unwillingness or inability to control them. From the state's perspective, *macetas* represent an affront to socialist legality. Their existence calls into question the capability of the state to manage the society and the economy. Although a number of *macetas* have been imprisoned and the government in February 1999 announced another major campaign to reduce illegal economic activities, the problem is far from resolved. Many continue to operate. Third, the informal economy is not limited to subsistence-related activities; it has spread to include more traditional "illegal" activities such as gambling, suggesting that a socialist mafia is in the making. Fourth, Manolito Café, like the following case, required *socios* in the workplace who secured the coffee, diverted it from the state warehouse, and then sold it privately. Networks are being forged that act as independent agents and, as the next chapter argues, constitute a proto-civil society even when their civility is questionable.

In another case, *Golden Feathers,* nineteen workers at a transportation enterprise that distributed chicken from the state's slaughterhouse were indicted for stealing and selling the cargo on the black market. Unlike Manolito Café, who was well known to the police for previous offenses, the participants in Golden Feathers had been good citizens, and some were said to have been "exemplary workers" with no prior criminal record.[15] *Golden Feathers* proves that the informal economy is not the province of "bad people" but of everyday Cubans. The case confirms the existence of networks operating within state enterprises, between co-workers and *socios* who derail state policies. As the state's capability is compromised, so is the government's ability to govern in the long run.

The society is becoming increasingly defiant, and in the 1990s openly so. A culture of illegality permeates social life, socializing individuals into ways of breaking the law. Asked if she felt it was wrong to steal from her work-place (food, lightbulbs, or any other item), a Cuban mother said no. Stealing from the state was not stealing, she argued, adding that she would do anything necessary to provide for her kids.[16]

Gender, Informality, and the Question of Resistance

Because women traditionally have been responsible for placing food on the table and caring for their families, they have been in the forefront of the in-formal economy. But there are reasons other than the gendered division of labor for women's strategic role in the informal. Participation in the informal economy can be a full-time job. Because women have been less incorporated into the labor force and earn comparatively less than men, it makes economic sense for them to be active in the informal sphere. Since the home and the *barrio* (neighborhood) are the centers of the informal, the fact that women spend more time at home and in their neighborhoods facilitates communication with other women and the formation of solidarity based on empathy. *Socialismo* (the feminine form) is as important as *sociolismo,* if not more so.

With the deepening economic crisis of the early 1990s, men have had to assume greater shares of the duties related to feeding the family and providing for basic needs. Their role in the informal has grown as a result. Men seem to dominate the bigger for-profit operations like those of Manolito Café and Golden Feathers. It seems that men comprise the great majority of *macetas.* A division of labor along gender lines seems to be emerging in the informal economy, which closely parallels that of the official economy. Men engage in high-stakes economic dealings; women tend to concentrate on securing the immediate needs of daily life.

Sociopolitical, not only economic, informality has become more pro-nounced after the crisis of Cuban socialism in the 1980s. Alternative spaces for expression of self-identity and meaning have emerged or have been strength-ened in a process that has led to the creation of an incipient proto-civil society. Youth, artists, and intellectuals have become more critical and daring in their contestation of state ideology and praxis. Cubans of all walks of life are finding a voice and a space, as small as it may be, to call their own. Groups of farm-ers have formed independent cooperatives. Religious believers and women's groups have become increasingly proactive in self-help ventures.

Whether social informality and nonconformist lifestyles constitute re-sistance is not an easy question to answer. The difficulty stems from another basic issue: Is consciousness of resistance necessary for an act to be considered resistance? Is all pilfering resistance, not theft? Are alternative lifestyles (or deviance, according to some) a form of resistance? This last question presents an additional degree of difficulty: Can an individual resist simply by not being accepted as normal in society?

Not all informal behavior is resistance; neither is all deviance. What constitutes resistance must be understood contextually, since power is always contextual and relational. What appears as informal resistance is also, and usually concurrently, accommodation. Accommodation and informal resistance are the two sides of the same coin in the relationship between superior and subordinates. To decipher what they mean it is necessary to place those practices in specific contexts. Contextualization allows us to see that resistance (and deviance) is culturally and temporally defined and therefore contextually relative. If a state defines a certain behavior and a specific way of being as "counterrevolutionary," as the Cuban state does in the case of myriad activities and identities, the pursuit of those actions and those life spaces then constitutes a form of resistance. No consciousness of resistance is required. When you ask a Cuban why he or she participates in the black market, for instance, the response is not "I am *resistiendo*" (resisting) but "I am *resolviendo*" (making do, surviving). The consequences of this person's actions, however, have political import for the functioning of the state and people's perception of it. Informality and its emotional infrastructure are political not only in consequences but in cause as well.

Formality/Informality: The Symbiotic Relationship

The relationship between the formal and the informal in Cuban socialism is a complex and functional one. The formality of state centralization, ideological dogmatism, and central planning has fed, unwittingly, the proliferation of informal practices to the point that they permeate social life. With the decline of state economic capabilities, a process of informalization, destatization, and privatization has ensued.

The bureaucratic centralization of the economy and its near-collapse has led to the expansion of the informal economy. Although participation in the black market is considered a political as well as an economic crime, Cubans resort to it every day because the state economy cannot provide the daily necessities. Government policies since the 1980s have also contributed to the rise of informal economic behavior. The overture to international tourism has generated a host of informal activities around hotels, airports, and attractions, wherever tourists are. Among the most striking is *jineterismo,* a type of prostitution that caters to foreigners. Other Cubans sell contraband cigars and provide a variety of services, from unlicensed taxis to room and board. A new version of Liborio, the Cuban picaresque figure, has emerged, roving around tourist resorts, following the dollar trail. However, the *jinete* (hustler, mediator, and facilitator) is not a phenomenon circumscribed to the tourist industry or dating to the 1990s exclusively.

According to Jorge F. Pérez-López, the *jinete* "is an individual whose strength is an ability to develop social relationships that will lead to being able to obtain goods and services in short supply." [17] *Jinetes* have existed in Cuba since the 1960s and have facilitated the operation of firms in the socialist system that "rewar[d] those who are friendly with government officials." [18] Informal economic activity has helped the regime weather the economic storm of the late 1980s and 1990s. The state has been unable to eradicate informal economic practices (theft, graft, bribes, corruption, among others) in part because the raison d'etre of informality is the state itself, in part because informality is functional, and in part because supervisors and police turn a blind eye (as they themselves are usually involved).

The symbiotic relationship between formality and informality is not only an economic one. Formality has bred informality generally, underscoring a cultural propensity toward *lo informal*. In the religious arena the less institutionalized religions, such as *santería* and certain sects of Protestantism that use homes as centers of worship, experienced a great resurgence earlier than the more institutional ones, such as Catholicism. Their growth is partially a response to the formal dogmatic interpretation of Marxism-Leninism that shunned believers until the early 1990s. Cubans sought in the informal a refuge from the formal.

State Attacks on Formality and Informality

The Cuban government has tried to battle the insidious effects of both formality and informality. Although formalism is an integral part of the modern state, it tends to rob the political system of the esprit that animates support for it, especially if excessive formality undermines its efficiency and the efficacy of its officials. The Cuban government's effort at combating both has had an ironic twist: when it has tried to formalize, informality increased at the grassroots; when it attempted to deformalize (as in the fifth UJC Congress), the government resorted to new formalism (i.e., new legal codes and institutions).

Periodically since the 1960s Cuban leaders have announced campaigns to deformalize political participation and reduce bureaucracy. In practice both

formalization and deformalization have coexisted and oscillated in emphasis. The reasons behind the attempts at deformalization of the early 1990s
(beginning with "Sin Formalismo" and continuing with the *llamamiento,* or
appeal, to the 1991 PCC congress) were twofold. First, through deformalization the regime hoped to incorporate segments of the society that had been
alienated in the past or had become disenchanted with the regime, thereby increasing the participation of Cubans in the political structures of the regime.
This was the motivation behind the 1992 decision to permit religious believers to join the Communist Party. The cosmetic changes within the UJC had a
similar intent. Behind the attempt to reinvigorate official institutions was the
interest in attracting younger Cubans to the fold. The government's actions
are based on the recognition that its institutions must accommodate a society
that is much more variegated than in the past. To that end, in the early 1990s
the government started to advocate unity within diversity. At a time that the
party and the state were fighting for their survival, expediency and flexibility
rather than purity and dogmatic rigidity briefly became a priority. The shift
constituted a considerable, albeit short-lived, accommodation to the society.
By early 1996 the top leadership signaled a return to formality and control in
a speech by Raul Castro condemning reformist intellectuals.

The second reason behind deformalization was emotional in character,
to inject the masses and the political system with the revolutionary fervor of
earlier times. The revolution required an emotional infrastructure to triumph
over Batista as well as to sustain itself in power. Realizing that the Cuban
masses were losing that loving feeling, Fidel and other leaders emphasized
themes and leitmotivs that pulled at the heartstrings of Cubans, specifically
nationalism in its Cuba-the-besieged-island variant and the glories of the revolutionary struggle. Since the 1980s the government launched two major campaigns to do just that.

Fidel Castro's speeches of the mid-1980s justifying the Rectification
Campaign, collected under the title *Por el camino correcto* (By the Correct
Road), called for genuine emotional commitment to the "revolution" and the
fatherland at the same time that institutional formality was being strength-
ened. Without the revolution there would not be an independent *patria* (fatherland). At a time of economic downturn and dwindling political support, the
call for *conciencia* (consciousness), *optimismo* (optimism), *idealismo* (idealism),
dignidad (dignity), *sacrificio* (sacrifice), and *lucha* (struggle) was an attempt to
reignite the politics of passion and the crusade for absolute moral ends (i.e.,
socialism in a sovereign Cuba). In the process the ills that plagued Cuban
society, including informality, would be combated: "Because this star [of the

Revolution] shines so much more for us, it has more lights. . . . She requires all, demands all: our effort, our energy, each minute, each second of our lives; it demands sweat, sacrifices, our blood, the lives of any of us. This is what we have always felt." [19] To achieve the ultimate goal no sacrifice was too much, no compromise was possible: "We must be much more intransigent." [20] Only through passion would the revolution be saved.

The second major effort was in 1990 in preparation for the fourth congress of the Communist Party. The call for the congress, known as *el llamamiento,* encouraged Cubans to eschew dissimulation, rote repetition, and formulaic participation by venting their feelings about the political system in public gatherings designed for that purpose. Revolutionary socialism would be reanimated in the process. Like Rectification, *el llamamiento* failed, when the top leadership of the party, surprised at widespread discontent manifested during the grievance sessions, opted to close the space for debate rather than leave the doors open for authentic and autonomous participation. The fourth and fifth party congresses (1991 and 1997 respectively) were tightly choreographed affairs. The institutions of the state and their leaders proved to be incapable or unwilling to engage in the necessary reforms that would reactivate popular support, because doing so might threaten their own positions.

Instead the political system has relied on periodic international crises to drum up nationalist passion among Cubans. The conflict with the United States has served this purpose well. One of the incidents that illustrates the use of crises to stir emotional responses on behalf of the nation-state is the February 1996 downing of two civilian aircraft belonging to the Miami-based Brothers to the Rescue, an organization of civilian pilots—mostly Cuban-American—who searched for and rescued *balseros* from the Florida Straits. Planes flown by the head of the organization on several previous occasions had entered Cuban airspace, humiliating the Cuban military. On February 24 two of the Brothers' unarmed planes were shot down over international waters as they approached the island. The incident not only detoured U.S.-Cuban relations, which up to that point seemed to be improving moderately under the Clinton administration, but aroused intense passion both on the island (especially among hard-liners) and among Cuban exiles.

Crises such as this one heighten the senses, charge the emotions, and render politics exhilarating. For a brief time after the incident, the politics of passion succeeded in mustering support for the regime, although many Cubans were also appalled at the action of the Cuban military. But, with time and repetition, the politics of passion have diminishing returns, particularly when the leadership casts what should be routine technocratic phenomena, such as the sugarcane harvest, in terms of do-or-die, a matter of devotion, a crusade for survival. Resorting to *conciencia* instead of addressing material and policy issues in an effort to improve the abysmal performance of the economy tends to have a detrimental effect on people's support in the long run.

If political formality has been problematic in terms of dampening support for the regime, social informality has been the greatest challenge the Cuban government has had to confront. Although the official discourse presents informality as a security threat, the state has been hard pressed to keep it at bay. Selective repression is the most the state can do since the practice is not only pervasive but also, ironically, beneficial to the regime in some ways. The nature of the informal is such that it does not lend itself to defeat by conventional mechanisms. Moreover, the material and emotional needs that *lo informal* satisfies are so crucial that people are willing to run significant risks.

The Cuban government has been losing the war against informality. In spite of the repressive mechanisms adopted, economic crimes have soared in the 1990s. According to a Cuban source, "Those most frequently committed were embezzlement, misappropriation, failure to protect government economic units, receiving stolen goods, and illegal economic activity."[21] The National Assembly has struggled to combat the wave of economic criminality and social informality in general. These efforts notwithstanding, officials have continued to complain about pervasive "social indiscipline." State organs have been instructed to revamp their ideological work with, and vigilance of, the grassroots. New parasecurity groups were organized to respond to the problem, among these the Popular Councils (municipal-level units that deal with special issues, including economic crime), the National Commission of Social Prevention and Attention, the Unified Vigilance and Protection System, and the *patrullas campesinas* (peasant patrols) that protect crops from thieves.[22] A new campaign was launched in early 1999 increasing the penalties for a host of informal practices.

Criminalization has not been the only course of action pursued. Confronted with widespread practices that were impossible to root out completely and that at the same time were beneficial to the people, and indirectly to the regime itself, the government decided to legalize several of the activities once considered unacceptable. In the period between the mid-1980s and mid-1990s the state decriminalized the *paladares* (family-run restaurants in homes) and the holding of dollars and approved self-employment in more than one hundred labor categories. Although hard-liners within the PCC found many of the decisions anathema to Marxist dogma, the pragmatists apparently won. Through formalization of the informal the government was able to monitor and regulate the once-illegal practices while appearing to give breathing room to the people and securing additional revenue for itself (through taxation, licensing requirements, and fees and by capturing dollars from the black market and funneling them into government coffers through state foreign exchange houses).[23]

The new state policies basically codified social behavior. The reason for accommodation, ironically, was to exert some measure of control over the informal sector. Legalization of the informal resulted in state regulation of it. What was once informal now became formalized. What was permissible had changed as a result of the probing of people at the grassroots, in the margins. Ordinary Cubans, engaged in the pedestrian but vital task of *resolver,* helped to redefine the rules of the game while not being totally in control of it. In fact, the regulations imposed on the informal economy proved unpalatable to many Cubans. Those who had operated somewhat free from government controls in the past now had to secure permits and pay heavy fees that made their endeavors hardly profitable. Many left these activities, while most found ways to bypass state regulations and to continue to operate informally.

The Ambivalent Impact of Informality

Informality has challenged the Cuban state by carving a sphere outside its control. Maximalist states try to eradicate informal practices not only because these thrive outside official purview but also because they pose an obstacle to it. The informal requires a personal, affective, and emotional infrastructure that runs counter to the norms of those types of regimes. In one-party states, like Cuba, the informal assumes a larger and potentially more dangerous role precisely because informality flourishes in relation to state regulation. The state's efforts to penetrate society, regulate social relations, and extract resources have been weakened by informal behavior. From this vantage point, the state is less powerful than one would think from looking at other indicators, and the society is stronger.

Informality represents a challenge to the regime in the private sphere, among loved ones, where alternatives to the government can be expressed. It is there, in the politics of affection, that divergent worldviews are articulated and hidden transcripts developed. The feelings that compel informal behavior are problematic for Cuban socialism, for they can fuel resistance by underscoring vital expressions of meaning, identity, and affect other than those supportive of and endorsed by the political order. And through the politics of affection the state's ability to control the economy is challenged, as the networks of affection serve as channels of appropriation and distribution of resources outside, but intimately tied to, the official economy.

The rise of informality is a result of the failure of the ideology and the practice of state socialism in a context of economic crisis after 1985. Once promises failed to materialize, Cubans searched for material goods and meaning, identity, and affective attachments in other venues, mainly private ones. Once the standard operating procedures of the state fell prey to inefficiency and inefficacy, individuals turned to friends, family, and *socios* to try to get things done, put food on the table, and create a sense of self.

The informal gives individuals a lifespace, constrained as it usually is, at the same time that it provides flexibility to a centralized economic and political system, especially during periods of economic scarcity. But the emotional infrastructure of *lo informal* does not mount a frontal attack on the political system. The fear of being sanctioned makes individuals resort to covert measures instead of overt defiance. By rendering social life more domestic and less political (in the traditional sense of the word), the informal tends to restrict interactions to small groups. The accompanying retreat from the public provides the state with ample room to maneuver as a seemingly "apathetic" segment of the population will not challenge the regime directly. The resulting retreat to the private that has occurred as state-sponsored mobilization becomes discredited does not threaten the center of power immediately.

Cubans conformed less because they had stopped believing in the state's promises, in part as a result of the state's reduced capacity to fulfill them after the 1980s. The relative loss of state effectiveness (including in the area of internal security) has contributed to the exponential multiplication of everyday forms of resistance. Informality has had an impact on the state's ability to govern and on its legitimacy. It is likely to have serious implications for Cuba's political future as well. Its impact has been ambivalent though. While it erodes legitimacy, as people break the law on a daily basis, it secures practical legitimacy insofar as people do not challenge the formal trappings of the regime directly. By "performing" compliance, Cubans have contributed to legitimating the government's authority.

The impact on governability is similarly dual. *Lo informal* is functional to the regime to the extent that it supplies material and nonmaterial goods, services, and attachments that the state cannot provide. Insofar as it is functional, it provides flexibility while not threatening the government's hold on power at the macro level. Informality, nevertheless, challenges the state's control at the micro level, at the level of *la calle* and *la vida cotidiana* (daily life). Government policies become increasingly difficult to implement if informal factors derail them. How can the government set targets for economic production if absenteeism plagues all sectors and pilfering from the state factories and warehouses is rampant? Ultimately the survival of the regime is at stake, for it cannot accomplish the tasks it has set for itself. As the gap between state promise and performance widens, state-society relations become more difficult to manage. The moral pillars of socialism itself are put to the test as inequality has increased and the moral sins of the past (corruption, prostitution, *amiguismo*) make a thundering comeback.

The contradictory repercussions of informality on the state is clearly seen in the black market. While the black market might be more efficient than the state in supplying goods and services that are not readily available, there are costs to the regime. Those costs include inefficiency in economic planning and distribution, the loss of goods and revenues—especially much-needed hard currency—and the erosion of government credibility. The government's inability to stem the tide of informal social and economic relations shows that it is much more vulnerable than the strength of the PCC, the apparent unity of the elite, the support of the armed forces, and the size of the openly organized opposition indicate. The Cuban state is not as strong as it appears in theory, in much of the scholarship, or even in the eyes of most Cubans. From the perspective of what goes on in daily life, the Cuban regime continues to hold the reins of power at the macro level while slowly losing control of the micro level, of the social and informal level of society, of *la calle y la casa* (the street and the home).

Conclusion

Lo informal acts paradoxically like an escape valve for social pressure while also building it up through networks and hidden transcripts. Citizens who are constantly preoccupied with making ends meet have limited time, energy, and resources to devote to the "big" issues of "high" politics. In this way the informal reduces pressure. But the informal also provides the space and the group feelings necessary to elaborate hidden transcripts containing the hopes and disappointments of thousands of others. Those hidden transcripts are necessary to vindicate change sometime in the future. By revealing the politics of the grassroots vis-à-vis the state, the informal sheds light on the social dynamics of inertia and potential change in one-party states.

The informal captures those emotions that can threaten political order, if and when they erupt into the public arena. Hidden transcripts, liminal practices, and marginal actors are an emotional infrastructure that can become

a social movement. What appeared to be the overnight crumbling of socialism in Eastern Europe and the Soviet Union was in fact an incremental cor-
rosion of the entire system in no small measure due to socioeconomic informality. For the longest time the corrosive impact of informality was only
perceptible in the sphere of daily life; the party, the state bureaucracy, and the
police seemed to be unaffected.

The politics of affection (and disaffection) expressed in *lo informal* have
overtaken the politics of passion that guided the revolution of 1959. In the
informal one finds the desire for a better tomorrow and the disenchantment
with what has been, combined with a culture of illegality and instrumentalism. In the informal sphere ordinary Cubans try to do the best they can in a
very difficult situation, resorting to family and friends and also to the "everything goes" normativity of one of Cuba's predominant political cultural paradigms. In the process Cubans challenge the socialist nation-state, presaging a
similar challenge to any other regime that takes its place. In the informal lies
both the tendency toward social incivility and the tendency toward civility,
for the politics of affection may contribute to the formation of civil society.
In *lo informal* the ground has been laid for change but also for continuity, a
troublesome harbinger of what may come.

7

BUT WILL YOU LOVE ME TOMORROW?

Passion, Affection,
and Civil Society
in Transition

Will the informality pervasive in Cuban socialism and the politics of affection that sustain it contribute to political transition on the island? In what ways will *lo informal* tend to facilitate or inhibit change? Do the politics of affection contribute to the formation of civil society and democratization? I address these questions here by looking to the future of Cuban politics from the vantage point of passion and affection. To start, I pose a basic, albeit neglected, question in the literature on transitions and institutionalism: Where does civil society emerge from? The question intersects issues of institutions, behavior, and political culture. Answering it helps to locate one possible source of regime change in one-party states such as Cuba.

The informalization of Cuban society, in tandem with the politics of affection, is evidence of the growing gap between state and society, the state's limitations in exerting social control at the grassroots level, and the formation of a proto-civil society that tends to contribute to political transition. In the long run, however, the political culture of passion, affection, and *lo informal* will have a contradictory impact on political transition and democratization. The politics of passion and affection will exert their influence on governance and social life in a way that undermines democratic norms once, and if, democracy is established on the island.

In answering the question posed above, I depart from the assumption that political culture will help to shape political outcomes but that it will not be the only factor determining what is to come. This position echoes Giuseppe

Di Palma's claim about the indeterminacy of politics: "In political matters, particularly in matters of regime change, causal relations are only probable and outcomes uncertain. We can make broad probabilistic predictions about categories, but we cannot make firm predictions about individual cases. In any single case, unless relevant circumstances cumulate in the extreme, the end result is not inescapable."[1] He adds that "whatever the historical trends, whatever the hard facts, the importance of human action in a difficult transition should not be underestimated."[2] Any discussion about the future must be by definition tentative, probabilistic. That is why I avoid teleological and romantic approaches. On the contrary, while no particular future is guaranteed, the cultural tendency to construe politics through passion and affection will tend to reappear, perhaps with a vengeance during and after the transition. The only romanticism evident in this interpretation rests on the acknowledgment that the emotional will help to shape Cuba's future in ways that sustain and subvert liberal democracy and civil society.

Democracy, Civil Society, and Political Culture

By liberal democracy I mean a system of government that at a minimum meets the following criteria: (1) it holds regular competitive elections among competing parties; (2) it guarantees civil liberties, including those of political and social minorities; (3) it observes and is based on the rule of law; and (4) it has a public space known as civil society in which individuals, groups, and associations exercise their rights. This public sphere has two main dimensions: quantitative/institutional and qualitative. The quantitative/institutional dimension refers to the number, type, and size of organizations that constitute civil society and the legal framework that "permits social self-organization and defines the terms of the state-society relationship."[3]

The qualitative dimension depends mainly on the institutions and the political culture of society in general and civil society in particular; its orientation, its character, the identity of the actors and their goals, values, and procedures. The attitudes, feelings, and behavior characteristic of the participants are part and parcel of the qualitative aspects of democracy and civil society, but they have not received the attention they deserve. The qualitative is the slippery texture of the social. Together with the institutional foundation, the qualitative basis of civil society imbues it with unique features in particular contexts. By neglecting political culture and its emotional constructions, one would miss an important dimension that differentiates politics and civil society in different settings. Trust, for instance, contributes to the civility of civil society and to its "social capital." Not all societies operate in the same context of trust, nor do they have the same qualitative dimensions of social capital.

Like democracy, civil society is not an easy concept to define given its mixed intellectual genealogy, its variegated nature in different contexts, its normative subtext, and the resulting lack of consensus in the literature.[4] Civil society is *part* of the social world from which it emerges. Not all domestic society conforms to civil society. One can distinguish civil society from economic society (firms), from political society (political parties), and from society at large (of which civil society is a subset), but they are all interrelated through the sociocultural. For my purpose here I adopt a minimalist definition: civil society is the sphere of social interaction in which voluntary organizations operate "freely" to represent a variety of identities and interests, including social, cultural, political, and economic ones. Traditionally civil society has been perceived as the arena between the state and the family, that is, between the political and the nonpolitical. I, like Jean Cohen and Andrew Arato, among others, do not accept that division because it neglects the role of the personal, the familiar, and the intimate in crafting social life and thus in contributing to civil society.[5]

The subtext of civil society is predominantly a liberal one that values individualism, the market and free enterprise, and sociopolitical diversity. This does not preclude the existence of corporatist or state ties with the organizations that constitute civil society. All states regulate nonstate organizations to some degree. By the same token, the relationship between the state and the components of civil society assumes a wide range of modalities, not excluding corporatist or semicorporatist ones, even in liberal democracies. The relationship between the state and civil society is not mainly or exclusively oppositional. The presumed autonomy of civil society is overstated in theory, resulting in the unwarranted supposition that the main feature of civil society-state relations is opposition and separation. Although the articulation of "autonomous" interests is a necessary condition for civil society, the notion of autonomy should be used advisedly, because the lines between what is independent and not are often blurred.

Civil society and democracy are mutually constituting phenomena: each helps to mold the other. Civil society shapes democracy through voluntary organizations that represent a panoply of interests, by allowing individuals to exercise their rights as citizens, and by transmitting values throughout the political system. Democracy sets the contours of civil society by establishing norms that legalize the rights of civic organizations and, possibly, by institutionalizing democratic civic values. The same relationship applies between the social sphere and civil society. The social influences the character of civil society, and civil society also helps to define social relations. Unlike other definitions that claim that civil society constitutes an arena in which voluntary associations can operate "free from both family influence and state power,"[6] the one I favor sees the relationship among family and friends, civil society, and government/state as much more porous. Civil society is forged by personal worldviews and relations typically confined to the private sphere. For example, the genesis of many small private firms is the family; the origin of human rights groups in one-party states is to be found among friends. The private is a link to the public; the social and the political are intimately associated.

State-Society Relations in the 1990s and Beyond

By the 1990s something of significance had changed in state-society relations in Cuba. While the PCC remained predominant, a variegated society had been increasingly manifesting itself, initially in informal ways and slowly thereafter in an organized fashion. Throughout the decade a process of informalization, destatization, and privatization of life has been under way, testing the limits of the state's reach. As a consequence, the state has lost the kind of control it once exerted over *la calle*, the economy, and some of its mass organizations). Mass organizations saw their importance dwindle along with their resources after the economic crisis of the late 1980s and 1990s; so did their ability to attract, co-opt, and sanction Cubans. At the grassroots, Cubans, especially since the 1980s, have resorted to the informal and the politics of affection to survive, underscoring the process of informalization, privatization, and destatization.

The reasons for this triple process are several. State policies clearly contributed to its dynamics. The Special Period in Times of Peace, the harshest phase of the austerity program begun in 1986, closed factories, laid off workers, opened the economy to tourism and foreign investment, and expanded the legal space for self-employment.[7] The economic crisis forced the state to assume less responsibility for the well-being of the population, creating greater room for other agents to act. A degree of liberalization and decentralization by default and by commission ensued. But destatization was not only imposed by dire economic conditions. In fact, it was the policy of choice among reform-minded members of the party and the state. Economic decentralization, on the one hand, and the attempt to reinvigorate Cuban socialism (by recognizing pluralism and increasing representation and participation), on the other, reflected a new mental map among sectors of the political elite and other groups in society (intellectuals, professionals, students, and ordinary Cubans). Leaders of state and party agencies and mass organizations responded to the crisis by attempting to shed their official status, a process aided in the late 1980s by state policy itself that put the label "nongovernmental organization" (NGO) on a host of official institutions. As explained below, NGO status offered both political and economic rewards.

Throughout society informalization and privatization were also the result of ordinary Cubans' need to *resolver*. Through their informal practices and their politics of affection the grassroots have been contributing to the redefinition of state-society relations and the possible emergence of civil society. Other Cubans started to organize their own NGOs, and the few associations not under official government control experienced a renaissance as the state and the socialist economy confronted a major material and ideational crisis.

Civil Society: Its Origins

Although civil society has played either a leading or a secondary role in regime change, few scholars have tried to locate the seeds of civil society in one-party states before they assume an organized form. Most accept the notion of the "resurrection" of civil society. But before its resurrection, where does the life of civil society begin? Three main schools of thought in social movement and democratization theory have addressed how and why groups are formed, but they do not specifically identify where they emerge from, particularly in one-party states. According to the first, "structures of opportunity"— that is, reduced risks and increased space for social organizations—allow for the establishment of formal groups and determine the ebb and flow of social movements and civil organizations. The second school emphasizes the role that individuals concerned with new issues and new identities play in establishing associations and social movements. Individuals join forces to defend "lifespaces." A third group of scholars focuses on a group's ability to secure and mobilize resources as the key to the creation and success of organizations.[8]

The predominant perspectives not only neglect to pinpoint where these groups "hide" before they assume organizational form, they also fail to account for the role that the affective—the informal and the emotional—plays in group formation. The literature on feminist mobilization is a partial exception, as it has highlighted the interrelationship of the personal and the political. What is missing in the literature on civil society, social movement theory, and transitions, specifically in the case of former communist systems, is the connection between the private sphere of everyday life, the informal practices of domestic society, and the emergence of organizations in civil society. One of the reasons that this gap exists in the literature is that scholars traditionally assume a strict demarcation between the private (i.e., family and friends) and the public. From that position, they conclude, as Zbigniew Rau does in his study on former communist states, that civil society "reemerged from nothingness."[9] His conclusion is unacceptable, for one cannot get something out of nothing; if civil society reemerged, it must have existed somewhere before.

Several scholars of socialism have recognized that a variegated society is to be found in the informal spheres of social life.[10] What is still missing is the recognition that individuals do not establish groups and organizations due exclusively or primarily to the opportunities available, or due to the life-spaces (as defined traditionally) they seek to create, or as a result of resources accumulated. An a priori step is missing that would link the affective to the formation of groups.

So where does civil society emerge from? It emerges initially from the politics of affection in everyday life. Affection and passion (along with interest) are primary building blocks of groups and, by extension, of social movements and civil society. The deepest roots of organizations are found in the private and in the personal, in the sphere of everyday informal politics and their networks of affection. The politics of affection and disaffection, usually perceived as the private realm of life, are the initial arena where the public is mediated, dealt with, and reacted to. They carry identity and interests, emotion and reason, bundled together.

Alberto Melucci's proposition that social movements "operate mainly in the pre-political terrain of everyday life" provides a theoretical connection between the informal (or in Melucci's term, "the subterranean") and the politically visible. Although Melucci focuses on late-capitalist complex societies, his emphasis on the "hidden forms of organization . . . outside civil society" and "underneath the state" which individuals create to deal with the "uncertainties" of daily life is applicable to socialist Cuba.[11] Through these networks individuals question and challenge official codes of conduct and form alternative frameworks, an indispensable stage before movements become "political."

In contrast to other theories, Melucci's helps to detect the limitations of state control, connects individual motivation to collective action, and shows that social movements do not emerge from nothingness. Apparent atomization of society (à la Kornhauser) is just that, apparent. As individuals interact with each other in the informal sphere of daily life, collective expectations and identities are constructed, outside, underneath, and even within the state, which serve as shared mental frames of reference and sources of networks. One of the components of this process of collective identity and action in its formative stage is that individuals make, in Melucci's words, "emotional investments" in one another that enable them "to recognize themselves in each other." [12] Melucci concludes that "in this sense collective action is never based solely on cost-benefit calculations and a collective identity is never entirely negotiable." [13] Contrary to my argument and in tension with his own, Melucci concludes that the affective cannot be considered political because it functions according to a different logic. The logic of the emotional in its social setting is not necessarily prepolitical or outside politics, as Melucci concludes. He exaggerates the boundary of what is political and not, ironically, after he transgresses it. In the final analysis his position falls into the binary opposition private/public (which his theory initially problematizes) and, moreover, views the emotional as "natural" rather than meaningfully constructed in society, culturally relative, and carrying instrumental as well as affective and moral purposes.

While one possible response to the question of where civil society emerges from in one-party states is the politics of affection and the informal practices of society, one must take into account that both structures of opportunity and resource capability will determine whether groups will achieve formal institutional standing. In authoritarian and totalitarian contexts the principal source of change in the structure of opportunity is a weakened or reformist state, especially when the latter eases the restrictions on and the cost of forming independent associations. The inability to muster resources (material and otherwise) renders the prospects for institutionalization and mobilization dim.

When individuals in their private lives and among close-knit groups of friends attempt to establish their autonomy (morally, politically, culturally, economically, spiritually) from the state, the seeds of civil society are sowed. This process coincides with what Marcia A. Weigle and Jim Butterfield call the defensive stage of civil society development, "in which private individuals and independent groups actively or passively defend their autonomy vis-a-vis the party-state." [14] According to them, the development of civil society in posttotalitarian states proceeds in a linear and progressive trajectory: from the initial defensive stage, to an emergent one in which autonomous groups place limited demands in a wider social arena on a reforming state, to a mobilization stage in which the independent forces offer alternative forms of governance to that of the party-state, and, finally, to an institutional setting in which laws are enacted to guarantee the rights and responsibilities of independent social actors. The process hinges on the particular time and characteristics of the regime and the society in question.[15]

Although Weigle and Butterfield do not acknowledge the role that affective networks and their emotional software play in the genesis of the emergent stage, they recognize that independent activity can emerge from *within* the totalitarian regime basically because the "increasing gap between private and public values and interests [leads] to calls for the 'self-defense' of society."[16] Informal autonomous activities may eventually result in a systemic crisis as multiple illegal and unofficial groups and networks reject the official channels of participation. Not all informal activities in the former socialist countries, however, became officially "public." On the contrary, they continued to be "submerged," manifesting the retreat to the personal and the private (if the traditional dichotomy can be upheld). "Retreat" symbolized a defense of the autonomy of the person vis-à-vis a state that expects mobilization and politicization, in line with Hirschman's theory of shifting involvements.[17] "Retreat" is at times accompanied by the need to find real community—with the affective attachments the concept implies—outside state-sponsored organizations.[18]

Civil Society in the 1990s

Is civil society emerging in Cuba in the 1990s? Is this possible under the socialist regime? Scholars from divergent ideological perspectives have answered the question differently. Some see the seeds of civil society taking root in the economic reforms the government has implemented. Others highlight pressure from below and organizations that have distanced[19] themselves or broken away from state and party control.[20] Others, more sympathetic to the regime, have argued that civil society exists *a la cubana*: that is, within the mass organizations of the party and the socialist state, even though some advocate greater representation and participation.[21]

At the end of the 1990s there is a diverse domestic society in Cuba but not a full-fledged civil society. This does not mean that the regime's mass organizations are negligible sociopolitical actors. Mass organizations in Cuba have been significant subjects and agents of politics. Their importance resides in two different areas: as mechanisms of politics (which includes arenas for debate and articulation of contending interests at different junctures as well as instruments of socialization, implementation of state-directed policies, and arenas of leadership recruitment) and as potential sources of civil society formation in the future. I consider it an error of judgment, though, to argue that civil society, as defined above, has existed in socialist Cuba.

What one finds on the island in the 1990s is a proto-civil society some-where between a defensive and an emergent stage, following Weigle and Butterfield's model. By proto-civil society I mean the increasing number and visibility of small, and not so small, groups and institutions voicing different interests and identities within and without the framework of the party and the state. As the state enacted economic reforms after Rectification and lost its ability to control *la calle* as it once did, *lo informal* expanded. Together these factors opened a space for additional and alternative groups to form and com-pelled Cubans to seek sources of economic welfare and meaning and identity outside official channels. But the process of defense and emergence, contrary to what Weigle and Butterfield present, has not been linear, automatic, or easy. After 1996 the state adopted a hard-line strategy in an attempt to eliminate pockets of civil society, thwarting some of the emergent groups (particularly among intellectuals and human rights activists) as a result.

The following sources feed proto-civil society: the state (including the PCC and its extensive bureaucratic apparatus), the informal groups and prac-tices of society (which respond largely to the logic of the politics of affec-tion), and the small set of nongovernmental actors that has survived during the socialist period, principally religious organizations. Another source of civil society formation is transnational: Cuban-American exiles (and their host of organizations) and international NGOs and governments that are supporting a variety of NGOs on the island (what constitutes an NGO in the Cuban case is not always clear).

The state is a breeding ground for future civil society in two princi-pal ways: through its policies and through its bureaucracies. Within state bureaucracies (as well as within the PCC) lie different networks (based on af-fection or interest) that are likely to coalesce as factions or formal associa-tions if the structure of opportunity is propitious. From these bureaucracies and subgroups future leaders and associations that will compose civil society will emerge. The individuals, groups, bureaucracies, and interests the social-ist state now contains will not disappear totally after the transition. They will be redefined and rearticulated in the new context, similar to what occurred in former communist and authoritarian regimes worldwide. Among these will be labor (including farmers), technocrats, intellectuals, party cadres that have already started to assume leadership positions in the joint venture sector of the economy, university students, and women. Party-affiliated economists and intellectuals have increasingly voiced alternative visions and are poised to en-gage in self-directed activities that have greater financial and professional re-wards. Several officials and party members have abandoned their positions to pursue independent and dissident activities. Among the latter are professional journalists, teachers, economists, farmers, and doctors. Others, like the Grupo de los Cuatro, have publicly broken with the regime and have expressed their dissent, ending up in prison as a result.

The threefold process of informalization, destatization, and privatization has been under way since the 1980s and has entailed a twofold contestation of the boundaries between the public and the private. While private homes have become centers of cultural encounters (*tertulias*), *paladares*, and houses of worship (*casas culto*), public spaces have become "privatized" in peculiar ways. Artists (such as the group Arte Calle) exhibit their nonsanctioned works in the streets of Havana (hence the name of the group), religious processions fill the streets, *jineteras* beckon potential customers in the main boulevards, and young people gather at the Malecón to listen to rock music. Public institutions have harbored individuals and sponsored events that push the line of the permissible. Such is the case of La Casa de la Cultura Roberto Branly in Havana. Popularly known as El Patio de María (María's Backyard), the state organization has been renamed by the vox populi after the woman who, against official odds, opened its doors to disaffected teenagers.

Another modality of destatization is reflected in the attempts by mass organizations and other agencies of the state and the PCC to gain relative autonomy. This has been the case of the Asociación Nacional de Agricultores Pequeños (National Association of Peasants; ANAP) and of the social science research centers once under the control of the Central Committee (the case of the Centro de Estudios de América is the most notorious).[22] NGO status would provide flexibility in decision making and access to transnational sources of much-needed funding. Artists and intellectuals have been leaders in this regard. In the 1990s films, books, journals, and the visual arts have been produced independent of the state, at times in conjunction with foreign contributors. This process redefines the relationship between the state and its organs and the state and society in small but significant ways.

State policies have contributed to the creation of semiautonomous groups in society: joint ventures, the self-employed, the informal cottage industry that has grown up around the tourist sector, businesses and cooperatives, among others.[23] As the Cuban state undertook economic reforms leading to a modicum of liberalization, it unwittingly created the space for additional semi-independent organizations and increasing informality in decentralized areas of the economy. Economic reforms, however, are insufficient to create a civil society, as the case of China demonstrates.[24]

Lo informal, with its politics of affection, is a major source of independent associations on the island. Ties of friendship and kinship, networks of *socios,* the underground economy of affection, and patron-client relations foster necessary conditions for the emergence of civil society. Trust and collaboration outside the channels of the state are important dimensions for the creation of civil society, as is the recognition of multiple identities, passions, and interests in domestic society. As individuals resort to their closest friends and family members to satisfy daily and existential needs, the defensive and emergent stages of civil society are in the making.

In addition to the informal networks of affection, three types of organizations have been operating in Cuba. They differ in their relationship to the state, in their affective foundation, in their normativity, and in their interests. A useful typology is based on their autonomy vis-à-vis the state: controlled governmental organizations (congos), government-oriented nongovernmental organizations (gongos), and NGOs. Congos are the mass organizations of the state and the PCC. Born out of the politics of passion after the revolution of 1959, they are based on Marxist assumptions of the role and capability of the state. Because of the economic and ideological difficulties confronting Cuban socialism and the economic rewards that NGO status can offer, some congos have attempted to distance themselves from the official centers of power. Congos have not been immune to the general crisis affecting the system and have lost the power and appeal they once commanded. A few have found renewed importance in times of economic decline (i.e., the ANAP) and, consequently, have gained a measure of relative autonomy. The government, realizing the institutional challenges it confronts, has attempted to create new organizations and revamp participation in the older ones.[25]

Compared to the congos, the gongos are of recent creation, dating to the early 1990s. Their establishment suggests the emergent phase of civil society. Gongos are semicorporatist organizations. The government has granted them legal standing through the Ley de Asociaciones (Law of Associations), which regulates "independent" associations. The law requires that an official state bureaucracy endorse the petitioning organization and serve as its sponsor. The sponsoring institution guarantees nominal supervision over the new association as well as its ideological conformity. To secure the endorsement of a state agency, a personal (affective) relationship between the individual proposing a new association and the official in charge of the state agency is necessary. As a result gongos are headed by individuals with close personal contacts with party and state officials. The personal dimension is a sine qua non of the formation of gongos. They have been allowed to exist principally because their leaders enjoy moral and affective capital. The Instituto Félix Varela, the now-defunct Fundación Pablo Milanés, and the Centro Martin Luther King are prime examples of gongos. The Sociedades Anónimas, quasi-private economic enterprises, created in the 1990s, are not considered gongos because their function is exclusively economic.

Both the personalism and the corporatism inherent in gongos tend to erode as gongos strengthen institutionally, secure funding from international agencies, develop a constituency of their own, and stake their autonomy. Gongos have established relationships with international donors in an attempt to operate as bona fide NGOs. The Instituto Félix Varela has undertaken activities unprecedented in Cuba, for example, a debate on postmodernism and concerts to raise funds for development programs. While gongos might eventually transform themselves into NGOs, several congos are moving in the direction of becoming gongos in an effort to expand their autonomy and efficacy and secure international financial support. If the economy and the state continue in crisis, one can expect greater distancing of the official organizations from the PCC and the state, resulting in an increase in the number of gongos. If the state continues to be unable to support activities to the extent it once did, PCC members and officials will find it beneficial to form their own gongos, but it is unclear whether the leadership would allow that trend to unfold.

NGOs, with few important exceptions, are also relatively recent. They include human rights, religious, fraternal (e.g., Masons), and professional organizations. They are "dissident" groups insofar as they do not conform to the ideology of the regime, challenge the monolithic communist state, and present alternatives to the status quo. Although they are relatively small, they carry immense symbolic resonance. In spite of government controls and repression, they have been multiplying in the 1990s, reaching close to two hundred organizations in the area of human rights alone. The most active and significant NGO, because of its national reach and its international connections, is the Catholic Church. Despite exogenous and endogenous limitations, the Church has flourished since the late 1980s. It is the only NGO that has a national presence and relative economic power (it distributes food and medicines through CARITAS). The Catholic Church has dozens of lay groups throughout the island that are engaged in a number of religious and civic activities and has succeeded in attracting thousands of Cubans to its fold. The liveliness of the Catholic religious community, evidenced by the rise in attendance at mass, baptisms, and vocations and the growing number of Church publications, is unparalleled in Cuban history. At strategic moments, the Church has confronted the Cuban government on political issues such as human rights and economic reform.

That religious organizations are spearheading the revival of formal civil society is not surprising. Churches, although crippled after 1959, continued to operate; they had an infrastructure and the moral capital on which to grow. Further, Cubans, like others living in periods of uncertainty, have sought the affective solace that religion offers. Like their counterparts in communist regimes, in religion they have found an alternative to the official ideology, a source of answers to existential questions.

Most, if not all, of the recently created professional and human rights NGOs have a personal affective basis. Their roots are located in groups of friends and family members. Human rights groups and independent professional organizations—journalists and economists have been the most active—have been established among friends, family members, and acquaintances who trust each other. In a very real and practical way friendship gave birth to the human rights movement on the island.[26] Opposition to the regime was cultivated among these small circles of *amigos, aseres* (popular slang for "buddies"), *hermanos* (brothers, meaning "close buddies") and *compañeros* (partners, comrades). The personal and the affective forged solidarity and trust, leading to common political positions. Friends provided the comfort and support necessary to withstand grave risks and suffering.

Although one could argue that taking those risks was not rational (given the costs attached—imprisonment, exile, loss of employment), individuals pursued their goals largely out of personal affective and experiential motivations and normative convictions. An affective rationality is manifest. Activists felt that they were justified because the system was unjust. A deep sense of injustice compelled them, as did the experience of parents, friends, and other relatives who had been engaged politically in the past. Some of the leading human rights activists in Cuba had relatives who had previously participated in political activities (e.g., Ricardo Bofill and Vladimiro Roca).[27] Firsthand knowledge of what it means to be involved in the public arena is an additional personal dimension that influences who becomes engaged in the public sphere.

International events, as well as developments within Cuban socialism, filtered through a personal affective prism, contributed to the creation of the first independent organizations on the island in the early 1970s. The experience of the Prague Spring and the reform movement in Hungary, for example, had an impact on many young revolutionaries who started to question the course that Cuban socialism (and that of the Soviet Union) was taking. Books distributed through the underground, such as those by Solzhenitsyn, made many reconsider their positions. Likewise, decades later the ideas of perestroika and glasnost in the Soviet Union and democratization throughout Africa and Latin America contributed to the rise of a dissident movement in Cuba.

Dissidents were motivated by feelings and interests anchored in ideals and born out of the discrepancy between theory and practice in Cuban politics. Their passion was both a judgment of the failures of the system and an affirmation that there ought to be and could be something better. They pursued their agenda passionately. The more they were besieged by authorities and opponents, the stronger their commitment and the tighter the bonds between group members. Yet these individuals and groups manifested the personalism and fragmentation typical of Cuban political life at the same time that they sought the establishment of a moral political community that would abide by human rights standards. Bitter rivalries within human rights movements soon appeared, making unity difficult to manage and even more difficult to sustain.

Lo informal as an Uncivil Source of Civil Society

As a source of civil society formation lo informal presents challenges for the civility of society and the institutions of government. The logic of the informal does not correspond to the tenets of liberal democracy or to the norms of modernity. Informality has its own epistemological and ontological outlook that tends to thrive as it undermines official rules. Ironically the practices associated with lo informal approximate the notion of civility, solidarity, and friendship that Aristotle argued should characterize the relations between members of a political community. The main obstacle is that the politics of affection among small groups tend to inhibit the formation of larger associations in civil society. Moreover, informality fosters a culture of illegality in which bypassing legal norms is acceptable, encouraged, and admired. Because of the resilience of the culture of lo informal, what is likely to be established in Cuba in a post-Castro future will be democratic in form but not necessarily in practice, democracy but not in its liberal variant. The informal as a source of civil society formation carries within it antiliberal political cultural codes.

Transition and Posttransition Emotional Politics: Affection, Passion, and the Future

Most scholars pondering transition in Cuba have analyzed the possible scenarios of political change, playing a kind of Las Vegas odds (and odd) game. Much less has been written about the qualitative aspects of Cuba's politics in the future. How change comes about will affect the character of politics in general, but the most permanent qualities will not be determined by the process of transition itself but by other more enduring aspects of Cuban politics and political culture, namely, the politics of affection and passion. The conduct and character of political and civil society that will emerge on the island represents the greatest challenge to long-term liberal democracy there. The dilemma Cuba will face is not about the "resurrection" of a civil society but about what type of civil and political society will be resurrected. The bottleneck is not in the rise of voluntary associations, for they will multiply quickly once the state allows them to, but in the political culture of society.

In places where the politics of affection and passion are dominant features of political culture, civility tends to suffer. The politics of affection have a dual impact on civil society. On the one hand, they help to forge the bonds of groups that constitute civil society. On the other hand, the networks of affection retard the formation of a civil society because affection must be transcended to expand membership. That is, affection must be replaced or translated into nonparticularistic criteria.

Likewise, the politics of passion, with their propensity toward incivility, are likely to reemerge during transition and thereafter. Passion will revolve around issues of revenge—settling scores between alleged victims and victimizers—conflicts between those who left and those who stayed behind, class differences and material distribution, and perhaps race and gender as well. Passion can animate a social movement in its quest for a better *mañana*, but it can also lead to polarization and uncompromising positions, putting into question democratic stability, procedures, and norms and rendering elite pacts more difficult to engineer.

Therefore, the politics of affection and passion will help to construct civil society at the same time that they threaten its expansion and its civility. Affection and its networks are likely to continue to bypass institutions and their norms, in favor of personal connections and opportunism and its "everything goes" justification. Passion and its penchant for a winner-take-all approach to politics bodes ill for the future as well. So does the general informality of Cuban society.

Transition will come at a time when most Cubans are exhausted by politics. They want, above all, to be free from government regulations, interference, and collectivist pursuits. Many Cubans will disengage from politics, to pursue private concerns. Disengagement from civil society does not bode well for democratic consolidation, as it gives more room for elites to make decisions and to be less accountable and for professional politicians to do as they will. Disengaged individuals will continue to pursue the politics of affection, with their corporatist character and indirect challenge to democracy. Apathy born out of disappointment with collective endeavors will rob civil society of vitality and representativeness. This is the pattern of retreat to the private that Hirschman identified as the shifting involvement syndrome.

Conclusion

Emotions are necessary, if insufficient and problematic, for transition and democratic consolidation. The dilemma is not easily resolved. Emotions are important as value judgments, for they allow a population to express its views and aspirations. But affectivity, especially if it turns into the politics of passion, is dangerous, for it implies a crusade against others who do not see things in the same light. Like passion, affection can undermine the legal equality of all citizens in favoring personal exceptions. Democratic transitions require elite pacts or a consensus on democratic values operationalized through institutions. But democratic institutions in Cuba will have to confront the political cultural challenge.

Is Cuba's political culture a hospitable ground for democracy? Are the legacies of colonialism, corporatism, failed democracy, authoritarianism, and maximalist socialism conducive to a democratic transition, or do they subvert democratic governance? The past, that amorphous concept, does not determine the future in an anonymous or linear unavoidable manner. People make choices along the way within particular structural constraints and forces that help to shape options. Cuba's past does not preclude a democracy, although the political culture of passion, affection, and informality tends to conspire against it. The competing paradigms typical of Cuban politics in the past—modern liberal, corporatist, and the informal—will continue to exert their influence on Cuban politics. During and after the transition the pursuit of high absolute moral ends through any necessary means—the politics of passion—will be combined with the politics of affection, in which personal exceptionalism provides the logic to bypass the formalities of state structures, procedures, and norms to fulfill personal passions and interests.

During and after the transition emotions will play their characteristic dual role—helping to construct and destroy political order. Combined with the clash of normative frameworks typical of Cuban political culture, they will put the nation-state, its modern tenets, and liberal democracy to the test once again. The long-term prospects for democracy are dimmed by the inhospitable political economy of the foreseeable future that will demand continued austerity. Democratization in Cuba will tend not to meet the academic standards of liberal democracy or the ideal expectations of most. The democratization that will unfold will be *a la cubana* and will not fit easily into liberal molds. If and when democracy is implemented in Cuba, it will encounter a strong tendency toward incivility in political and civil society in particular and in domestic society in general. That incivility will emanate from the politics of passion and the politics of affection.

If Robert D. Putnam is right, as I think he is, that civic-mindedness is a good predictor of democratic success and economic development, then one would conclude that the future of democracy in Cuba is hardly bright.[28] However, Putnam might be conflating two dimensions, the political and the economic, that should be treated as separate. The social capital needed for economic development might be found in societies that do not count with the social capital conducive to political democracy. The social capital of the politics of affection lends itself to small businesses, family enterprises, and networks that can contribute to economic growth. This seems to be the case for Cubans during the Republic, under the socialist government, and in the diaspora community in Miami. Therefore, we can expect a modicum of economic development on the island but not the "equivalent" measure of political democratic development.

Harry Eckstein argues that "balanced disparities" are required for democratic stability. One of those disparities is affective attachment and affective neutrality toward the political system.[29] If the issues confronted tend to be foundational and morally charged, politics tend to lose that balance and civil society tends to become uncivil as politics are pursued passionately. This is particularly the case when institutions are weak and a consensus on democratic values is missing. Moments of transition are prone to these types of political passions. During such processes collectivities are hard pressed to sustain balanced disparities.

Emotionally charged issues are part and parcel of the process of transition. The redefinition of the political community, revanchism, mixed feelings about the Cubans in Miami, the jockeying for positions of authority and economic privilege, the unresolved issues regarding property settlement, the painful economy of the near future, and the racial divide compound to make transition problematic and emotionally charged. Class differences will become increasingly marked, among a population that has been accustomed to a modicum of equality. The most problematic social sector is the youth, particularly the poorer youth, *los desvinculados* (the "unconnected"). The riots that occurred in Old Havana in summer 1994 are indicative of the social explosion that might occur in transition and might linger well after a regime change. World time offers one way to deal with these issues: free enterprise in a leaner state that provides a minimal safety net. But the Cuban people need, and expect, more. Their desire is based on a paradox: a smaller state that guarantees political and economic freedoms in addition to a modicum of material support. In the context of a bankrupt economy, these expectations seem doomed to remain unfulfilled.

The tradition of rhetorical inflation and demagoguery may find fertile ground during the transition. Retribution and settling of scores and property claims are main issues that can fuel the politics of passion as well. The shrinking of the safety net, the accentuation of class differences, and the probable rise in unemployment and criminality as a result will contribute to incivility. Market reforms, especially if ushered in under a merciless capitalism, will not only augment the pain of ordinary Cubans but also foster incivility and disenchantment with the new order. The euphoria of private enterprise might also validate the notion that everything goes in this system of relentless individualism, including corruption and gangsterism. Network capital will become increasingly important as former officials resort to their relations in an attempt to secure their financial positions in a postsocialist regime, which has been a common pattern in transitions from socialism elsewhere.[30]

Many of the problems of the transition and the posttransition revolve around a core problem: how to construct a political community in which there is no consensus of values. Complicating matters further, reconstruction of the Cuban nation-state will take place at a time when nation-states everywhere are increasingly challenged to do their jobs efficiently and credibly. Fundamental issues relating to the provision of a safety net and the definition of citizenship are unresolved in many countries. In sum, transitions, like revolutions, are affairs of the heart. Partly because of this emotionally charged situation, posttransition Cuba will be difficult to govern. The combination of high expectations, apathy and a retreat to the private, and social political divisions will make it so. A culture of illegality tends to flourish in such conditions. A *civil* society might prove elusive once again.

In a posttransition period the traditional aspects of Cuban political culture will take the modern notion of democracy to task. What will ensue is not liberal democracy as we know it from textbook definitions but a democracy *a la cubana*. Multiple factors will come into play to shape the contours of Cuban democracy: structural, international, elite, institutional, and sheer luck. Politics in general, and democracy in particular, are the result of multiple factors coming together simultaneously. Political culture will be one factor, among many, that will give the future political system its particular flavor. It will push Cuban politics once again in the direction of the politics of passion and affection and their characteristic incivility and informality, threatening the normative expectations of democracy.

The result is that change in Cuba will bring transition without necessarily ushering in transformation in the political culture. The high expectations for the transition may come to naught given the dire condition of the productive and political-cultural infrastructure. Cubans are likely to overestimate the actual short- to medium-term economic possibilities of transition while they simultaneously underestimate the recurrent patterns of behavior that challenge liberal democracy.

8

EPILOGUE

Passion and
Affection from
a Distance

Passion and affection are not exclusive to Cuban politics. On the contrary, emotions illuminate how people relate to the social and the political, what they consider important, and how they express and interpret interests and identities. Although natural in the sense of having a physical biological dimension, the emotions should be understood as cultural expressions that, while sharing similarities across different contexts, are marked by local specificities. Among Cubans living outside the island (also referred to as exiles, refugees, émigrés, migrants, the diaspora, the transnational community, and, in the United States, Cuban-Americans), politics have also been construed as passion and affection. The politics of passion and affection have characterized Cuban politics in the United States in several ways, reproducing in a new political and economic setting the cultural codes of the homeland.

The politics of passion are at the heart of exile politics the world over. In the Cuban case the post-1959 *exiliados* (exiled ones) were initially those who "lost" the civil war and later those who became disaffected with the revolution. The politics of passion have been integral to their opposition to the Cuban regime since 1959 and hegemonic in their thinking and practice. For many of those who were forced to leave or who opted to leave, the homeland constitutes a moral end for which they continue to struggle, if from a distance. The opposition to Fidel Castro's government has been construed as a crusade against evil. From this perspective, the revolution betrayed the noble ideals of the struggle against Batista and destroyed the fabric of the Cuban nation. Return to *la patria* represents a victory against the evil opponent; defeat of the

Castro regime would legitimize the exiles' righteousness and pave the way for the moral rebirth of the Cuban nation.

The following quote by one of the most visible Cuban-American leaders (and Fidel's nephew), Representative Lincoln Diaz-Balart, is a reflection of the prevalent conceptualization of Cuban exile politics: "We must do everything possible to accelerate the collapse of the dictatorship. This is the passion that drives me."[1] "We must do everything possible" echoes the instrumentality of Cuban politics and the absolute moral imperative that compels individuals to act; the combination leads to a typical manifestation of Cuban political culture in which the ends justify the means. The end—the collapse of the Castro regime and his demise—warrants all necessary means—violence, embargo, isolation, condemnation, and even censorship and physical attacks against those outside Cuba who do not toe the same line. No compromise is possible; one must be "vertical" in one's opposition.

That passion compels Cuban-American politics after four decades is and is not surprising. Although some scholars have argued that the exiles of yesteryear have become the immigrants of today, leaving behind their Cuban identity in favor of a hyphenated Cuban-American one, passion has not died even if the younger generations seem to be less passionate about the struggle.[2] As the journalist Pamela Constable remarked, "Such passions still dominate exile thinking."[3] Groups motivated by the politics of passion carry the moral imperative for hundreds of years, reproducing its codes from generation to generation. Over time the politics of passion have assumed different modalities, though, while sustaining its principal norms. In the early years (from 1959 to the early 1960s), Cuban refugees saw themselves as temporary exiles who would return after a military victory led by the United States, themselves, or both. The attempt to overthrow the Castro government through the invasion at the Bay of Pigs in 1962 epitomized this logic. The discourse of the politics of passion is captured in dozens of exile publications.[4] Throughout the years the language of passion has continued to represent Fidel and communism as the ultimate evils that must be combated, even through violence.

By the early 1980s, as the Cuban community had achieved considerable economic success and an electoral critical mass in southern Florida, the politics of passion found an institutional venue in the Cuban American National Foundation (CANF). Its leader, Jorge Más Canosa, spoke the language of passion—the search for a new moral Cuba—and pursued politics as a crusade against the corruption of that absolute national goal. Más Canosa embodied Cuban political culture and its codes of passion. With time, Más Canosa, the foundation, and its political action committee exercised considerable influence in Congress and the White House, specifically on U.S. policy toward

Cuba. CANF's efforts resulted in a number of policies, including the establishment of Radio and TV Martí to broadcast to the island, the Cuban Democracy Act of 1992, and the Helms-Burton Act that tightened the U.S. embargo in 1996.

Passion, not only generous financial contributions to both sides of the aisle in Congress, helps to explain the success of CANF's campaign to veto any attempt at normalization of U.S.-Cuban relations. Passion was instrumental in mobilizing support in the Cuban-American community (where hundreds of thousands attended the public rallies organized by CANF) as well as in Congress, where Más Canosa was treated with the deference usually reserved for heads of states (for he could not only deliver funds but votes as well). If resource mobilization is a determinant factor in the formation and achievement of a social movement, passion constitutes another type of strategic resource.

The politics of passion are not only a modality of political behavior but also a nonmaterial resource composed of a discourse and a moral capital that attracts (and detracts) followers. Passion also facilitates financial contributions to a political effort. CANF, for instance, had tens of thousands of members who contributed monetarily; membership in the foundation's board of directors required a donation of thousands of dollars. The foundation's financial contributions to both Republicans and Democrats combined with the nonmaterial capital enjoyed by Más Canosa helps to explain CANF's influence. The politics of affection also served as a source of network capital of vital importance for the formation of exile organizations. It explains the support that exiled Cubans gave to Más Canosa, their maximum leader—who they perceived as the anti-Castro—as well as Más Canosa's economic success. In sum, the ability of CANF to achieve its purpose in the policy arena resulted from the synergy of material and nonmaterial resources, in tandem with other factors.[5]

That Cuban-Americans never stopped pursuing politics as passion, even after the success of their lobbying efforts in the context of U.S. politics, is evidenced by opinion polls. Even in the face of the failure of military options and changed international conditions, Cuban-Americans never quite discarded the possibility of military action. In 1997 close to two-thirds supported the notion of U.S. military intervention on the island.[6] Their response suggests that the all-or-nothing, winner-take-all approach to politics—a trademark of the politics of passion—has not been abandoned. Cuban-American politics regarding the homeland continued to be compelled by deep emotional/moral streams four decades after the advent of the revolution. The "losers" still seek moral (and some even material) redress: the total elimination of the Castro regime, which would usher in a new Cuba, the Cuba that was supposed to be, the one that Martí dreamed of, the one embodied in the Constitution of 1940, democratic and progressive. In the same fashion that in Cuba "the winners" presented their social enterprise as the construction of a utopia, the exiles have projected an opposing utopia. Both sides claim that José Martí, the father of Cuban utopianism, is on their side.

What is surprising and ironic, but typical of Cuban politics, is that despite the success of Cuban-Americans as immigrants in terms of economic achievement—relying in no small measure on the politics of affection—the politics of passion still burn bright. Economic change has not translated into political-cultural transformation. Electoral fraud, embezzlement, and acrimonious vendettas have plagued city politics in Miami and Hialeah, the two principal Cuban-dominated urban centers in the United States. Max Castro has highlighted another dimension of the dissonance between political and economic achievement: the success of the immigrants contrasts with the failure of the exiles.[7]

The Politics of Affection and Their Impact on Miami-Cuba Relations

Not all Cuban-Americans have advocated the hard line of embargo and disengagement vis-à-vis the island, the main policy tools of the politics of passion. Younger segments of the population, recent arrivals, and some old-timers have endorsed an alternative course of rapprochement and engagement.[8] The differences, albeit important, are mainly of means, not of ends. Although multiplicity of opinions, tactics, and tone has characterized Cuban-American politics and its myriad groups (whose primary difference often is found in leadership and personality—an expression of the politics of affection—not necessarily in major ideological divergence), by the late 1990s the cleavages became pronounced as the island experienced a severe economic decline in the wake of the collapse of the Soviet Union.

While the politics of passion did not die, the politics of affection at the grassroots became politically and socially energized. Affection for family members, friends, and the Cuban people in general (whose living standard had plummeted as a result of the post-1986 economic crisis) motivated thousands of Cuban-Americans to send remittances to their relatives and friends in Cuba. Tens of thousands visited the island carrying medicine and dollars for food. Their remittances (estimated between $700 million and $800 million annually) became a partial substitute for the tattered socialist safety net and for lost Soviet assistance.

In the same way that the politics of affection and its networks expanded as a response to the deepening economic crisis on the island, transnational networks of affection increased in response to the suffering of the Cuban people.

In times of economic need family and friends resort to each other; affection and instrumentality were coupled in this fashion in the 1990s. The politics of affection made many Cuban-Americans challenge their preconceived notions that propelled the politics of passion. As one Cuban-American put it: "I have always supported the embargo, but when your eighty-two-year-old mother writes and says there is only enough soap to bathe once a week, it is very hard to maintain that position."[9] In the 1990s the politics of affection have confronted the politics of passion, revealing the dual codes that operate in Cuban and Cuban-American political culture. One of the results is that the politics of affection, notwithstanding the discourse of passion, have been able to mobilize individuals and groups in support of people-to-people contact with the island, especially after John Paul's visit to Cuba in 1998. The pope's message and the Cuban Catholic Church's position on behalf of national reconciliation legitimized reaching out to those on the other side, blurring the distinction between us and them, good and evil.

By the late 1990s the politics of affection coexisted with the politics of passion in terms of Cuban-Americans' views on Cuba. When asked if they endorsed the idea of visiting family and friends on the island, 70 percent responded affirmatively.[10] The duality is not as paradoxical as it may seem: a strong posture against the government and a soft one vis-à-vis the people. Such a dichotomy is not rife with tension and conflict. Specific policy initiatives might be interpreted by some as soft on both the people and the government and therefore demand opposition.

Such was the case in early 1999 when the Cuban government threatened to (and eventually did) cut telephone service between the island and the United States in retaliation for a U.S. court ruling that allowed family members of the Brothers to the Rescue pilots (who had been shot down by the Cuban Air Force in February 1996 in international waters) to be compensated from the funds that U.S. telephone companies owed their Cuban counterpart. The issue polarized the Cuban-American community and brought together the politics of passion and affection in a most convoluted way. One side argued, "The most important thing is that we are able to talk to our family [on the island]. There is nothing more important than that."[11] The logic of the politics of affection assumed the character of the politics of passion: "The common good must be above individual well-being, and in this case the common good is to maintain telephone service."[12] Others unfurled the traditional banner of passion: "If we kneel in front of the *chantaje* [blackmail] [of Fidel Castro] to cut the long-distance calls, tomorrow we will confront a bigger one. . . . Justice must be blind, and if there is a judgment against the Cuban government it is important that the U.S. government pursues that order without concern to the *chantajes* of Castro.[13]

The Politics of Affection and the Enclave

The politics of affection have been instrumental in the economic success of Cuban-Americans in Miami. Although scholars have debated the reasons for the economic success of Cuban-Americans,[14] the politics of affection per se, which created the social glue necessary for the establishment of small as well as large enterprises, have been an unrecognized part of that story. The networks and the affective realism of the politics of affection contributed to capitalism in the diaspora and the emergence of what Alejandro Portes and Robert L. Bach called "the Cuban enclave" in Miami.[15]

Portes and Bach have argued that "immigrants do not arrive on the shores of the United States as isolated individuals clutching only their personal resources as tools for resettlement. Rather, in addition to individual capacities, immigrants have access to the resources of the larger social groups of which they are part."[16] Social networks, based on ethnicity and country of origin, are one of those resources migrants can access. Portes and Bach acknowledged that "as a form of social affiliation, ethnicity involves special bonds among people of similar origins."[17] The "special bonds" are intrinsically affective, either in terms of co-nationals or family and friends. The aid that family and friends gave the recent arrivals was one of the crucial "supportive mechanisms at work in the enclave." Economic achievement "was significantly determined by the early support of family and friends and by employment in Cuban-owned firms."[18]

The politics of affection have facilitated the incorporation of Cubans into city government, other elected positions, and civic organizations. The logic of the politics of affection has also been manifested in less savory ways: a degree of "corruption" in public life that ranges from charges of electoral irregularities to defamation of political opponents, from bribery to welfare fraud. This sort of corruption is not the monopoly of Cuban-Americans; far from it, as Chicago and Boston amply demonstrate. But the politics of affection and the norms of *lo informal* tend to facilitate and justify these practices outside Cuba as they do inside the island, before, during, and most likely after socialism. These bonds of affection seem to thrive among ethnic communities or in-groups (again, Boston and Chicago offer interesting comparisons) and facilitate and justify means that are not morally acceptable otherwise. As the Cuban-American experience shows, the principal characteristics of the politics of affection and the culture of informality remain intact regardless of economic and political regime, even if their outcomes may differ in different political and economic systems.[19]

In the future both the politics of passion and the politics of affection in the Cuban-American community will intersect with political change on the island, molding the process. Passion and affection will tend to express themselves in opposite directions: passion might polarize the situation while affection might work toward reconciliation. But the politics of passion and affection may also contribute to change in other ways. Passion might provide the normativity for an alternative future, while affection might undermine the institutional procedures of the new state. During the uncertainty and dislocation that transitions bring, the politics of affection will underscore the expanded role that networks play in moments of institutional change. As a result of the cycle of shifting involvement, the politics of affection will assume greater relevance during the period of transition. In the process the politics of affection will contribute to economic innovation as small family firms are established, many supported by capital from Cuban-Americans.

Conclusion

One of the conundrums of the modern nation-state is that it is caught between competing demands: the need to craft an affective attachment to (and among) the citizenry, on the one hand, and the need for technocratic performance on the basis of efficiency and standard operating procedures, on the other. The intellectual constructs of modernity—especially the reductionism inherent in rational choice theory and traditional versions of liberalism in general—do not provide the necessary conceptual tools to address the dilemma. Neglecting the emotional bases of politics and the intimate relationship between reason and passion misses the practical and theoretical significance of the affective in creating local, national, and transnational communities and in both subverting and undergirding principal projects of modernity. A vital conceptual dimension that could enrich social theory goes unrecognized as a consequence.

Since modern times the architects of social science literature have built its edifice without an explicit emotional foundation, particularly in political science and economics, and are surprised when their constructs sometimes crumble (e.g., the failure of the literature on communist regimes to point to potential forces for change in the society). The rational actor model has exerted its dominance in a fashion that has excluded central aspects of human experience, blinding us to factors that have a marked impact on state-society relations and intrastate politics; *Homo economicus* reigns supreme. Even Weber and his heirs contributed to the weakness of the modern conceptualization by positing binary oppositions between instrumental reason and rational logic, failing to recognize that the affective is intimately conjugated with the instrumental and the moral, the private and the public.

All major ideologies and approaches to social science tend to hide the emotions by presuming them. By bringing them out, we recuperate some of the intellectual roots of modernity. Emotions are present in the metanarrative of modernity, but in hiding, with sporadic sightings here and there. If we are to understand human beings, the ultimate social agents, and how they/we deal with long-standing and recent social issues such as identity, revolutions, and ethnic cleansing, we need to incorporate the affective into politics.

In this book I have argued that the emotions have their own rationality that must be understood in culturally specific ways. A holistic understanding of self-interest, realism, and rationality would incorporate the emotional and in the process would shed light on political culture and social developments in particular localities. I have attempted to show that the material and the affective/ideational help to shape each other in specific settings following a logic of affective realism. Like affection and reason, they are interwoven rather than diametrically opposed. *Reason* is not the antonym of *emotion*. Rationality is not the opposite of emotionality. In human daily interaction affective realism, with economic and noneconomic import and its own norms, predominates. To find the politics of emotions and their reasons, one must look at the informal relations of everyday life and analyze their social, economic, and political expressions, meanings, and ramifications.

The practical aspects of the politics of emotions are a permanent concern not only for poor traditional societies but for industrialized and postindustrial ones as well. No society escapes the challenge of community building, as recent developments in suburban areas of the United States and in Yugoslavia demonstrate. Modernization itself produces a breakdown of the bonds of collective life, but that does not mean that all the affective links between individuals disappear, should do so, or are not to be replaced. Nor does modernization entail an abandonment of particularistic criteria or deepseated emotional currents in politics.

But rescuing the emotions is not enough. In bringing them back and out, we should also recognize that we need to reconceptualize them in two main ways: we need to avoid the classical dichotomies that make the emotional irrational (and the realm of women, the poor, and others) and acknowledge the variety of effects, often contradictory, that emotions have on social life.

Emotions sustain and undermine order, create and destroy civil and political society, support and erode democracy and authoritarianism, contribute to economic growth and its limits, and help to explain change and continuity. Emotions have their reasons and their multiple impacts on politics and society, depending on other, intervening socioeconomic factors and cultural tendencies.

The Cuban case shows that what appear to be negative emotions in other modalities might contribute to what in modern times has been portrayed as positive. This is the case with the contribution of affection to economic growth, revolutionary change, the construction of nationalism, capital accumulation, and the emergence of civil society. However, what erects and sustains many of the tenets of political modernity also challenges them. In Cuba the politics of passion and affection have subverted the modern nation-state, democracy, and socialism. The politics of passion and the politics of affection at times have sustained each other (as they did in the revolutionary struggle and the revolutionary government's early years in power), but mostly they have undermined the goals of the collectivity. The politics of affection typical of *lo informal* challenge the utopias pursued through the politics of passion. The logics and norms of each tend to clash, leading to less than stellar results for the state and modern political programs in the long run.

But emotions are not all; they do not explain everything. They do not tell the whole story of social life (if any such overarching and monocausal narrative is possible, desirable, or accurate). The politics of passion and affection are but a meaningful part of politics, a complement to the story that needs to be told, or better still, retold with feeling.

NOTES

Chapter 1

1. Albert Hirschman, *The Passions and the Interests* (Princeton: Princeton University Press, 1977).

2. Marc Granovetter, *The Sociology of Economic Life* (Boulder, Colo.: Westview Press, 1992).

3. This discussion is based on Hirschman, *The Passions and the Interests.*

4. Adam Smith, *The Theory of Moral Sentiments* (Indianapolis: Liberty Classics, 1976).

5. Benedict Anderson, *Imagined Communities: Reflections on the Origin and Spread of Nationalism* (London: Verso, 1991).

6. Stephen Holmes, *Passions and Constraint: On the Theory of Liberal Democracy* (Chicago: University of Chicago Press, 1995), 26–27.

7. Ibid., 1.

8. Stephen Holmes, "The Secret History of Self-Interest," in *Beyond Self-Interest*, ed. Jane S. Mansbridge (Chicago: University of Chicago Press, 1990), 268.

9. See, e.g., James C. Scott, Carl Landé, Laura Guasti, and Steffen W. Schmidt, eds., *Friends, Followers and Factions* (Berkeley: University of California Press, 1976).

10. E. Victor Wolfenstein, *The Revolutionary Personality: Lenin, Trotsky, Gandhi* (Princeton: Princeton University Press, 1967).

11. Harold Lasswell, *Power and Personality* (Westport, Conn.: Greenwood Press, 1976). See also T. W. Adorno, Else Frenkel-Brunswik, Daniel J. Levinson, and R. Nevitt Sanford, *The Authoritarian Personality* (New York: Norton, 1969).

12. Gabriel Almond and Sidney Verba, *The Civic Culture: Political Attitudes and Democracy in Five Nations* (Princeton: Princeton University Press, 1982), 5.

13. Ibid., 488.

14. Harry Eckstein, *Regarding Politics: Essays on Political Theory, Stability, and Change* (Berkeley: University of California Press, 1992).

15. Lucian W. Pye, *Politics, Personality, and Nation Building: Burma's Search for Identity* (Westport, Conn.: Greenwood Press, 1976).

16. Ibid., 16.

17. Ibid., 18.

18. Ibid.

19. See Max Weber, in H. H. Gerth and C. Wright Mills, eds. and trans., *From Max Weber: Essays in Sociology* (New York: Oxford University Press, 1958).

20. For a full discussion of this point, see Robert Frank, *Passions within Reason: The Strategic Role of the Emotions* (New York: Norton, 1988).

21. Amitai Etzioni, quoted in Jane S. Mansbridge, ed., introduction to *Beyond Self-Interest* (Chicago: University of Chicago Press, 1990), 18.

22. Mansbridge, *Beyond Self-Interest,* ix.

23. Amelie O. Rorty, ed., *Explaining the Emotions* (Berkeley: University of California Press, 1980).

24. Robert Frank, "A Theory of Moral Sentiments," in Mansbridge, *Beyond Self-Interest,* 73.

25. Catherine A. Lutz, *Unnatural Emotions: Everyday Sentiments on a Micronesian Atoll and Their Challenge to Western Theory* (Chicago: University of Chicago Press, 1988), 15.

26. Ibid., 5.

27. Neil L. Smelser, "Vicissitudes of Work and Love," in *Themes of Work and Love,* ed. Neil L. Smelser and Erik H. Erickson (Cambridge, Mass.: Harvard University Press, 1980), 106.

28. Ibid.

29. The discussion that follows is based on Robert C. Solomon, *The Passions* (Garden City, N.Y.: Anchor Press, 1976).

30. Solomon, *The Passions, 15.* Emphasis in original.

31. Robert C. Solomon, "Emotions and Choice," in Rorty, *Explaining the Emotions, 263.*

32. Ibid., 258.

33. Ibid.

34. Jürgen Habermas, *The Philosophical Discourse of Modernity: Twelve Lectures* (Cambridge, Mass.: MIT Press, 1987), 16–17.

35. Jon Elster, "Sadder but Wiser: Rationality and the Emotions," *Social Science Information* 24, no. 2 (1985): 399.

36. Jerome Kagan quoted in Frank, *Passions within Reason,* 81.

37. William Kornhauser, *The Theory of Mass Society* (New York: Free Press, 1959), 16.

38. Francis Fukuyama, *Trust: The Social Virtues and the Creation of Prosperity* (New York: Free Press, 1995), 10.

39. Robert D. Putnam, *Making Democracy Work: Civic Traditions in Modern Italy* (Princeton: Princeton University Press, 1993).

40. See Fukuyama, *Trust,* Chap. 3.

41. Fukuyama, Huntington, Eckstein, and Lasswell made a similar point years ago.

42. Edward Banfield, *The Moral Basis of a Backward Society* (New York: Free Press, 1967).

43. Glenn Cuadill Dealy, "Two Cultures and Political Behavior in Latin America," in *Democracy in Latin America: Patterns and Cycles,* ed. Roderic Ai Camp (Wilmington: Scholarly Resources, 1996), 46–66.

44. Emile Durkheim, *The Division of Labor in Society* (New York: Free Press, 1964); and Elliot Leyton, ed., *The Compact: Selected Dimensions of Friendship,* Social and Economic Papers No. 3 (St. John's: Memorial University of Newfoundland, 1974).

45. Stuart Eisenstadt and Louis Roniger, *Patrons, Clients and Friends: Interpersonal Relations and the Structure of Trust in Society* (Cambridge: Cambridge University Press, 1984), 6.

46. See Robert Boyd and Peter J. Richerson, "Culture and Cooperation," in Mansbridge, *Beyond Self-Interest,* 111–132.

47. Goran Hyden, *Beyond Ujamaa in Tanzania: Underdevelopment and an Uncaptured Peasantry* (Berkeley: University of California Press, 1980).

48. See Larissa Lomnitz and Ana Melnick, *Chile's Middle Class: A Struggle for Survival in the Face of Neoliberalism* (Boulder, Colo.: Lynne Rienner, 1992).

49. Ayse Gunes-Ayata, "Clientelism: Premodern, Modern, Postmodern," in *Democracy, Clientelism and Civil Society,* ed. Louis Roniger and Ayse Gunes-Ayata (Boulder, Colo.: Lynne Rienner, 1994), 24.

50. Hirschman, *Shifting Involvements,* 121–130.

51. For a general theoretical discussion of the role of trust in society, particularly from a social and political perspective, see Eisenstadt and Roniger, *Patrons, Clients and Friends.*

52. Eisenstadt and Roniger, *Patrons, Clients and Friends,* 40.

53. Eisenstadt and Roniger, *Patrons, Clients and Friends,* has helped my thinking on this specific process; see 288–292.

54. James C. Scott, *Domination and the Arts of Resistance: Hidden Transcripts* (New Haven: Yale University Press, 1990).

55. Gunes-Ayata, "Clientelism," 19–28.

56. See the discussion of a similar point in Samuel P. Huntington, *The Clash of Civilizations and the Remaking of World Order* (New York: Simon and Schuster, 1996), 77.

57. Quoted in Eisentadt and Roniger, *Patrons, Clients and Friends,* 18.

58. Barrington Moore, *Injustice: The Social Bases of Obedience and Revolt* (New York: Pantheon Books, 1978), 18.

59. Alejandro Portes, *The Informal Economy: Studies in Advanced and Less Developed Countries* (Baltimore: Johns Hopkins University Press, 1989).

60. See, e.g., James C. Scott, *Weapons of the Weak: Everyday Forms of Peasant Resistance* (New Haven: Yale University Press, 1988).

61. See Eisenstadt and Roniger, *Patrons, Clients and Friends.*

62. Jeremy Boissevian, *Friends of Friends: Networks, Manipulators and Coalitions* (New York: St. Martin's Press, 1974).

63. Stuart Henry, ed., *Informal Institutions: Alternative Networks in the Corporate State* (New York; St. Martin's Press, 1981), 2–3.

Chapter 2

1. Anthony Maingot, "The Real and the Ideal in Cuban Political Culture," in *Transition in Cuba* (Miami: Cuban Research Institute, Florida International University, 1994), 289–335. See also Rafael Rojas, "Viaje a las semillas: Instituciones de la antimodernidad cubana," *Apuntes Postmodernos* 4 (Fall 1993): 3–20.

2. Roland H. Ebel, Raymond Taras, and James D. Cochrane, *Political Culture and Foreign Policy in Latin America* (Albany: State University of New York, 1991), 28–29.

3. Ibid.

4. Rosario Rexach, Introduction to Jorge Mañach, *Historia y estilo* (Miami: Editorial Cubana, 1994), xiii.

5. Maingot, "The Ideal and the Real in Cuban Political Culture," 468–525.

6. Homi Bhaba, "Narrating the Nation," in *Nationalism*, ed. John Hutchinson and Anthony Smith (New York: Oxford University Press, 1997), 306–312.

7. Ramiro Guerra y Sánchez, José M. Pérez Cabrera, Juan J. Remos, and Emeterio S. Santovenia, *Historia de la nación cubana* (Havana: Editorial Historia de la Nación Cubana, 1957), xi.

8. Ibid., xvi.

9. Ibid., xv.

10. Herminio Portell Vilá, *Historia de Cuba en sus relaciones con los Estados Unidos y España* (Miami: Mnemosyne, 1969), 13.

11. Ibid.

12. Cintio Vitier, *Ese sol del mundo moral* (Mexico: Siglo XXI, 1975).

13. Luis Marino Pérez, "La indisciplina en los pueblos," *Cuba Contemporánea* 2, no. 1 (May 1913): 28.

14. Enrique José Varona, "Nuestra indisciplina," *Cuba Contemporánea* 4, no. 1 (January 1914): 13.

15. Eduardo Benes, "La psicología del partido político," *Revista Bimestre Cubana* 15, no. 3 (September–October 1920): 203–208.

16. Rafael Estenger, "Cubanidad y derrotismo," *Revista Bimestre Cubana* 3 (May–June 1940): 385.

17. Ibid., 387.

18. Ibid.

19. Ibid., 388.

20. Ibid.

21. Mario Guiral Moreno, "Malcriados y descorteses," *Revista Bimestre Cubana* 48 (December 1941): 389.

22. Mario Guiral Moreno, "Aspectos censurables del carácter cubano," *Revista Bimestre Cubana* 4, no. 2 (February 1914): 121–163.

23. Guiral Moreno, "Malcriados y descorteses," 189.

24. Nelson Valdés, "Cuban Political Culture: Between Betrayal and Death," in *Cuba in Transition: Crisis and Transformation*, ed. Sandor Halebsky and John M. Kirk (Boulder, Colo.: Westview Press, 1992), 207–228.

25. Ibid.

26. See Jules R. Benjamin, *The United States and the Origins of the Cuban Revolution* (Princeton: Princeton University Press, 1990).

Chapter 3

1. Louis Pérez, *Cuba: Between Reform and Revolution* (New York: Oxford University Press, 1995), 212.

2. Ibid., 213.

3. Marifeli Pérez-Stable, "Estrada Palma's Civic March: From Oriente to Havana, April 20–May 11, 1902," *Cuban Studies/Estudios Cubanos* 29 (forthcoming).

4. Hugh Thomas, *Cuba* (Barcelona: Ediciones Grijalbo, 1973), 618.

5. Benes, "La psicología del partido político," 208.

6. Carlos Márquez Sterling and Manuel Márquez Sterling, *Historia de la isla de Cuba* (New York: Regents, 1975).

7. José Sixto de Sola, "El pesimismo cubano," *Cuba Contemporánea* 3, no. 4 (December 1913): 273–303.

8. I owe this interpretation to Marifeli Pérez-Stable, who helped me to see the optimistic side of Sola's argument.

9. José Antonio Ramos, *Manual del perfecto fulanista: Apuntes para el estudio de nuestra dinámica político-social* (Miami: Editorial Cubana, 1995).

10. Pérez, *Cuba*, 214.

11. Ibid., 219.

12. Márquez Sterling and Márquez Sterling, *Historia de la isla de Cuba*, 170.

13. Ibid., 217.

14. Fernando Ortiz, *La decadencia cubana* (Havana: La Universal, 1924), 10.

15. Ibid., 18.

16. Fernando Ortiz, *Entre cubanos: Psicología tropical* (Havana: Editorial de Ciencias Sociales, 1987), 15.

17. Ibid., 233.

18. Ibid., 186–188.

19. Hugh Thomas and Anthony Maingot have made a similar point.

20. For the less positive side of the Constitutional Convention, see the coverage in *Carteles*.

21. Jorge Mañach, "La crisis de la ilusión," in *Pasado vigente* (Havana: Editorial Trópico, 1939), 16.

22. Jorge Mañach, "Norma y decencia," in *Pasado vigente*, 29.

23. Jorge Mañach, "Raíces del absentismo," in *Pasado vigente*, 113.

24. Eduardo R. Chibás, reprinted from *Bohemia* in E. Vignier and G. Alonso, eds., *La corrupción política y administrativa en Cuba* (Havana: Editorial Ciencias Sociales, 1973), 234.

25. Ibid.

26. For additional development of this point, see Maingot, "The Ideal and the Real in Cuban Political Culture."

27. *Diario de la Marina*, January 7, 1959, 15A.

28. Cesar García Pons, "La voz de la libertad," *Diario de la Marina*, January 6, 1959.

29. Ibid.

30. Ibid.

31. Marifeli Pérez-Stable, *The Cuban Revolution: Origins, Course, and Legacy* (New York: Oxford University Press, 1999).

32. For a full explanation of this process, see Pérez-Stable, *The Cuban Revolution*.

33. Carmelo Mesa-Lago, "Assessing Economic and Social Performance in the Cuban Transition of the 1990s," *World Development* 26, no. 5 (1998): 857–876.

34. Zoe Valdés, *La nada cotidiana* (Barcelona: Emecee Editores, 1995). English translation: *Yocandra in the Paradise of Nada* (New York: Arcade, 1995).

Chapter 4

1. For a survey of the interpretations, see Jorge I. Domínguez, "Politics in Cuba 1959–1989: The State of Research," in *Cuban Studies since the Revolution*, ed. Damián J. Fernández, (Gainesville: University Press of Florida, 1992), 95–118.

2. For an initial study of this phenomenon, see my "Political Religion and Revolution in

Cuba," in *The Religious Challenge to the State,* ed. Matthew C. Moen and Lowell Gustafson, (Pittsburgh: Temple University Press, 1992), 51–71, on which parts of this chapter are based.

3. *Diario de la Marina,* January 6, 1959, 2a.

4. *Bohemia,* January 11, 1959, 5.

5. Ibid., 92.

6. Ibid., 139.

7. Manuel Fernández, *Religion y revolución en Cuba: Veinticinco años de lucha ateista* (Miami: Saeta Ediciones, 1984), 22; John M. Kirk, *Between God and the Party: Religion and Politics in Revolutionary Cuba* (Gainesville: University Press of Florida, 1989), 176.

8. Kirk, *Between God and the Party,* 176.

9. Fernández, *Religion y revolución en Cuba,* 22.

10. Ibid.

11. David E. Apter, "Political Religion in the New Nations," in *Old Societies and New States,* ed. Clifford Geertz, (New York: Free Press, 1963), 61.

12. Clifford Geertz, "Ideology as a Cultural System," in *Ideology and Discontent,* ed. David E. Apter (New York: Free Press, 1964), 64.

13. Andrés Suárez, "Cuba: Ideology and Pragmatism" in *Cuba: Continuity and Change,* ed. Jaime Suchlicki, Antonio Jorge, and Damián Fernández (Miami: Institute of Interamerican Studies, 1985), 129–146.

14. *Diario de la Marina,* January 6, 1959, 1A, 6A.

15. Rafael Cepeda, "Fidel Castro y el reino de Dios," *Bohemia,* July 17, 1960, 110.

16. Carlos Franqui, *Cuba: El libro de los doce* (Mexico City: Era, 1966).

17. *Bohemia,* January 11, 1959, 28.

18. Anita Arroyo, *Diario de la Marina,* January 8, 1959, 4A.

19. Enrique Pérez-Serantes, "La Divina Providencia ha escrito en el cielo de Cuba la palabra triunfo," *La Quincena,* January 1959, 18.

20. *Bohemia,* January 11, 1959, p. 69.

21. Manuel Fernández, "Presencia de los católicos en la revolución triunfante," *La Quincena,* January 1959, 10.

22. *La Quincena,* March 6, 1959.

23. Cepeda, "Fidel Castro y el reino de Dios."

24. Interview with Natividad Torres, Cambridge, Mass., June 1989.

25. Nelson Valdés has made this point.

26. Eddu Nitya, *La suprema revelación, precedida por oda a la revolución, una nota liminar, y las siete reglas del perfecto espiritista, con Fidel ante la humanidad* (Havana: Tipografía Ideas, 1961).

27. Lloyd Free, *Attitudes of the Cuban People toward the Castro Regime in Late Spring 1960* (Princeton: Institute for International Social Research, 1960), 5.

28. Ibid.

29. Ibid.

30. *Bohemia,* January 11, 1959, 147.

31. Comment made by Andrés Suárez to the author.

32. *Diario de la Marina,* January 6, 1959, 2a.

33. Agustín Tamargo, "Fidel: No nos falle," *Bohemia,* January 18–25, 1959, 24.

34. *Bohemia,* January 11, 1959, 68.

Chapter 5

1. An earlier version of parts of this chapter appeared under the title "Growth in Cuba: Resistance and Accommodations," in *Conflict and Change in Cuba*, ed. Enrique Baloyra and James Morris (Albuquerque: University of New Mexico Press, 1993), 189–214.

2. For a discussion of these four dimensions, see Seymour Martin Lipset, *Political Man* (New York: Doubleday, 1959).

3. Rolando Zamora Fernández, *El tiempo libre de los jóvenes cubanos* (Havana: Editorial de Ciencias Sociales, 1984), 19.

4. Karl Mannheim, *Essays on the Sociology of Culture* (London: Routledge and Kegan Paul, 1967), 4.

5. For comparative perspectives and discussion of these points, see Seymour Martin Lipset, "University Students and Politics in Underdeveloped Countries," in *The Seeds of Politics: Youth and Politics in America*, ed. Anthony M. Orum (Englewood Cliffs, N.J.: Prentice Hall, 1972), 285–326.

6. M. Kent Jennings and Richard G. Niemi, *The Political Character of Adolescence: The Influence of Families and Schools* (Princeton: Princeton University Press, 1974). Emphasis in original.

7. Anita Chan, *Children of Mao: Personality Development and Political Activism in the Red Guard Generation* (Seattle: University of Washington Press, 1985), 190.

8. Frank Musgrove, *Youth and the Social Order* (Bloomington: Indiana University Press, 1964), 3.

9. Fidel Castro, quoted in Allen Young, *Gays under the Cuban Revolution* (San Francisco: Grey Fox Press, 1984), 3.

10. *Granma*, April 2, 1987, 3.

11. *Bohemia*, March 30, 1962, 45.

12. *Bohemia*, April 8, 1977, 59.

13. *Bohemia*, October 26, 1979, 43.

14. *Juventud Rebelde*, January 1, 1989, 2.

15. Ibid.

16. For an overview of the issues of study regarding Cuban youth in the 1990s, see María Isabel Domínguez, "Las investigaciones sobre la juventud," *Temas*, no. 1 (January–March 1995): 85–94.

17. *Informe al Congreso* (Havana: Unión de Jóvenes Comunistas, 1992).

18. Ibid.

19. See Bert Hoffman, ed., *Cuba: Apertura y reforma económica, perfil de un debate* (Caracas: Nueva Sociedad, 1995).

20. All quotes are from the Foreign Broadcast Service, Latin America (FBIS-LAT), August 31, 1990, 7–12.

21. FBIS-LAT, August 11, 1970, 10.

22. *Somos Jóvenes*, no. 134, 1990.

23. *Somos Jóvenes*, no. 137, 1991.

24. *Moncada*, May 1987, 42–43.

25. *Somos Jóvenes*, no. 135, 1991, 18–21.

26. Nara Araujo, "The Sea, the Sea, Once and Again: Lo cubano and the literature of the novísimas," in *The Elusive Nation*, ed. Damián Fernández and Madeline Cámara (Gainesville: University Press of Florida, forthcoming).

27. Holly Ackerman, "The Balsero Phenomenon, 1991–1994," *Cuban Studies/Estudios Cubanos* 27 (1997): 169–200.

Chapter 6

1. For how this operated in the case of the Soviet Union, see Raymond A. Bauer, Alex Inkeles, and Clyde Kluckhohn, *How the Soviet System Works: Cultural, Psychological and Social Themes* (Cambridge, Mass.: Harvard University Press, 1964); and Judith Sedaitis and Jim Butterfield, eds., *Perestroika from Below: Social Movements in the Soviet Union* (Boulder, Colo.: Westview Press, 1991).

2. See Larissa Lomnitz and Ana Melnick, *Chile's Middle Class: A Struggle for Survival in the Face of Neoliberalism* (Boulder, Colo.: Lynne Rienner, 1992).

3. Susan Eckstein, *Back to the Future: Cuba under Castro* (Princeton: Princeton University Press, 1996).

4. Ibid.

5. Moore, *Injustice*, 18.

6. Scott, *Weapons of the Weak*, 29.

7. See James C. Scott, *The Moral Economy of the Peasant: Rebellion and Subsistence in Southeast Asia* (New Haven: Yale University Press, 1976).

8. See Scott, *Domination and the Arts of Resistance.*

9. Joel S. Migdal, *Strong Societies and Weak States: State-Society Relations and State Capabilities in the Third World* (Princeton: Princeton University Press, 1988), 4–5. Emphasis in original.

10. Bauer, Inkeles, and Kluckhohn, *How the Soviet System Works*, 76.

11. See the reference to network capital in Chris Hann, "Philosophers' Models on the Carpathian Lowlands," in *Civil Society: Theory, History, Comparison*, ed. John A. Hall (Cambridge: Polity Press, 1995), 177.

12. See Jorge F. Pérez-López, *Cuba's Second Economy* (New Brunswick, N.J.: Transaction Press, 1995), for a list of expressions related to the informal economy and for a discussion of the second economy. See also Carlos Paz Pérez, *De lo popular y lo vulgar en el habla cubana* (Havana: Editorial de Ciencias Sociales, 1998).

13. Most of the examples are the result of interviews conducted in Havana and Pinar del Rio, Cuba, during my visits, particularly in June 1996.

14. FBIS-LAT, February 28, 1992.

15. FBIS-LAT, February 24, 1992.

16. Personal interview, Coral Gables, Fla., 1994.

17. Pérez-López, *Cuba's Second Economy*, 97.

18. Ibid., 102.

19. Fidel Castro, "Tenemos el deber sagrado de no estar satisfechos jamás," in *Por el camino correcto* (Havana: Editora Política, 1987), 71.

20. "Tenemos que ser mucho mas intransigentes," in *Por el camino correcto*, 1.

21. FBIS-LAT, March 12, 1992.

22. *Granma*, December 27, 1991.

23. Susan Eckstein makes a similar point in *Back to the Future.*

Chapter 7

1. Giuseppe Di Palma, *To Craft Democracies: An Essay on Democratic Transitions* (Berkeley: University of California Press, 1990), 4.

2. Ibid., 9.

3. Marcia A. Weigle and Jim Butterfield, "Civil Society in Reforming Communist Regimes: The Logic of Emergence," *Comparative Politics* (October 1992): 3.

4. John A. Hall, ed., *Civil Society: Theory, History, Comparison* (Cambridge: Polity Press, 1995).

5. Jean Cohen and Andrew Arato, *Civil Society and Political Theory* (Cambridge, Mass.: MIT Press, 1992).

6. Zbigniew Rau, Introduction to *The Reemergence of Civil Society in Eastern Europe and the Soviet Union,* ed. Zbigniew Rau (Boulder, Colo.: Westview Press, 1991), 1.

7. Carmelo Mesa-Lago, "Cambio de regime o cambios en el regimen? Aspectos políticos y económicos," *Revista Encuentro* 6–7 (Fall–Winter): 36–43.

8. Doug McAdam and John McCarthy, eds., *Comparative Perspectives on Social Movements* (Cambridge: Cambridge University Press, 1996).

9. Ibid., 7.

10. See, e.g., Robert Ryback, *Rock around the Bloc: A History of Rock Music in Eastern Europe* (Oxford: Oxford University Press, 1990).

11. John Keane and Paul Meir, Preface to Alberto Melucci, *Nomads of the Present: Social Movements and Individual Needs in Contemporary Society,* ed. J. Keane and P. Meir (Philadelphia: Temple University Press, 1989), 1, 3.

12. Ibid., 35.

13. Ibid.

14. Weigle and Butterfield, "Civil Society in Reforming Communist Regimes," 1.

15. Weigle and Butterfield, "Civil Society in Reforming Communist Regimes."

16. Ibid., 5–6.

17. Hirschman, *Shifting Involvements.*

18. See Barbara Lowenstein and Malgorzata Melchior, "Escape to Community," in *The Unplanned Society: Poland during and after Communism,* ed. Janine R. Wedel (New York: Columbia University Press, 1992), 173–180.

19. Gillian Gunn, "Cuba's NGOs: Government Puppets or Seeds of Civil Society?" Georgetown University Cuba Briefing Paper Series (7), 1995.

20. Ibid. See also Damián Fernández, "Civil Society in Transition," in *Transition in Cuba* (Miami: Cuban Research Institute, Florida International University, 1993).

21. See, e.g., Haroldo Dilla Alfonso, "Pensando la alternativa desde la participación," *Temas,* no. 8 (December 1996): 102–109.

22. Maurizzio Giuliano, *El caso CEA* (Miami: La Universal, 1998).

23. Archibald M. Ritter, "Entrepreneurship, Microenterprise, and Public Policy in Cuba: Promotion, Containment, or Asphyxiation?" *Journal of Interamerican Studies* 40, no. 2 (1998): 63–94.

24. David L. Wank, "Bureaucratic Patronage and Private Business: Changing Networks of Power in Urban China," in *The Waning of the Communist State: Economic Origins of Political Decline in China and Hungary* (Berkeley: University of California Press, 1995), 153–184.

25. Marifeli Pérez-Stable, "The Invisible Crisis: Stability and Change in 1990s Cuba," in

Cuba Today: The Events Taking Place in Cuba and the Ensuing Issues for Canadian Policy (Ottawa: Canadian Foundation for the Americas, 1999), 23–29.

26. See my "Democracy and Human Rights: The Case of Cuba," in *Democracy and Human Rights in the Caribbean,* ed. Ivelaw I. Griffith and Betty N. Sedoc-Dahlberg (Boulder, Colo.: Westview Press, 1997), 97–112.

27. See my "Democracy and Human Rights."

28. Putnam, *Making Democracy Work.*

29. Eckstein, *Regarding Politics.*

30. Endre Sik, "Network Capital in Capitalist, Communist, and Post-Communist Societies," Working Paper no. 12, Kellogg Institute, Notre Dame University, February 1995.

Chapter 8

1. Pamela Constable, "New Voices of Exile," *Boston Globe Magazine,* July 25, 1993, 22.

2. See, e.g., Gustavo Pérez Firmat, *Life on the Hyphen: The Cuban American Way* (Austin: University of Texas Press, 1994).

3. Constable, "New Voices of Exile."

4. See the *periodiquitos* at the Cuban Collection, University of Miami Library; and Maria Cristina García, *Havana USA: Cuban Exiles and Cuban Americans in South Florida, 1959-1994* (Berkeley: University of California Press, 1996).

5. See my "From Little Havana to Washington, D.C.: The Impact of Cuban-Americans on U.S. Foreign Policy," in *Ethnic Groups and U.S. Foreign Policy,* ed. Mohammed E. Ahrari (New York: Greenwood Press, 1987).

6. Guillermo J. Grenier and Hugh Gladwin, "Executive Summary," *FIU 1997 Cuba Poll* (Miami: Florida International University, 1997), 2.

7. Max Castro, "Presentation to the U.S. Southern Command", Miami, Fla., March 31, 1999.

8. Grenier and Gladwin, "Executive Summary."

9. Rui Ferrera, *El Nuevo Herald,* February 16, 1999, 1 (my translation).

10. Grenier and Gladwin, "Executive Summary."

11. Ferrera, *El Nuevo Herald.*

12. Ibid.

13. Ibid.

14. See Sylvia Pedraza, "Cubans in Exile, 1959-1989: The State of the Research," in *Cuban Studies since the Revolution,* ed. Damián Fernández (Gainsville: University Press of Florida, 1992), 235-257, for a review of these different interpretations.

15. Alejandro Portes and Robert L. Bach, *Latin Journey: Cuban and Mexican Immigrants in the United States* (Berkeley: University of California Press, 1985).

16. Ibid., 201.

17. Ibid., 204.

18. Ibid., 216.

19. See Alejandro Portes and József Böröcz, "The Informal Sector under Capitalism and State Socialism: A Preliminary Comparison," *Social Justice* 15, no. 3 (1988): 17-28.

BIBLIOGRAPHY

Periodicals

Bohemia
Cuba Contemporánea
Diario de la Marina
El Nuevo Herald
Foreign Broadcast Information Service
Granma
Juventud Rebelde
La Quincena
Moncada
Revista Bimestre Cubana
Somos Jóvenes
Temas

Books, Chapters, and Articles

Ackerman, Holly. "The Balsero Phenomenon, 1991-1994." *Cuban Studies/Estudios Cubanos* 27 (1997): 169-200.

Adorno, T. W., Else Frenkel-Brunswik, Daniel J. Levinson, and R. Nevitt Sanford. *The Authoritarian Personality*. New York: Norton, 1969.

Almond, Gabriel, and Sidney Verba. *The Civic Culture: Political Attitudes and Democracy in Five Nations*. Princeton: Princeton University Press, 1982.

Anderson, Benedict. *Imagined Communities: Reflections on the Origin and Spread of Nationalism*. London: Verso, 1991.

Apter, David E. "Political Religion in the New Nations." In *Old Societies and New States*, ed. Clifford Geertz, 57-104. New York: Free Press, 1963.

Araujo, Nara. "The Sea, the Sea, Once and Again: Lo cubano and the literature of the novisimas." In *The Elusive Nation,* ed. Damián Fernández and Madeline Cámara. Gainesville: University Press of Florida, forthcoming.

Baloyra, Enrique, and James Morris, eds. *Conflict and Change in Cuba.* Albuquerque: University of New Mexico Press, 1993.

Banfield, Edward. *The Moral Basis of a Backward Society.* New York: Free Press, 1967.

Bauer, Raymond A., Alex Inkeles, and Clyde Kluckhohn. *How the Soviet System Works: Cultural, Psychological and Social Themes.* Cambridge, Mass.: Harvard University Press, 1964.

Benes, Eduardo. "La psicología del partido político." *Revista Bimestre Cubana* 15, no. 3 (September–October 1920): 203–208.

Benjamin, Jules R. *The United States and the Origins of the Cuban Revolution.* Princeton: Princeton University Press, 1990.

Bhaba, Homi. "Narrating the Nation." In *Nationalism,* ed. John Hutchinson and Anthony Smith. New York: Oxford University Press, 1997.

Boissevian, Jeremy. *Friends of Friends: Networks, Manipulators and Coalitions.* New York: St. Martin's Press, 1974.

Boyd, Robert, and Peter J. Richerson. "Culture and Cooperation." In *Beyond Self-Interest,* ed. Jane S. Mansbridge, 111–132. Chicago: University of Chicago Press, 1990.

Castro, Fidel. *Por el camino correcto.* Havana: Editora Política, 1987.

Cepeda, Rafael. "Fidel Castro y el reino de Dios." *Bohemia,* July 17, 1960, 110.

Chan, Anita. *Children of Mao: Personality Development and Political Activism in the Red Guard Generation.* Seattle: University of Washington Press, 1985.

Cohen, Jean, and Andrew Arato, *Civil Society and Political Theory.* Cambridge, Mass.: MIT Press, 1992.

Dealy, Glenn Cuadill. "Two Cultures and Political Behavior in Latin America." In *Democracy in Latin America: Patterns and Cycles,* ed. Roderic Ai Camp, 46–66. Wilmington: Scholarly Resources, 1996.

Dilla Alfonso, Haroldo. "Pensando la alternativa desde la participación." *Temas,* no. 8 (December 1996): 102–109.

Di Palma, Giuseppe. *To Craft Democracies: An Essay on Democratic Transitions.* Berkeley: University of California Press, 1990.

Dominguez, Jorge I. "Politics in Cuba 1959–1989: The State of Research." In *Cuban Studies since the Revolution,* ed. Damián J. Fernández, 95–118. Gainesville: University Press of Florida, 1992.

Domínguez, María Isabel. "Las investigaciones sobre la juventud." *Temas,* no. 1 (January–March 1995): 85–94.

Durkheim, Emile. *The Division of Labor in Society.* New York: Free Press, 1964.

Ebel, Roland H., Raymond Taras, and James D. Cochrane. *Political Culture and Foreign Policy in Latin America.* Albany: State University of New York, 1991.

Eckstein, Harry. *Regarding Politics: Essays on Political Theory, Stability, and Changes.* Berkeley: University of California Press, 1992.

Eckstein, Susan. *Back to the Future: Cuba under Castro.* Princeton: Princeton University Press, 1996.

Eisenstadt, Stuart, and Louis Roniger. *Patrons, Clients and Friends: Interpersonal Relations and the Structure of Trust in Society.* Cambridge: Cambridge University Press, 1984.

Elster, Jon. "Sadder but Wiser: Rationality and the Emotions." *Social Science Information* 24, no. 2 (1985): 375–406.

Fernández, Damián. "Democracy and Human Rights: The Case of Cuba." In *Democracy and Human Rights in the Caribbean*, ed. Ivelaw I. Griffith and Betty N. Sedoc-Dahlberg, 97–112. Boulder, Colo.: Westview Press, 1997.

———. "From Little Havana to Washington, D.C.: The Impact of Cuban-Americans on U.S. Foreign Policy." In *Ethnic Groups and U.S. Foreign Policy,* ed. Mohammed E. Ahrari, 115–134. New York: Greenwood Press, 1987.

———. "Political Religion and Revolution in Cuba." In *The Religious Challenge to the State,* ed. Matthew C. Moen and Lowell Gustafson, 51–71. Pittsburgh: Temple University Press, 1992.

———. "Youth in Cuba: Resistance and Accommodation." In *Conflict and Change in Cuba,* ed. Enrique Baloyra and James Morris, 189–214. Albuquerque: University of New Mexico Press, 1993.

Fernández, Manuel. "Presencia de los católicos en la revolución triunfante." *La Quincena,* January 1959, 10.

———. *Religion y revolución en Cuba: Veinticinco años de lucha ateista.* Miami: Saeta Ediciones, 1984.

Frank, Robert. *Passions within Reason: The Strategic Role of the Emotions.* New York: Norton, 1988.

———. "A Theory of Moral Sentiments." In *Beyond Self-Interest,* ed. Jane S. Mansbridge, 71–96. Chicago: University of Chicago Press, 1990.

Franqui, Carlos. *Cuba: El libro de los doce.* Mexico City: Era, 1966.

Free, Lloyd. *Attitudes of the Cuban People toward the Castro Regime in Late Spring 1960.* Princeton: Institute for International Social Research, 1960.

Fukuyama, Francis. *Trust: The Social Virtues and the Creation of Prosperity.* New York: Free Press, 1995.

García, María Cristina. *Havana USA: Cuban Exiles and Cuban Americans in South Florida, 1959–1994.* Berkeley: University of California Press, 1996.

Geertz, Clifford. "Ideology as a Cultural System." In *Ideology and Discontent,* ed. David E. Apter, 47–76. New York: Free Press, 1964.

Gerth, H. H., and C. Wright Mills, ed. and trans. *From Max Weber: Essays in Sociology.* New York: Oxford University Press, 1958.

Giuliano, Maurizzio. *El caso CEA.* Miami: La Universal, 1998.

Granovetter, Marc. *The Sociology of Economic Life.* Boulder, Colo.: Westview Press, 1992.

Grenier, Guillermo J., and Hugh Gladwin. "Executive Summary." *FIU 1997 Cuba Poll.* Miami: Florida International University, 1997.

Guerra y Sánchez, Ramiro, José M. Pérez Cabrera, Juan J. Remos, and Emeterio S. Santovenia. *Historia de la nación cubana.* Havana: Editorial Historia de la Nación Cubana, 1957.

Guiral Moreno, Mario. "Aspectos censurables del carácter cubano." *Revista Bimestre Cubana* 4, no. 2 (February 1914): 121–163.

———. "Malcriados y descorteses." *Revista Bimestre Cubana* 48 (December 1941): 373–391.

Gunes-Ayata, Ayse. "Clientelism: Premodern, Modern, Postmodern." In *Democracy, Clientelism and Civil Society,* ed. Louis Roniger and Ayse Gunes-Ayata. Boulder, Colo.: Lynne Rienner, 1994.

Gunn, Gillian. "Cuba's NGOs: Government Puppets or Seeds of Civil Society?" Georgetown University Cuba Briefing Paper Series (7), 1995.

Habermas, Jürgen. *The Philosophical Discourse of Modernity: Twelve Lectures.* Cambridge, Mass.: MIT Press, 1987.

Halebsky, Sandor, and John M. Kirk, eds. *Cuba in Transition: Crisis and Transformation*. Boulder, Colo.: Westview Press, 1992.

Hall, John A., ed. *Civil Society: Theory, History, Comparison*. Cambridge: Polity Press, 1995.

Hann, Chris. "Philosophers' Models on the Carpathian Lowlands." In *Civil Society: Theory, History, Comparison,* ed. John A. Hall, 158–182. Cambridge: Polity Press, 1995.

Henry, Stuart, ed. *Informal Institutions: Alternative Networks in the Corporate State*. New York: St. Martin's Press, 1981.

Hirschman, Albert. *The Passions and the Interests*. Princeton: Princeton University Press, 1977.

———. *Shifting Involvements: Private Interest and Public Action,* Princeton: Princeton University Press, 1982.

Hoffman, Bert, ed. *Cuba: Apertura y reforma económica, perfil de un debate*. Caracas: Nueva Sociedad, 1995.

Holmes, Stephen. *Passions and Constraint: On the Theory of Liberal Democracy*. Chicago: University of Chicago Press, 1995.

———. "The Secret History of Self-Interest." In *Beyond Self-Interest,* ed. Jane S. Mansbridge, 267–286. Chicago: University of Chicago Press, 1990.

Huntington, Samuel P. *The Clash of Civilizations and the Remaking of World Order*. New York: Simon and Schuster, 1996.

Hyden, Goran. *Beyond Ujamaa in Tanzania: Underdevelopment and an Uncaptured Peasantry*. Berkeley: University of California Press, 1980.

Jennings, M. Kent, and Richard G. Niemi. *The Political Character of Adolescence: The Influence of Families and Schools*. Princeton: Princeton University Press, 1974.

Kirk, John M. *Between God and the Party: Religion and Politics in Revolutionary Cuba*. Gainesville: University Press of Florida, 1989.

Kornhauser, William. *The Theory of Mass Society*. New York: Free Press, 1959.

Lasswell, Harold. *Power and Personality*. Westport, Conn.: Greenwood Press, 1976.

Leyton, Elliot, ed. *The Compact: Selected Dimensions of Friendship*. Social and Economic Papers no. 3. St. John's: Memorial University of Newfoundland, 1974.

Lipset, Seymour Martin. *Political Man*. New York: Doubleday, 1959.

———. "University Students and Politics in Underdeveloped Countries." In *The Seeds of Politics: Youth and Politics in America,* ed. Anthony M. Orum, 285–326. Englewood Cliffs, N.J.: Prentice Hall, 1972.

Lomnitz, Larissa, and Ana Melnick. *Chile's Middle Class: A Struggle for Survival in the Face of Neoliberalism*. Boulder, Colo.: Lynne Rienner, 1992.

Lowenstein, Barbara, and Malgorzata Melchior. "Escape to Community." In *The Unplanned Society: Poland during and after Communism,* ed. Janine R. Wedel, 173–180. New York: Columbia University Press, 1992.

Lutz, Catherine A. *Unnatural Emotions: Everyday Sentiments on a Micronesian Atoll and Their Challenge to Western Theory*. Chicago: University of Chicago Press, 1988.

McAdam, Doug, and John McCarthy, eds. *Comparative Perspectives on Social Movements*. Cambridge: Cambridge University Press, 1996.

Maingot, Anthony. "The Ideal and the Real in Cuban Political Culture." In *Transition in Cuba*. Miami: Cuban Research Institute, Florida International University, 1994.

Mañach, Jorge. *Historia y estilo*. Miami: Editorial Cubana, 1994.

———. *Pasado vigente*. Havana: Editorial Trópico, 1939.

Mannheim, Karl. *Essays on the Sociology of Culture*. London: Routledge and Kegan Paul, 1967.

Mansbridge, Jane S., ed. *Beyond Self-Interest*. Chicago: University of Chicago Press, 1990.

Marino Pérez, Luis. "La indisciplina en los pueblos." *Cuba Contemporánea* 2, no. 1 (May 1913): 26–35.

Márquez Sterling, Carlos, and Manuel Márquez Sterling. *Historia de la isla de Cuba*. New York: Regents, 1975.

Melucci, Alberto. *Nomads of the Present: Social Movements and Individual Needs in Contemporary Society*. Philadelphia: Temple University Press, 1989.

Mesa-Lago, Carmelo. "Assessing Economic and Social Performance in the Cuban Transition of the 1990s." *World Development* 26, no. 5 (1998): 857–876.

———. "Cambio de regime o cambios en el regimen? Aspectos políticos y económicos." *Revista Encuentro* 6–7 (Fall–Winter): 36–43.

Migdal, Joel S. *Strong Societies and Weak States: State-Society Relations and State Capabilities in the Third World*. Princeton: Princeton University Press, 1988.

Moore, Barrington. *Injustice: The Social Bases of Obedience and Revolt*. New York: Pantheon Books, 1978.

Musgrove, Frank. *Youth and the Social Order*. Bloomington: Indiana University Press, 1964.

Nitya, Eddu. *La suprema revelación, precedida por oda a la revolución, una nota liminar, y las siete reglas del perfecto espiritista, con Fidel ante la humanidad*. Havana: Tipografía Ideas, 1961.

Ortiz, Fernando. *Entre cubanos: Psicología tropical*. Havana: Editorial de Ciencias Sociales, 1987.

———. *La decadencia cubana*. Havana: La Universal, 1924.

Paz Pérez, Carlos. *De lo popular y lo vulgar en el habla cubana*. Havana: Editorial de Ciencias Sociales, 1998.

Pedraza, Sylvia. "Cubans in Exile, 1959–1989: The State of the Research." In *Cuban Studies since the Revolution*, ed. Damián Fernández, 235–257. Gainsville: University Press of Florida, 1992.

Pérez, Louis. *Cuba: Between Reform and Revolution*. New York: Oxford University Press, 1995.

Pérez Firmat, Gustavo. *Life on the Hyphen: The Cuban American Way*. Austin: University of Texas Press, 1994.

Pérez-López, Jorge F. *Cuba's Second Economy*. New Brunswick, N.J.: Transaction Press, 1995.

Pérez-Serantes, Enrique. "La Divina Providencia ha escrito en el cielo de Cuba la palabra triunfo." *La Quincena*, January 1959, 18.

Pérez-Stable, Marifeli. *The Cuban Revolution: Origins, Course, and Legacy*. New York: Oxford University Press, 1999.

———. "Estrada Palma's Civic March: From Oriente to Havana, April 20–May 11, 1902." *Cuban Studies/Estudios Cubanos* 29 (forthcoming).

———. "The Invisible Crisis: Stability and Change in 1990s Cuba." In *Cuba Today: The Events Taking Place in Cuba and the Ensuing Issues for Canadian Policy*, 23–29. Ottawa: Canadian Foundation for the Americas, 1999.

Portell Vilá, Herminio. *Historia de Cuba en sus relaciones con los Estados Unidos y España*. Miami: Mnemosyne, 1969.

Portes, Alejandro. *The Informal Economy: Studies in Advanced and Less Developed Countries*. Baltimore: Johns Hopkins University Press, 1989.

Portes, Alejandro, and Robert L. Bach. *Latin Journey: Cuban and Mexican Immigrants in the United States*. Berkeley: University of California Press, 1985.

Portes, Alejandro, and József Böröcz. "The Informal Sector under Capitalism and State Socialism: A Preliminary Comparison." *Social Justice* 15, no. 3 (1988): 17–28.

Putnam, Robert D. *Making Democracy Work: Civic Traditions in Modern Italy*. Princeton: Princeton University Press, 1993.

Pye, Lucian W. *Politics, Personality, and Nation Building: Burma's Search for Identity*. Westport, Conn.: Greenwood Press, 1976.

Ramos, José Antonio. *Manual del perfecto fulanista: Apuntes para el estudio de nuestra dinámica político-social*. Miami: Editorial Cubana, 1995.

Rau, Zbigniew, ed. *The Reemergence of Civil Society in Eastern Europe and the Soviet Union*. Boulder, Colo.: Westview Press, 1991.

Rexach, Rosario. Introduction to *Historia y estilo*, by Jorge Mañach. Miami: Editorial Cubana, 1994.

Ritter, Archibald M. "Entrepreneurship, Microenterprise, and Public Policy in Cuba: Promotion, Containment, or Asphyxiation?" *Journal of Interamerican Studies* 40, no. 2 (1998): 63–94.

Rojas, Rafael. "Viaje a las semillas: Instituciones de la antimodernidad cubana," *Apuntes Postmodernos* (Fall 1993): 3–20.

Rorty, Amelie O., ed. *Explaining the Emotions*. Berkeley: University of California Press, 1980.

Ryback, Robert. *Rock around the Bloc: A History of Rock Music in Eastern Europe*. Oxford: Oxford University Press, 1990.

Scott, James C. *Domination and the Arts of Resistance: Hidden Transcripts*. New Haven: Yale University Press, 1990.

———. *The Moral Economy of the Peasant: Rebellion and Subsistence in Southeast Asia*. New Haven: Yale University Press, 1976.

———. *Weapons of the Weak: Everyday Forms of Peasant Resistance*. New Haven: Yale University Press, 1988.

Scott, James C., Carl Landé, Laura Guasti, and Steffen W. Schmidt, eds. *Friends, Followers and Factions*. Berkeley: University of California Press, 1976.

Sedaitis, Judith, and Jim Butterfield, eds. *Perestroika from Below: Social Movements in the Soviet Union*. Boulder, Colo.: Westview Press, 1991.

Sik, Endre. "Network Capital in Capitalist, Communist, and Post-Communist Societies." Working Paper no. 12. Kellogg Institute, University of Notre Dame, February 1995.

Smelser, Neil L. "Vicissitudes of Work and Love." In *Themes of Work and Love in Adulthood*, ed. Neil L. Smelser and Erik H. Erickson, 105–115. Cambridge, Mass.: Harvard University Press, 1980.

Smith, Adam. *The Theory of Moral Sentiments*. Indianapolis: Liberty Classics, 1976.

Sola, José Sixto de. "El pesimismo cubano." *Cuba Contemporánea* 3, no. 4 (December 1913): 273–303.

Solomon, Robert C. "Emotions and Choice." In *Explaining the Emotions*, ed. Amelie O. Rorty, 251–281. Berkeley: University of California Press, 1980.

———. *The Passions*. Garden City, N.Y.: Anchor Press, 1976.

Suárez, Andrés. "Cuba: Ideology and Pragmatism." In *Cuba: Continuity and Change*, ed. Jaime Suchlicki et al., 129–146. Miami: Institute of Interamerican Studies, 1985.

Tamargo, Agustín. "Fidel: No nos falle." *Bohemia*, January 18–25, 1959, 24.

Thomas, Hugh. *Cuba*. Barcelona: Ediciones Grijalbo, 1973.

Valdés, Nelson. "Cuban Political Culture: Between Betrayal and Death." In *Cuba in Transition: Crisis and Transformation*, ed. Sandor Halebsky and John M. Kirk, 207–228. Boulder, Colo.: Westview Press, 1992.

Valdés, Zoe. *La nada cotidiana*. Barcelona: Emecee Editores, 1995.

Varona, Enrique José. "Nuestra indisciplina." *Cuba Contemporánea* 2, no. 1 (May 1913): 12–16.

Vignier, E., and G. Alonso, eds. *La corrupción política y administrativa en Cuba.* Havana: Editorial Ciencias Sociales, 1973.

Vitier, Cintio. *Ese sol del mundo moral.* Mexico: Siglo XXI, 1975.

Wank, David L. "Bureaucratic Patronage and Private Business: Changing Networks of Power in Urban China." In *The Waning of the Communist State: Economic Origins of Political Decline in China and Hungary,* ed. A. G. Walder, 153–184. Berkeley: University of California Press, 1995.

Weigle, Marcia A., and Jim Butterfield. "Civil Society in Reforming Communist Regimes: The Logic of Emergence." *Comparative Politics* (October 1992): 1–21.

Wolfenstein, E. Victor. *The Revolutionary Personality: Lenin, Trotsky, Gandhi.* Princeton: Princeton University Press, 1967.

Young, Allen. *Gays under the Cuban Revolution.* San Francisco: Grey Fox Press, 1984.

Zamora Fernández, Rolando. *El tiempo libre de los jóvenes cubanos.* Havana: Editorial de Ciencias Sociales, 1984.

INDEX

CPSIA information can be obtained
at www.ICGtesting.com
Printed in the USA
LVHW030236080821
694671LV00001B/39

9 780292 725201